# ALBERT OUTLER
# THE PREACHER

# ALBERT OUTLER THE PREACHER

*Sermons on Several Occasions*

Edited by Bob W. Parrott

ABINGDON PRESS

*Nashville*

Albert Outler the Preacher



This book is printed on acid-free paper.

**Library of Congress Cataloging-in-Publication Data**

OUTLER, ALBERT COOK 1908
Albert Outler, the preacher
1. United Methodist Church (U.S.)—Sermons.
2. Methodist Church—Sermons. 3. Sermons, American. I. Parrott, Bob W. II. Title.
BX8333.077A43 1988 252'.076 87-27546

**ISBN 0-687-00950-2 (alk. paper)**

Since the boxes containing these papers were stored away for several years, references for many quotations became misplaced. After a diligent search, most were located, but a few were not. Those few are noted "not cited."

Unless otherwise indicated, the biblical passages that appear in these sermons are Albert Outler's own translations from the Hebrew and Greek texts; italics also are those of the author.



Those noted KJV are from the King James Version of the Bible.

MANUFACTURED BY THE PARTHENON PRESS AT
NASHVILLE, TENNESSEE, UNITED STATES OF AMERICA

*To Carla Grace Outler,*
*whose quiet strength*
*blesses her husband*

# C O N T E N T S

# PREFACE

## An Egghead in the Pulpit

Some surely will ask why samples of unpublished sermon manuscripts of a retired professor of theology were retrieved and edited by a former student whose career has been cast in the pastorate. That is a good question, and its answer can be expressed in four parts.

In the first place, Albert Outler is no standard-brand professor of theology, as a host of his students and admirers (and a few nonadmirers!) will testify. Second, these texts should be read as "conversations" between the Christian tradition, grounded in the Bible, and successive "human scenes" in this last half of the twentieth century. Albert Outler has a special gift for gleaning wisdom from the Christian past while also scanning the nearer horizons for signs of Christian faith and hope. Third, these sermons demonstrate that, for all his manifold involvements (academic, ecclesiastical, ecumenical, cultural), Outler's heart always has been in the pulpit, attempting to heed Charles Wesley's dictum, "Unite the pair so long disjoined: knowledge and vital piety."

A fourth answer is quite practical: There seemed no other way for this material ever to see the light of day.

Throughout his career, and even now in retirement, Outler has been carried along by an unending rush of widely varied commitments that leave him no time (or so it seems to him) to stop and finish off many of his projects, once the occasions have passed. His was and is the dilemma of the perfectionist eager to "serve the present age," his calling to fulfill. He never could quite manage to put his message out to others and put it down on paper in the same time-span, in a manner that he could live with in the future.

Thus, while these sermons are indeed his, they were not written for publication, but are faithful notes written for the situations at hand. It is hoped that these published "sermons" will in part satisfy some of his friends who have deplored his habit of putting out but not putting it down.

Clearly, some sort of salvage operation was in order, and I felt a nudging Providence pointing me in that direction. The job needed to be done, and the question was put to me: Why don't you tackle it? "Dr. O" had been a beloved teacher, and our friendship has continued. He is a born egghead, forever involved in this or that academic or ecumenical assignment, each with its bulging files. But since I am a preacher, it was his *sermons* that interested me most. I had heard some of them; others I had heard about from people whose judgment I respected. I knew their shared verdict: Albert Outler is a preacher with a style all his own, a theologian who doesn't sound like one, a theologian who refuses to talk down (or up!) to his audience. And yet one who manages to communicate to thoughtful people, hold their attention with what some would call heavy stuff, and leave them turned on to the grace of God.

Thus a felt need on my part turned into a demanding project. I broached it to "Dr. O" and he consented, with two typical provisos: that he not be distracted from his work in progress (at the time, he was struggling with his four-volume series of "Sermons" in the bicentennial edition of *The Works of John Wesley*); and that I pay special heed "to clearing up the glitches" left behind in whatever manuscript texts I might select. This volume is the first fruits of that venture, a memorial of a sort, but more than that—a mirror of the mind and heart of a pioneering theologian/churchman whose many-sided ministries have given credence to his rhetoric.

These sermons were preached in churches in many different places across the world. This is the point to their subtitle, *Sermons on Several Occasions,* borrowed from Albert Outler's special mentor, John Wesley. They vary in their stages of completion, and I have made no effort to "finish" them. My concern was to edit, not to editorialize. Some do not read as well as they sounded; Albert Outler's impromptu asides belong to his legend. Rabbi Marc Tannenbaum once introduced him as "Methodism's leading stand-up comic." Some read more clearly than they sounded, because of Outler's habit of packing as much as he could (sometimes too much!) into every sermon. His speech is both scholarly and colloquial and mixes historical references with contemporary allusions in a manner that is as fascinating as informing. He has his own version of Dr. Fosdick's old nostrum about preaching with the Bible in one hand and the daily newspapers in the other; in Outler's case, it is the Bible and the sweep of church history! He ignored the reigning homiletic styles of his time as they came and went, just as he never could be neatly pegged with partisan labels such as liberal or conservative. One quickly notices how deficient these texts are in illustrations. Those came in lively improvisations of the moment, and most of those gems are lost.

But the heart of the matter remains. The essence of his axial theme resonates in every message: the sovereign grace of God revealed in Jesus Christ, empowered in human hearts (and thus in history) by the indwelling presence of the Holy Spirit. Amazing grace in all its modes, from prevenience to glory, has been Outler's theme: the luminous Mystery that enfolds and upholds our lives; the ethical imperative "to love God above all else"; the spiritual directive both "to live and to walk in the Spirit."

Knowledgeable Christians will recognize in these sermons the Methodist tradition in its broadest and most understandable form, and yet will further sense how comfortably at home Albert Outler has felt with other traditions of the Christian family (and in many interreligious settings as well). His leadership in helping Protestants to rediscover "tradition" and Roman Catholics to reemphasize the primacy of Scripture is one of the endeavors that has gratified him most.

Conserving and editing these sermons has been a daunting task and yet a rewarding one. It may be just as well that "Dr. O" was not able to do the job himself. For certainly he would have recast the texts extensively, which would have obscured to a great extent their original timeliness. I believe that as they stand they will be welcomed not only by those who have known the man in person, but also by those who may discover him for the first time in these pages.

My heartiest thanks are due, first of all, to my wife, Doris, whose diligent help and gentle criticism have been invaluable. "Dr. O" has commented often that her sense of how sermons come across in the pew is better than mine! My thanks to my secretary, Wava Fick, who typed and retyped (and retyped the retypes!). My thanks to the editors of Abingdon Press for their help in getting this book between covers. Special thanks are due Carla Outler, whose help with her husband's files made the job possible. And finally a salute to "Dr. O" for his unintervening interest along the way.

# 1

# *What Can We Pray For?*

## *An Introductory Comment*

This sermon is finely tuned to the truth of the way one communes with God. What can we pray for? We can pray for anything we deeply desire, as long as we offer both our request and our motives to God in prayer, for his decision.

Bishop W. N. Ainsworth told Albert Outler, following his undergraduate studies, that there would be no place for a Ph.D. in Georgia. And sure enough, when Outler wanted to return to the South and appeared with a Yale Ph.D. in hand, he was turned down. He found a job teaching at Duke Divinity School and then went back to teach at Yale.

Albert Outler said: "I was very much at home at Yale; I still am. But not at home in the region—in the sense that the university and the divinity school and the churches were almost hermetically sealed-off compartments. This meant you had to vault a wall whenever you went from the university to the church and then back again. I thought it was possible in the South to work with church and university simultaneously."

This sermon probably was delivered when Outler was Yale's Dwight Professor of Theology, during the period when he longed for the South, where he could serve in a broader fashion. And eventually his desire was fulfilled when he moved to Perkins.

## *The Sermon*

*Lord, teach us to pray (Luke 11:1).*

There are two dubieties about the efficacy of prayer. The one, we might call the doubt of unfaith: the growing suspicion that prayer does not really change things—that in an orderly world natural processes follow their own laws, against which prayer is powerless; or that at best, prayer is a psychological help, a kind of autosuggestion that may improve our tempers and motives, but without objective efficacy. The other is what we might call the doubt of faith: that prayer is superfluous—that since God knows our needs and is benevolent, it is only vain repetition to rehearse them before him; or that it would be greedy to press for more.

Both these doubts, however different their grounds, have the effect of paralyzing the life of prayer and devotion. If prayer is impotent, obviously the impulse to pray will grow weaker. And if prayer is superfluous, the impulse to pray can be piously suppressed.

Over against these two dubieties of prayer, there are also two credulities. One is the credulity of faith: the simple confidence that prayer is something like a cosmic drink dispenser into which you put your money, select your potion, push a button, turn a lever, and there you have it—complete with the correct change. I have heard pious reports of miraculous answers to prayer that assume just such a simple division of labor. You send in your order, God fills it—making some allowances for items not in stock—and both parties are reasonably satisfied with the deal!

The other, we might call the credulity of unfaith. This is the naive belief that what we have, or what we are to have, depends solely—or at least primarily—on our own efforts, plus our efforts in enlisting the efforts of others in our behalf. But this simple confidence—that God is a heavenly Sears-Roebuck, or that he is a coach and we the star players—also leads to a paralysis of the life of devotion. To believe naively in our own power leads to the dreadful tragedies of titanism, wherein the strong or greedy overreach themselves and go crashing down in ruin.

What then is left? What can we pray for? Why pray at all? What *is* prayer? These are honest questions, real questions to all spiritually minded men and women. They deserve an honest answer. And there is an answer, a biblical, Christian answer. But it is an answer that can be understood only as people come to understand the biblical, Christian conception of God and humans and their right relations.

Luke 11:1 tells us of the disciples' request that Jesus teach them a prayer. Obviously they had prayed before and knew something about the life of prayer, but it was a common custom for famous rabbis to compose special prayers for their disciples—a sort of badge of their group devotion. Jesus responded to their request by composing a prayer, no single phrase of which is wholly original, and yet the whole of which is a perfect model for the right mood, the right motives, and the right aims of authentic vital prayer. Its text is preserved in Matthew 6:9-13.

1. *Our Father.* Not Cosmic Boss, not Cosmic Flunky, but Ultimate Reality, disclosed to us as personal, fatherly love and will. This is the atmosphere of true prayer in which we address our Creator, in whom we live and move and have our being, without whose prevenient grace and power no part of our existence has any meaning.

2. *Hallowed be thy name.* The first impulse of true prayer, once the atmosphere is set, is the same as the chief end of worship and Christian life: "to glorify God and to enjoy him forever." It is to recognize and acknowledge the Father-God as also the Holy One. There is, in all of us, a deep sense of the holy, and we never quite get beyond the power of responding to the holy in awe and self-critical awareness of our human needs and faults.

3. *Thy kingdom come.* As soon as the holy is identified, our right reaction is to submit our desires and motives to the judgment and will of the holy Father-God. God's kingdom is his righteous rule in our hearts and minds, and this is the first and last thing that all good prayer is about.

4. *Thy will be done on earth.* Here is where prayer turns into action, for it is God's mysterious purpose that his will be done on earth freely and with love.

5. *On earth as it is in heaven.* God's will in heaven is done in knowledge and in joy—not from fear or greed. And so it may be done by the faithful here on earth—in joy, in love, without fear or greed.

6. *Give us this day our daily bread.* Here is the knowledge of human need. *Daily bread* is a phrase that covers all material needs. It is proper and right to pray for what we need—now that we offer our prayer, and our motives for that prayer, to the judgment and wisdom of God.

7. *Forgive us our sin.* It is a natural thing to want forgiveness, but it ought always to be prayed for on the condition that we forgive others. This is a subtle transformation of the second half of our Lord's summary of the law. There it is: "Thou shalt love thy neighbor as thyself "—which means we cannot love our neighbor unless we have some sort of proper or undistorted love of self. We cannot give love until we have received it. Here forgiveness, the highest and most effective form of love, depends upon our giving it before we can receive it. The proper aim of prayer is reconciliation, breaking down the barriers that distort our relations with God, with others, and with ourselves.

8. *And lead us not into temptation.* This is a strange request because it has an unexpected assumption. Temptation here refers to undue testing, or a struggle beyond our strength. It is a proper item of authentic prayer that, while we acknowledge our limitations and the value of fruitful tension and striving, we also should pray for exemption from tests too hard for us to bear. But note that even here our prayer assumes God's wisdom in knowing better than we the limits of our strength and the uses of adversity.

9. *But deliver us from evil.* The Greek word for *evil (peirasmos)* means *ordeal,* a trial that would put faith at risk. This is not cringing, but an honest petition to be spared a test we might flunk.

Thus, here in Jesus' prayer, minus the doxology (which was added later), we have our first question answered. What can we pray for? *Anything* we deeply and sincerely desire. Can we pray for even selfish things? Yes indeed, just as long as we offer both our prayer and our motives in prayer to God for his judgment and answer. It is a natural instinct to pray for the health and well-being of our loved ones and friends; for food, shelter, and clothing; for guarding and guiding; for help and protection. But these are all, in a way, selfish prayers if only the petition itself is offered and not the motive. When our selfish concerns are withdrawn from the reach of God's judgment, then obviously we have a form of magic—low religion.

But if our prayers, our deepest desires, and ourselves, all are offered together to God, who knows our needs, we literally may ask what we will. And what is more, as we grow in the habit and temper of good praying, our own sensitivities grow and are sharpened, and our requests become more and more appropriate and moral and right.

But what good does prayer do? What does it accomplish? The first right answer is: Who knows? Prayer certainly is not a form of manipulation of God. And prayer certainly is more than mere autosuggestion. Prayer is the highest instance of this strange mystery of our finite freedom and finite power, set and operating within the parenthesis of God's infinite freedom and infinite power.

Prayer is a *sharing* of God's power, not a wielding of it.

> More things are wrought by prayer
> Than this world dreams of. Wherefore, let thy voice
> Rise like a fountain for me night and day.
> For what are men better than sheep or goats
> That nourish a blind life within the brain,
> If, knowing God, they lift not hands of prayer
> Both for themselves and those who call them friend?
> For so the whole round earth is every way
> Bound by gold chains about the feet of God.[1]
>
> —Tennyson

The truth is, we don't know a lot about how spiritual and moral effects are achieved in the natural world, or in the realm of persons. We know we are affected by the thoughts, the wills, the deep desires of others—certainly to the degree that we know other persons and are known by them. But our knowledge of other persons is limited, and we are known by a limited number of persons—and that always partially.

But what if there were an Infinite Spirit who was Creator and Sustainer of every finite spirit, who received and judged and, as it were, redistributed our aspirations and prayers—purged and refined—and who, in the life of prayer and devotion, was the immanent power and presence that received our prayers and mediated the prayers of others to us? Sounds mysterious and speculative, you say? Sure—but what we know about being a person and the effects persons have on one another is pretty mysterious, too—however well we may explain it at the empirical and psychological levels. One thing is clear. The causal order we observe in nature and the order of interpersonal relations are not completely identical. God is present in nature to give it structure and process—but God is present in interpersonal relations to supervise our use of our God-given powers of freedom and love.

What, then, does prayer do? Well, it does not affect the causal order of nature—not as such. Prayer that aims at rescinding natural law for private interest is unworthy and goes unanswered. But the prayer of faith opens up the channels of personal interaction between ourselves and God, God and ourselves, and ourselves and others—all in and through the active presence and power of God's Holy Spirit.

Christian prayer is *not* magic; it is our faithful communion with God-the-Father-revealed-in-Jesus-Christ-our-Lord-and-Savior. Such communion is sharing—and in sharing we project our sincere aspirations, and we receive new and usually disturbing light about our sins and shortcomings. In sharing we express our hopes and fears, and we receive the assurance that nothing that can befall us will separate us from the love of God in Christ Jesus.

In prayer, we do not inform God of what he does not yet know.

In prayer, we do not cajole God into doing what he is unwilling to do.

In prayer, we do not recite our wishful thinking as though it were an accomplished *deed*—or a daydream about the virtues of a never-never land.

In good prayer, we open our hearts to God, to whom all hearts are open. We make our desires known to God, to whom all desires and needs are known. With God, we can be honest and candid, because, even if our secrets are not hidden, we can be confident that God is neither shocked nor hostile in that knowledge of us.

There is a grand passage in Fenelon—one of the truly great masters of Christian prayer and devotion—that describes the mood and motive of true prayer:

> Tell God all that is in your heart, as one unloads one's heart, its pleasures and its pains, to a dear friend. Tell Him your troubles, that He may comfort you; tell Him your joys, that He may sober them; tell Him your longings, that He may purify them; tell Him your dislikes, that He may help you to conquer them; talk to Him of your

> temptations, that He may shield you from them; show Him the wounds on your heart, that He may heal them; lay bare your indifference to good, your depraved tastes for evil, your instability. Tell Him how self-love makes you unjust to others, how vanity tempts you to be insincere, how pride disguises you to yourself as to others. If you thus pour out all your weaknesses, needs, troubles, there will be no lack of what to say. You will never exhaust the subject. It is continually being renewed. People who have no secrets from each other never want for subjects of conversation. They do not weigh their words, for there is nothing to be held back; neither do they seek for something to say. They talk out of the abundance of the heart, without consideration, just what they think. Blessed are they who attain to such familiar unreserved intercourse with God.
>
> *(not cited)*

What then can we pray for? *Anything* we deeply desire—as long as we offer our prayers *and* our motives to God's wisdom and love. For our prayer is our communion with God, and its quality depends upon the quality of our faith in God. Thus we pray in the name of Jesus Christ our Lord. Amen!

Now a final word about the kinds of prayer. There are many kinds, and we are all prejudiced, at least a little, toward one kind or another. This shows how tempting it is to suppose that the human fashion of prayer affects the efficacy of prayer.

I happen to believe that forms, and even postures, matter in prayer—not because they affect God's willingness to bless us, but because we are creatures of matter, as well as of spirit, and that bodily forms affect the clarity and the purity of spiritual acts and aspirations.

But prayer is mostly a personal relation—and ought to be as constant, normal, spontaneous, and varied as the forms of creation and grace.

A wise disciple of Paul gave sound advice to young Christians about this: "I desire then that men should pray anywhere and everywhere, lifting holy hands without anger or competition" (I Tim. 2:8).

Lord, teach *us* to pray and, in our prayers, teach us the true meaning of faith and obedience, and endow us with the true blessings of wisdom and truth. This we pray in Christ's name and in his Spirit.

# 2

# *Our Hope for Years to Come*

## *An Introductory Comment*

This post–World War II sermon probably was preached while Albert Outler was at Yale, although it could have been later. It illustrates an important thesis for him: "Life in this present is life in the presence of God. . . . This is why we might speak of the gift of faith and grace as the *gift of time*—time to work, time to love."

In recognition of his stewardship of the gift of time, in 1985 Albert Outler was given an award for excellence in the area of religion. The *Dallas Morning News* reported: "Fourteen outstanding men and women will be presented the fourth annual Awards for Excellence in Community Service for their significant contributions to the quality of life in Dallas. . . . We salute the recipients for their energy and dedication to making this city a great place to live!"

We have disavowed any reliance upon history as predictive of the future—and will now disavow any reliance upon prophecy as a technical control of things to come. The future is as inscrutable as the past is irrevocable. Moreover, it comes upon us, rather than just waiting out there to happen.

The freedom *toward* the future, supplied by an intelligent freedom toward the past, is not a knowledge that any future can be manipulated. It is, rather, the freedom of anticipation—of looking forward to possibilities, not toward prescribed programs. "It is not for you to *know* the future times and seasons," said Jesus, at the same time the angel had encouraged the disciples to *expect* and *await* the Parousia.

Why does God let this or that happen? Why does God do this or that? Such queries have their counterparts in the questions of eschatology: What on earth is God up to? Will he allow a thermonuclear war?—humankind to perish?—redemption to fail? What is the shape of things to come—in America, or wherever? Consider the functions and the limitations of rational *foresight*—what goes into the making of an educated guess about the future? There is therefore a crucial difference between this and the conviction that our destiny is in God's hands and that underneath *are* the everlasting arms.

I will not argue the question of clairvoyance—neither in the Bible nor in contemporary soothsaying. There was a great deal of foresight among many of the prophets, but it was *human* foresight, human reflection upon the live possibilities present in any knowledgeable analysis of the future, in light of the determinate past and the indeterminate present. Those were moments of insight. But what is unique in the prophets was their awareness of the quality and aim of God's active presence in his creation and in history, especially within the inner dynamics of his people—his particular *laos.*

How then does the historian with a vivid sense of God's dynamic action in the hearts and wills of people, in the spiritual dimensions of history—how does that historian look to the future? What is an honest and faithful *expectatio?* "We *look forward (expectavimus—prosdekomenon)* to the resurrection of the dead and the life of the *kosmos* to come."

The life of faith is life in the mystery of each present moment—the *real* present, the present "distended" so that it is more than a crossover between the past and the future. Life in *this* present is life in the presence of God *(coram Deo),* "unto whom all hearts are open." This is why we might speak of the gift of faith and grace as the *gift of time*—time to work, time to love, time to live—the time of our lives. God is not absent from other times, but present in them *to us* as those times are re-presented to us in recollection *(memoria)* and expectation *(expectatio).*

Therefore, let us learn to view all times in the light of faith's living present, when God is self-disclosed in love; when we discover our real freedom and destiny, robbed of its terrifying uncertainty. "O God, our help in ages *past,* Our hope for years to *come.*" Remembered help and expectant hope are equally dependent on *living* faith; and this faith is, at every moment and at every point in one's lifetime, equidistant from eternity. James Montgomery's hymn is heretical—as well as psychologically wrong:

> Here in the body pent,
> Absent from him I roam
> And nightly pitch my moving tent
> A day's march nearer home.
> —James Montgomery

We are, of course, people forever on the move, *homines viatorum.* Life is a pilgrimage from the cradle to the grave, but the validation of our pilgrimage must inevitably come from the faith in which it is upheld and enabled. A high moment in life is not a Q.E.D. (*quod erat demonstrandum:* "That is what we set out to show and here it is") at the end of some time-span. This is the good essence in that fine old Methodist notion of the perseverance of the saints: "New every morning is the love; Our waking and uprising prove." Only thus can we face the tragedies of life with faith unshaken—the future with hope and confidence. Only thus can we enjoy God's provident bounty.

It is in the face of the future that we can see the lineaments of one's real reliance, measure one's specific gravity in the amniotic fluid of existence. Thus we must be ever mindful of: (1) the superficiality and irrelevance of "optimism" *and* "pessimism";

(2) the essential treason of any cry of doom, as well as the demonic character of orectic (wishful) thinking (e.g., "Ye shall be as gods," etc.); (3) any sense of safety in novelty, change, and the distractions of "progress"; (4) the paralysis of nerve and the desiccations of life; (5) the courage to live and to die, which comes from the acceptance of being in *God's hands,* at his disposal, and amenable to his purposes:

> Our shelter from the stormy blast
> . . . . . . . . . . . . . . . . . . . . . . . . . . . .
> Be thou our guide while life shall last,
> And our eternal home!
>
> —Isaac Watts

# 3

# *The New Commandment*

## *An Introductory Comment*

Albert Outler was a delegated observer at the Vatican II Council in Rome, Italy; this sermon was delivered at the English Methodist Church in Rome on December 1, 1963, the week after the assassination of President John F. Kennedy on November 22. It was an unedited handwritten copy, obviously done on the spot. The paper looked as though it came from a hotel writing pad.

When faced by the challenge of the moment, Outler used the "new commandment" in John 13:34. He had already found that text validated by several Roman Catholic cardinals and bishops. They had loved him as they were loved by Christ, and he had witnessed through their lives the truth of what he preached.

The temptation, however, was to love him because of his courtly manners and his charisma. People would follow him to restaurants just to hear him order from the menu in Georgia-accented Italian.

## *The Sermon*

My text is the whole thirteenth chapter of the Gospel According to John, plus three verses from chapter 15 (vs. 9, 12, 17). I presume to offer you so much Scripture in one gulp, in contrast to the small sips to which we are accustomed, because the Fourth Evangelist clearly thought he needed this much context in which to focus his awareness that Jesus Christ not only taught the primacy of love, but revealed himself as the dynamic source of love's power—of our power to love, the source of whatever serenity we may have.

If we study this chapter carefully and compare it with the first three Gospels, we get a most remarkable impression. This story of Jesus washing the feet of the disciples and making this action a paradigm of their relations toward one another, stands *here* precisely in the place of the accounts of the Last Supper in Matthew, Mark, and Luke. Like those accounts, it is placed just after the close of Jesus' public ministry and just before the climactic drama of the passion, death, and resurrection. Like those accounts, it records Jesus performing a symbolic rite and commanding his disciples to reenact it among themselves thereafter. Like them, it has a similar plot—the disciples are depicted as not really comprehending at the time what was going on. There is the same interweaving of the themes of Peter's big-hearted blindness and Judas's myopic bitterness. And finally, like them, the point of the whole text is the unfathomable mystery of God's love for both his inept and his rebel children—and the terms on which all of them may come to know what life is all about, or else fall prey to hollowness, demonry, or tedium.

Hear it, then, with ears open to a word from the Lord to you, here and now, and whatever future there may be for any of us. [Scripture passage read with emphasis.]

We may, of course, decide for ourselves how it happened that foot washing did not become a dominical sacrament. Or at least, we will be careful hereafter when someone says we Christians should take our liturgical cues from Scripture—and hence have only two sacraments, because that's all the Lord ordained! For the moment, though, I am willing to set *that* fascinating puzzle aside.

The other distinctive practical point to our story, of course, is the so-called *new* commandment: "A new commandment I give to you, that you love one another; even as I have loved you" (John 13:34RSV). This is obviously connected to John 15:9: "I have loved you as the Father has loved me." Here, then, is a dynamic linkage of the sources and channels of authentic love. We are to love as we are loved by Christ, who loves us as he is loved by the Father. This is the secret—not of the *idea of* love, but of the *power to* love.

It would have been perfectly natural for the minds of these men, when they heard the notion of a *new* commandment, to leap instantly to the *old* commandment—the commandment in Deuteronomy to love God with one's whole being, with the parallel commandment in Leviticus 19:18 to love one's neighbor as one's self. Jesus solemnly declared that on the combination of these two commandments (as in Matt. 22:34-40, Mark 12:28-31, Luke 10:25-28) hang all the Law and the Prophets—which is to say, all true religion and morality. The more critical among them must have asked themselves, What's new about *this* commandment? How does it differ from the *old* ones? That is still a good question, and its answer provides a basic understanding of the gospel.

The law of love is the law of life. There is no clearer or more profound truth than this. The world is perishing for want of love, and this has been so through all the muddled centuries of blood and glory that lie behind us. It has never been truer of any age than of our own era of "progress" and comparative affluence, in which demoralization spreads like a cancer through the various nations and cultures of the world—when virtue and self-discipline are sniffed at or despaired of by an age of antinomianism. The distillate of this ancient hatred finally condenses into an assassin's bullet that shatters the hearts of people of goodwill around the world and leaves us all with the horrid realization that hatred is the real alternative to love and community and social order. This is what all lovelessness was tending toward, was aiming at, all along.

Mrs. Outler and I are from Dallas, and we have lived for years in an atmosphere of rabid pressures from the far left and the far right. You would not know, at this distance, that there also has been a struggle within that atmosphere, a struggle against ideological terrorism—unremitting and fairly effective—and it has come from the universities, from the eggheads, from the large-hearted Christians and Jews. Integration was won for Dallas quietly. It was the one major city in the South that made the transition without disgrace. There is still a free university in Dallas—this against odds that some of our glib detractors have never faced, day in, day out, year in, year out. Just yesterday we received copies of two public statements from our university, one from its president, the other from the Theological Faculty to the Mayor. A paragraph from the first is worth reading here—so far from the scene:

> The bullet hit our President, but the rifle was aimed at our nation and the civilized world. It was aimed in hate and fear and lovelessness. Whoever aimed it had lost his faith in freedom—but he is a product of a demoralized community, here and around the globe. Indeed, our own lovelessness and bigotry helped aim that rifle and we ought to be sensitive to its horrible recoil against our shoulders.

But the mystery of evil consists in the shocking paradox that the love that is our only conceivable redemption in tragedy, in our inhumanity, in the equal horrors of wickedness and meaninglessness, is not to be had upon order or command. It does not follow as a consequence of the *opinion* that love is our highest good and God's summary imperative. We simply do not love others, or even ourselves, because we *ought,* because we are ordered to—not even because we know in our heads that it is a good thing to do.

This is the exquisite irony of a great deal of very high-minded, socially sensitive religion—some that goes by the name of Christianity. I've known people who try to love their neighbors (and others as well) by patterns of compulsive good will, the grim determination to love them no matter what. We know relentless do-gooders who serve the myriad causes of justice in self-righteous dutifulness ("radical obedience" is the current pious label). We know how they aim to carry out the reform program of the Magnificat on their own—"He hath pulled down the mighty from their seats, and exalted them of low degree" (Luke 1:52 KJV).

Now mind you, this is clearly on the right side of things—love is the first and the last commandment. The Leviticus understanding of our neighbors tells us they are due our love *on the ground* of our common humanity. This is elemental: It is the warp of all morality worth the name, just as righteousness is the woof of that same morality.

But we may even try to love on order, and fail. The *old* commandment to love comes nearer to bringing us under *judgment* than it does to cleaning out our hearts and restoring in our wills the power to love. Loving on order does not free us from self-deception. We may delude ourselves that we are loving, simply because we speak well of love.

Jesus knew this. And he knew that his abundant budget of high and valid moral teachings would be turned into one or the other extreme of works-righteousness—moralism, or what Wesley called "furious *solidifianism.*"

And so the new commandment is tied to an existential reality that the disciples knew at first hand—and that we, too, can know (albeit in a different way) at first hand: "Love one another *as I* have loved you"—as you have *been* loved, as I have been loved. The power to love comes from the knowledge of being loved—really loved: cared for, understood, provided for, disciplined, forgiven—not being possessed or patronized, not being managed or handled as a commodity, or a statistic, or as a "case."

One thing modern psychotherapists agree on is that this experience of being really loved is the shared basis of mental health, of personal self-understanding, of creative human relations. We all know this, more or less, and we all could give testimony to the various ways in which the love that has been given us is the stuff and energy of the love we have been able to give to others.

And so Jesus called on his disciples to love one another out of gratitude to him—and he gave them a sacramental demonstration to guide them. Here, in this faintly embarrassing act of footwashing (set as a sort of climax against the background of all they already had experienced of his love for them and for others) they could realize how truly his love was gracious, humble, confident.

He had made it plain that the primal source and energy of all love is God—that God's grace is God's love in human existence (that God's love in action is what we mean by grace, nothing less or more).

He made it equally plain that love does not work by merit, or rank its subjects in any sort of pecking order. Our Lord knew at least as much as any aristocrat about human inequality as a bare, irreducible fact: he refused to draw the false conclusion that some right of rank or place or status goes with either high or low degree.

So he washed Peter's feet and those of the others—and everybody felt as awkward as we would if we were about to do such a thing here and now. It is a great comfort for folks to have proper places (high or low), to stay in them, and to keep others in theirs. "But it shall not be so among you," he said.

The love with which Jesus loves us is a confident love. His incredible mission had been to call people into God's kingdom and prepare the way for the community of the church. Humanly speaking, his love had not achieved any remarkable results, nor could any have been predicted, as the odds stood just then. But he was supremely confident—and it turns out he was supremely right! And this has been the power of life in the body of Christ ever since: The unselfish, humble, confident love that comes from God is offered back to God in worship, and proffered to our neighbors in service.

Grace is gratitude, and the life of gratitude is the truly gracious life. Gratitude is the proper, right, real response to love, to our being loved by God and being blessed by God's love through the agencies and surrogates by which it comes to us.

And it has an inbuilt compass for life's direction, a sort of barometer to measure life's pressures (one that tells you whether the pressure is up or down), even though it does not always provide a detailed set of rules for this and that. To love as we have been and are being loved is to love unselfishly, which means to care and be helpful. To love is not to act on some broad principle, but to be a helpful resource in the presence of need. It is to love humbly, having the disposition to be glad when others have preference—not because of their merit or our demerit, but because in the long run, no one suffers from lovelessness who seeks the good of others. It is to love confidently, because the justification of love, as of life itself, is not in our hands or records, but in the hands of God, who *is* love and whose sovereign grace is the sole bulwark and redemption of all creation.

And so, benumbed and outraged as we are by the tragedy in Dallas, and fearful as we may be of what it portends, we can go on with our lives and tasks of loving—not as we *ought,* but as we already have been and are still loved—secure in our faith that "God is the ruler yet."

Even so, come quickly, Lord Jesus!

# 4

## *The Heart of the Gospel*

### *An Introductory Comment*

lb02602 This, the first of The Francis Sermons, was preached at Highland Park United Methodist Church in Dallas, Texas, on October 5, 1969, and also at The First United Methodist Church in Peoria, Illinois, on March 9, 1969. Albert Outler preached the good news that "God loves us in a very special way, and Christ is all the proof we need of it. *This* is the heart of the gospel."

Here Outler preaches as an evangelist. The biblically grounded, Christ-centered truth which he proclaimed made its way through him to the people.

He first preached this sermon in the worship setting in which he was most comfortable—a congregation in a university community. A faculty member who came to hear him that day said, "Al, that's better than you normally do!"

He said of Duke, the first university in which he taught, "I was there seven years—and those were my formative years. Our children, Frances Gertrude (Trudy) and David, were born there, and I came to realize that by nature and instinct I am a university man. I teach in the school of theology, but there has to be a context of a university."

## *The Sermon*

*God was in Christ, reconciling the world [and us] to himself (II Cor. 5:19).*

My purpose in this place is both audacious and quite simple: I want to talk to you about Jesus Christ—about his meaning for our lives and all human life. That is to say, I want to preach the gospel—the good news of what God in Christ has done and is doing; how God can make our lives truly and fully human. I want to talk about the Christian experience of new life in Christ and what that can mean to any and all who will hear and heed this good news.

There is a familiar closure to many ritual prayers in all the churches. It is the phrase, "Through Jesus Christ our Lord"—or some variant. It points to the fact that Christian prayer is rightly offered *to* God the Father *through* Jesus Christ the Son, *in* the Holy Spirit. My hope, in this sermon and those that follow, is that we will come to understand this phrase in a new and fresh way, so that when we hear it again it will have more meaning for us; and that it will seem natural and right to offer our prayers *from* our hearts *to* our God "*through* Jesus Christ our Lord."

We begin where everybody is today—in a world in deep trouble, shaken to its foundations, uncertain and fearful of its future. These are days of tumult and confusion—in the world, in the church, in our hearts and lives. Many of the old landmarks—of good taste, of social order, of customary morality and political harmony—have toppled or are toppling. Strange notions are being hawked abroad; every news broadcast brings some new alarm. Radical slogans fly about: "God is dead"; "the church is done for"; "sex is merely recreational"; "pot and LSD are good clean fun"; "everyone is free to do his own thing" (as Timothy Leary has formulated the heart of the "*new* gospel"). The news about "Alice's Restaurant" has finally reached *Newsweek* and *Time,* with both running the same feature story on youth and drugs.

The world is wracked by war; our cities are tinderboxes; the generation gap brings tragedy on all sides; the nation is being torn apart. We have lauded or excused violence; we are now being destroyed by it. We have lauded or excused "freedom"; we are now being drowned in the abuses of freedom.

Our splendid achievements in technology and business have generated our confidence that we can make ourselves secure. And yet, it is just this manufactured security that now is threatened, and we find ourselves doubly insecure. Every human advance we have made is vulnerable to misuse and corruption. What anyone can do can be undone, and much of it is being undone before our very eyes.

In such a time, the fearful withdraw, and the aggressive gird themselves for reckless battle. The rebels rush to extremes on opposite ends of the spectrum, freaking out with self-righteous hurrahs. The unthinking are baffled and bemused. Nobody at all sensitive can remain undisturbed. The anchors of faith and hope are dragged along in the hurricane of rapid social change. That ominous prophecy of Hebrews 12:27 is being acted out in these latter days before our very eyes: "Those things that can be shaken will be shaken, so that the unshakable may remain."

But what *is* unshakable? What will remain when these seismic shocks are over? Certainly we already know that much of what we took for granted as being as immovable as the eternal hills has turned out to be perishable and passing. Much of the old theology, the old mores of class and race and sex, the old pecking orders in national and international affairs, our old traditions of authority and civility—these are gone or are going. Worst of all, there are many who still identify these old familiar patterns with Christianity itself, and therefore assume—some in glee, some in grief—that with the passing of "the old regime" Christianity and the church are done for. What they ignore is that Christianity and the church have survived such crises before—some even more ominous than ours today.

Actually, of course, Christianity was born in crisis, in a vast upheaval of a world grown old—a time of frightful turmoil and anxiety, of confusion and alienation, startlingly like our own in many essential respects. Christianity survived the ridiculous odds against it—not because of its organization or its ritual or its theology, but chiefly by having and sharing its gospel, its good news about God and human destiny in the face of bad news. The Christians had a heart-lifting, mind-clearing, will-strengthening message: that God had done for them what they could not do for themselves. That is, God had taken the initiative in reconciling the rebellious, anxious, and uptight, bringing them into new relationships with himself, with themselves, and with others—a trustful, secure faith and life-style.

This gospel was preached and lived and proved in the experience of the little communities of Christians that dotted the map of the Graeco-Roman world.

The gospel, as first preached and ever since, has had a great many derivative ideas and satellite institutions added to it, which all too often have been identified with church authority. The first Christians developed visible structures, and those structures have gone on developing—necessary supports but also occasionally serious detriments to the gospel and to the Christian mission in the world. In the fourth century, for example, Christians accepted the union of church and state—then took fifteen centuries to discover what a fatal mistake *that* was. The gospel, from the beginning, has included both the vision of God on earth and also those practical programs which make Christianity applicable and effective in the world. It includes the high adventures of theological reflection and ethical insight. It entails all manner of outreaching endeavor in mission and service—all the good causes with which we are or ought to be involved—here in this church and in all the churches.

And yet in its final essence the gospel is none of these—not the church, not theology, not social action. It is, rather, an utterly personal, utterly simple, eternally true word from God to us: that God loves us—all of us—in a very special way; that he calls us to love him above all else and to love our neighbors as ourselves. And this word of God's special love is buttressed by the life and death and resurrection of Jesus Christ, the proof and demonstration of God's boundless love, the love that transforms and redeems. God loves us!—and Jesus Christ is his decisive revelation of that love. God calls us to love—and Jesus Christ is the decisive pattern of the way in which we can love. God's love was manifested in a human life—in the life of "the man of God's own choosing." It was revealed in a life like our own lives ought to be but are not—a life of faithful obedience and unmeasured love, of sacrificial death and triumphant resurrection, a life that now can be seen as the pivot and hinge of all human history, past, present, and future. This gospel of God's unfaltering, invincible love has a name (Jesus Christ), a date (the days of Pontius Pilate), a place (Palestine), a historical career (Jesus' mission in Galilee), a tragic death (Jerusalem), and a glorious victory (Easter and Pentecost). It was all very obscure, unimpressive, readily misunderstood and misinterpreted, and yet it has been utterly decisive—not only for the first disciples, but for all who thereafter have followed in their train.

This gospel of God's reconciling love, God's offer of reconciliation to us, God's invitation for us to be reconciled to him and to one another—"for us and for our salvation." This, indeed, is what salvation means: to live and work and prepare to die in God's felt presence, assured of his love and goodwill, prompted by *his* love to give loving devotion to others in their need. *God* loves you; God loves *you;* God *loves* you—and Jesus Christ is the proof of all this, no matter how you accent the sentence. Accept this love; be reconciled; live in reconciliation; live to reconcile others. It's as simple as that, as profound as that, as marvelous as that!

The gospel of Christ is intensely personal, and yet it is always aimed at persons in community. The first great event in Christian history was the gathering of the church, Christ's Body—a community of men and women whose love for God had been called out by the overwhelming demonstration of God's love for them. The first fruit of God's reconciling love was a new community of persons reconciled to God and to one another, a community of hope and security in God's love revealed in Christ.

Life apart from God is tragic and doomed to meaninglessness. Life on its own curves back upon itself in a self-centered circle. Life that is arrogant or anxious, that rebels against God's sovereignty, that dreads God's wrath, that tries to evade God's judgment or ignore his demands—life like that finally loses its sense of meaning and destiny. Life in defiance of God is the ultimate tragedy. Life apart from God is the ultimate loneliness. Life in disobedience to God is the ultimate evil.

The gospel is the good news that none of this has to be. None of it is what God intends for our existence. The gospel is the good news that God has acted in Christ to allow us to turn away from fear to faith, from guilt to trust, from anxiety to hope, from estrangement to reconciliation. Jesus Christ is the proof of all this. In Christ we are confronted with God—with the revelation of God's unmerited love and favor, with the demonstration in human history of God's upholding and sustaining grace. And yet also in Christ we are confronted with one of our very own humankind, one who has tested the heights and depths of human glory and despair, and has shown us that both are suffused with God's loving Providence.

In this twin miracle of the Word of God made flesh and dwelling in our midst, we find all the clues we need to the personal character of God and to the mystery of our own existence. As we live with Christ and learn from him, we come closer and closer to that full and joyous communion with God which gives us the energy of Christian dedication and the assurance of meaningful life. This, actually, is what Christianity is all about: life lived in utter trust that God loves us, just as we are and in spite of what we have been; in the trustful confidence that God really intends to give us hope and glory. Trying to live this wonderful good news in all of life's hard situations is difficult—too difficult indeed to manage on our own without the daily renewal of our faith, and this is what God gives us as we commune with him daily in trustful prayer, with open hearts. But this good news is still true, still the heart of the gospel, still our best hope in earth or heaven.

God loves us in a very special way, and Christ is all the proof we need of it. *This* is the heart of the gospel. But we can prove it also in our own hearts, in our own lives, when we open our hearts to love, to God's love; when we cleanse our lives of all conscious malice; when we reach out to share in God's good causes of love, justice, and peace in this world, now.

Christ is the revelation and demonstration of this marvelous mystery—in his life and teachings, in his death and resurrection, in his grace and continuing power to transform our lives—"For our high priest is not one who was exempt from our weaknesses and our sufferings, but was tested and tried [in his faith] just as we are, apart from mortal sin [which is no part of our human essence, either]. Therefore we can be confident and secure whenever we come to the throne of God's grace, and we can always be assured of mercy and help in every time of need" (Heb. 4:15-16).

> Almighty God, our heavenly Father, who of thy great mercy hast promised forgiveness of sins to all them that with hearty repentance and true faith turn to thee: Have mercy upon us; pardon and deliver us from *all* our sins; confirm and strengthen us in all goodness; and bring us to everlasting life; *through Jesus Christ our Lord. Amen.*[2]

# 5

# *The Table of Our Lord*

## *An Introductory Comment*

This "Table of the Lord" homily, heard on Worldwide Communion Sunday, October 5, 1969, was the second of The Francis Sermons delivered by Albert Outler at Highland Park United Methodist Church. He reminds his audience that just as Jesus, the Lord of Glory, is Brother to us all, so also are we all brothers and sisters in him.

"And so the memory of an ancient past becomes the means of renewing Christ's real presence in our midst—this is the essence of the Eucharist. *Here and now,* for *you and me*—the Lord of Glory comes to serve as Host."

This sense of communion is essentially the same as the one he feels in a favorite piece of music: "Fauré's *Requium* ends, not with the normal requium, but with the hymn of the angels, welcoming the soul into Paradise." Reflecting on that *Requium,* he added, "That's what I would want at my funeral!"

## *The Sermon*

A moving scene is depicted in two short verses in the fourth chapter of Luke's Gospel (vss. 40-41). This text has been turned into one of our most beautiful hymns—which, sadly, is unfamiliar to many, partly because there are so few *evening* services of worship anymore!

At even, ere the sun was set,
  The sick, O Lord, around thee lay;
O in what divers pains they met!
  O with what joy they went away!

Once more 'tis eventide, and we,
  Oppressed with various ills, draw near;
What if thy form we cannot see?
  We know and feel that thou art here.

O Savior Christ, our woes dispel;
  For some are sick, and some are sad,
And some have never loved thee well,
  And some have lost the love they had;

And none, O Lord, have perfect rest,
  For none are wholly free from sin;
And they who fain would serve thee best
  Are conscious most of wrong within.

O Savior Christ, thou too are man;
  Thou hast been troubled, tempted, tried;
Thy kind but searching glance can scan
  The very wounds that shame would hide.

Thy touch has still its ancient power;
  No word from thee can fruitless fall;
Hear, in this solemn evening hour,
  And in thy mercy heal us all.
—Henry Twells

This is Worldwide Communion Sunday, and in just a few minutes now, we will join with the rest of Christendom in celebrating it here in this church—yet another of the countless congregations throughout the world that today have done likewise.

This particular Sunday began some twenty hours ago at the

International Dateline in the western Pacific—and the earliest celebrations at the Lord's Table were in palm-thatched chapels in Fiji, Samoa, and Micronesia. Then, as the day fled westward round the globe, other Christians in other countries gathered in their churches to invoke the living presence of Christ in his sacrament and to receive his healing power in their hearts and lives—in Japan, the Philippines, Asia and Australia; in Turkey and Greece and Russia; in Africa, Europe, and the Americas—Christians of every race and color, of all languages, dress and custom, in every conceivable circumstance of life and fortune. Christians, as we know, are a minority in the world, but on such a day as this we loom larger than usual because of our self-conscious community, generated and sustained by this universal sacrament of God's love in Christ.

It takes no great imagination to bring to mind the wide range of differences in the form and manner of the eucharistic observances during this Worldwide Communion Sunday—different languages and liturgies, different doctrines and interpretations—and the sad fact remains that even on a day like this, we have not been able to bridge the chasm that still separates Christians at the holiest of our holies. Even so, there is a common experience in *all* these services—an experience we are about to share with those other Christians—a meeting with Jesus Christ at his Table, an experience of the renewal of the very essence of our Life in Christ, in the simple act of eating a simple meal together.

The liturgies that have been developed throughout the ages for Holy Communion are often elaborate, and the rhetoric of the prayers is often stilted and archaic. Some of us find the ritual and rhetoric truly meaningful and deeply moving; others do not. But the essence of it all is utterly simple: a bit of bread and a thimbleful of wine or grape juice, blessed in Christ's name, then shared by a group of people who bear Christ's name and thus, by Christ's promise, receive his real presence into their hearts and lives. When people share a meal, even the simplest meal, they are related to their host in a very special way. Here at the Table of the Lord, we too may be related to Christ in the Spirit by a special act of faith and hope—in a solemn, joyful, and mysteriously efficacious feast that feeds the hungers of our hearts.

Our sharing in this Sacrament is, in the first place, an exercise in memory: "Do this in remembrance of me." As the prayers are said and as the elements are passed and shared, our memories will turn back to that first Eucharist "on the night in which Jesus was betrayed," and also to the whole of his earthly life and ministry. We will recall the mystery of his birth and life and teachings; we will remember the strange and wonderful way he taught and lived out his message of God's sovereign grace; we will reconsider his distillation of the essence of biblical faith and ethics, his faithfulness under hideous pressure, his suffering and sacrifice on Calvary, his triumph over death. All this was far away and long ago—yet by the marvel of sacramental participation, here it all will be made freshly new. The revived memory of that strange man hanging on his cross—"for us and for our salvation"—does something to us if we are at all sensitive: Our hearts are stirred to guilt, and yet also to hope; our hearts are broken for our own sins and shortcomings, and yet also are healed by the vivid assurance here offered of God's *accepting* love, and of his *expecting* love as well. "Do this, in remembrance of me"—and as we do, Christ draws near in a truly personal and life-changing intimacy.

And so the memory of an ancient past becomes the means of renewing Christ's real presence in our midst—this is the essence of the Eucharist. *Here and now*, for *you and me*—the Lord of Glory comes to serve as Host; as the still and ever-living exposition of God's anguish for our sins and his strange way of dealing with us in our estrangements—from him and from one another. And in this presence, if we are fully and rightly aware of it all, the eucharistic miracle takes place. There is nothing magical or superstitious or even sacerdotal about it: Our words and actions will not *cause* the miracle to happen or prevent it. For the essential eucharistic miracle is the transformation of strangers into a Christian family, through their experience of community with Jesus Christ at the Table of the Lord. He is Brother to us all, and as we know him as brother, we know one another as brothers and sisters in him. Many of us scarcely know each other here in this church—and this will not change as far as outward reality is concerned. But if, as we pray and commune and receive Christ's living Spirit, we find ourselves more open to the fact that the strangers here are actually and truly our brothers and sisters—and that all those for whom Christ died, here and everywhere, are also part of our Christian family, then we must so act toward them, or else live out a lie and self-deception: What is this but a miracle, a life-transforming experience of love and the imperatives of love!

But the Communion does even more than recall the past and transform the present. It looks ahead to the future in hope and lively expectation. In a world like this, the future is bound to be fearful—and if our future hopes are pinned on what we can do for ourselves, our prospects are irredeemably tragic. Our only lively hope, in this world and the next, is in God, who created us in a love that will not let us go; who sustains us with a love that does not reject us even when we reject him—and that aims to bring us to full self-realization in communion with *him,* in this life and in the life of the world to come. This Sacrament is the token and pledge of that promise of God and of our faith in that promise. It is the means of grace by which our trust is renewed and our faith in God deepened and clarified.

Here then, we meet together at the Table of the Lord, with *Christ himself* as our healing host. Here we meet together in the train of millions of other Christians—with millions yet to follow us—to eat and drink, in celebration of what God has done for us and what he has promised still to do. Here we meet together in a simple ceremony of offering and sharing, to let these commonplace symbols of bread and wine manifest God's grace and our faith.

We will share in this token meal in the manner of many in the Reformation churches—that is, in the pews rather than at the altar rail. This custom may be unfamiliar to many in our Methodist tradition, but it has much to commend it in terms of convenience and economy of time. Besides, there is an important symbolic meaning in the act of receiving the elements from a neighbor and passing them on to another neighbor. In any case, of course, it is not the form that matters. We could even spill a tray of cups and no great harm would be done. What *we* do here is far less important than what *God* does here—and that depends more on his grace and our faith than on our ritual actions.

And yet those actions are psychologically helpful, and I earnestly hope that we attend to them closely and participate in them seriously. Let us listen to the words; consider the actions; open our minds and hearts to the healing, mending, reconciling, invigorating powers of the Spirit, who is abundantly here present.

Confident in our belief in this sacred memorial, this real presence, and this deathless hope, let us therefore heed and hearken to an ancient bidding that calls us to the feast—the invitation to prepare ourselves in repentance and confession for God's forgiving and healing love:

> Ye that do truly and earnestly repent of your sins, and are in love and charity with your neighbors, and intend to lead a new life, following the commandments of God, and walking from henceforth in his holy ways: Draw near with faith, and take this holy Sacrament to your comfort, and make your humble confession to Almighty God.[3]

# 6

# *Through Jesus Christ, Our Lord*

## *An Introductory Comment*

This homily, the third in the series of Francis Sermons, delivered October 6, 1969, best expresses Albert Outler's Christology:

"As we come to Jesus and seek to learn from him, we discover some strange effects he has upon us. He will not 'stay put,' at arm's length. We may try to hold him 'out there' and speculate about him—then, suddenly and somehow, the relationship changes, and *he* becomes the inspector and judge and assessor of *our* existence." The one appraised becomes our appraiser!

"In Christ's presence, we cannot remain neutral—he has a way of drawing us to the point of decision: for him or against him, for faith or against faith, for discipleship or for alienation."

As a willing participant seeking to learn more about Christ, Albert Outler is placed under his searching eyes.

Outler knows that he is known by Christ and accepted and loved by God. When asked how he would tell a child about the most profound truths of God, he said: "I would say, 'You are loved by God.' "

## *The Sermon*

The truth of Christ is as simple as the fact of love, but that, in itself, is an unfathomable mystery. Its meaning is therefore forever old and forever new, unplumbed and inexhaustible. It has been interpreted differently in different times and circumstances, but in every age the central fact has stood out above all theory, supreme above all rivals. Christ is and always has been, literally and uniquely, the man for all seasons: from the first century, Anno Domini, which saw the origins of Christianity and the church; from the second century, in which the gospel made its uncertain way among the Gentiles; through all ages past, in the present, and for all the ages yet to come. Our Christian confidence is forever focused in Jesus Christ—in his revelation of God's redemptive love, in his gift to us of a lively hope for human future.

"Yesterday, today, and forever"—this means that every "today" must try to understand and interpret the Christ of yesterday and look ahead toward Christ's coming in future glory. Christ is forever the same—it is our awareness and understanding of him that vary from time to time. It is the perennial task of the church to face the essential reality of Christ and to provide contemporary interpretations that will help make this reality as alive to us in our time as he was to those who knew him in the days of his flesh.

From the beginning, people have found the Christian message hard to believe and still harder to explain. Paul said, "We preach Christ as having been crucified, a stumbling block to the Jews and sheer nonsense to the Gentiles" (I Cor. 1:23). It is easy to understand why this should have been so. Jews were conscientious monotheists—they had come by their monotheism the hard way! To them the ascription of saving power to Jesus of Nazareth was bound to seem idolatrous; hence it was a scandal and offense to their faith in one God. The Gentiles, for their part, had no great trouble believing a doctrine about the divine presence in a human existence, but the claim that such a divine being had suffered an ignominious death upon a Roman cross was literally nonsense, like a four-sided triangle or a one-handed clap. It could not be! Therefore, it had not happened the way the disciples were telling it.

In the face of such incomprehension the Christians had to preach and explain their message about Jesus—God's Christ, our Lord and Savior, "the power of God and His wisdom." They had to demonstrate this gospel in their life together, as well as explain it to their critics. That is why the confession, "Jesus Christ is Lord and Savior to the glory of God the Father," is so absolutely basic, then and now. For if we sincerely believe in Jesus' Lordship and saving power, we then have a firm grip upon the christological *fact,* even if we lack a neat and tidy theory to account for it. In those early days, faith preceded understanding. And it still does.

The gist of the earliest understandings was that Jesus was a man of God's own choosing, the unique creation of a human self to mediate God's revelation and grace, a man who was God's Word (God's ordering influence) in an actual human life. To put it in a single phrase, as Paul did, "God was in Christ." This is to say that all of God that was relevant to the human situation of sin and estrangement was present and active in this man, Jesus of Nazareth. "God was in Christ"—not as a second god or demigod, but as God *himself.* There is but one God: the God and Father of our Lord Jesus Christ. This means at least two things: First, in Jesus of Nazareth, we have to do with the saving love and power of the one true and living God—no less; yet also, in the selfsame Jesus of Nazareth, we have to do with one of our own kind—a historical being essentially like ourselves. We who live in these later ages have as much access to the Christ-event as did the very first Christians, because we have the witness of those first Christians to the historical event and, even more crucially, to its perennial and personal meaning.

This explanation depends on an elemental Christian assumption: that Jesus Christ shares with God the Father in his ultimate mystery—for God's reality is a mystery beyond our final probing, no matter how ingenious. But equally real and important, Jesus also shares our own human mystery—for each of us is an unplumbed mystery. And so the formula arose in the creeds: "Of the very same reality as God himself; of the very same reality as we ourselves." In this double reality, so the Christian theologians came to say, there are two "natures," two energy-systems, two operations—one human, one divine—and these two operations or energy-systems constitute a single personal unity. Thus, in one, single, integrated person, there were two dynamic activities, divine and human, and the two must not be confused; they must not be switched around;

they must not be separated; they must not be divided. Within this broad frame of reference, Christian teachers may roam about in their reflections and speculations. They may formulate any sort of theory that fits these facts and their own Christian experience—and this is what they have proceeded to do in every age since. And this is what we are still doing in our current age of theological bedlam. The search for a sound doctrine of Christ in modern terms still goes on, the search for a theory to fit the data—data of the New Testament, of the Christian tradition, and of the experience of modern people in the modern world.

All too often, however, these modern images of Christ that successively 'modern' generations have turned up from time to time have been at utter variance with the character portrayed in the Gospels. There was, for example, the bloodthirsty Christ of the Crusades, who inspired two centuries of savage holy war. There was the schizoid Christ of the wars of religion in the seventeenth century—when in the name of Christ, Protestants and Catholics fought each other so fiercely that all Europe was reduced to a shambles, and sensitive men and women turned to secularism as a more humane alternative.

It is also important to realize that over the long pull, the predominant accent in Christian teaching about Jesus has almost always been on his *divine* nature, on the supernatural Savior, on Christ the wonder-worker. The humanity of the historical Jesus was rarely denied, but usually relegated to an inferior level. The image of Christ as prophet—his denunciations of the status quo, his call for social and political reform—was easily muffled by a society that preferred the church to serve as a pious prop for the feudal system. Thus Christ the King was identified with earthly pomp and power. The portraits of Jesus became more and more regal, more and more transcendent. This, incidentally, is what really accounts for the growth of the cult of Mary and the special role of the clergy as mediators between the faithful and the remote Christ. *They* had a sort of private, preferred access to this inaccessible Judge; they could get help from a forbidding, stern ruler, whereas the rest of us were excluded from any such intimacy. Thus began the system of ecclesiastical bribery and superstition against which the Reformation rose in wrath.

But then the tide turned once again as the medieval world gave way to the modern world in the eighteenth century. The key to this radical change was our new estimate of ourselves, our newfound confidence in the human prospects for the good life, achieved here and now by *human* effort.

Christianity, in reaction to the triumphs of the new secular humanism, found itself reemphasizing the *human* nature of Jesus once again—and then, with typical extravagance, running to the opposite extreme. We went back to the Gospel narratives to discover the *real* Jesus—the moral hero, the great Teacher of righteousness, who fused the quintessence of Jewish ethics and Greek wisdom into a religion of neighborly love—*The First Gentleman*, as Edward Everett Hale put it in the title of his book on the life of Jesus.

With this overemphasis on humanity came a shift in the liberal interpretation of human salvation. From the classical stress on justification by faith alone, liberal theology moved over to the opposite stress—salvation by way of our human imitation of the human Christ—adopting his faith in God as our faith and following his moral precepts and parables as our life patterns. These liberal images of Christ coincided with a great epoch of soaring hopes that inevitable upward progress would place us on the cosmic escalator—the last such epoch humanity has known!

But when those soaring hopes were shattered—as they have been by two world wars, a savage depression, and a world still in flames and with fresh torments—the christological pendulum swung back yet again; this time from the Jesus of history to the Christ of faith. This epoch of neoorthodoxy lasted a full generation, from about the time I entered seminary until quite recently. Now it is on the wane, and in its place has come, on the one hand, another wave of liberalism, and on the other, a new radicalism. The new liberals (Bultmann, Bornkamm, Pannenberg) have revived an interest in the historical Jesus in a very special form. For them, he is the human symbol of our open future before God, the psychological clue to a free faith in God's great love for us. In order to defend their view, they have felt themselves compelled to discard the otherworldliness in the traditional pictures of Christ. This they called demythologizing, which does not mean the denial of the *symbolic* truth of the otherworldly elements in the New Testament, but only of their *literal* truth in any strictly empirical sense.

To the left of these new liberals there is a yeasty group of radicals, ranging all the way from Jim Pike (of tragic memory) to Leslie Dewart, Harvey Cox, Tom Altizer, and Bill Hamilton. The importance of this group is the extraordinary furor it has generated—a very small spasm convulsing a very large body. Yet even in the midst of their attempted demolition of traditional Christianity, these people kept for themselves a shrine of reverence for the spirit of Jesus amidst the ruins. "God is dead," they say, but add that *Jesus* is still very much alive and relevant. This, incidentally, is a weird testimony to the unquenchable vitality of Jesus Christ—for today's "moderns" as well as for those of any age.

What with all this tide-turning and pendulum-swinging—in which the young are tempted to confuse the latest word with the *final* word—the task of the thoughtful Christian has continued to be what it has been all along: to keep a firm grasp on the fact of Christ as *God* and *man*, and then hang loose to all competing interpretations. The endlessly unfinished business of theology is to keep striving for balance—for synthesis, for integrity—for the *whole* picture of the whole Christ: divine *and* human; the Savior of mankind; the man of God's own choosing; our Brother who is also our High Priest, "touched by the feelings of our infirmity, tempted at all points as we are, yet without sin" (just as we ought also to be without sin). Our continuing task, as theologians, preachers, laity (that is, the people of God), is to go on probing and pondering our own experience of Jesus Christ, who reveals God to us, and who also reveals *us* to ourselves!

The baseline for every Christian confession that Jesus Christ is Lord and Savior is the recognition that, in and through Jesus Christ, we have to do with the living God. This means that however we stretch our minds, we are still dealing with the mysterious. Yet we also confess, on the warrant of the Gospels themselves, that in Jesus Christ we have to do with an actual historical man (not humanity in abstraction, but a human self actually like ourselves—a human being with a known and knowable character). And because he shared our nature, he is our best clue to the hidden mystery of that nature. To know him is to know more about ourselves than we could otherwise ever know.

The trouble with the classical theories that attempted to "explain" this paradox of Jesus the Christ was that the older theologians were stuck with archaic psychological models of human nature: the duality, or separation of the mind from the body, some notion of two levels of incarcerated spirit and sinful flesh. The higher, or spiritual, pole of the self, they called spirit; the lower pole, they called body—and then they identified "person" with the spirit. Thus, the "person" of Jesus Christ was considered naturally divine, and his human nature was thought to be without human "personality."

In the modern world, however, the word *person* has a very different connotation. It means the unity and identity of a whole human organism, held together in its uniqueness and integrity. The person is not a *part* of the human organism; it *is* that organism, as organized by the mystery of its personal *identity*. This identity has at least three focuses: social, psychological, spiritual—the person I appear to be to others, the person I appear to be to myself, and the person I am known to be by God. These focuses may be widely different, although in a perfect human being in a sane society, all three would coincide.

In the case of Jesus—and this, again, is why the Gospels are so important to live with, not just to pick at—these three focuses of his human selfhood *did* coincide: (1) what he was to his more perceptive disciples; (2) what he understood himself to be; and (3) what God meant for him to be and do. The New Testament gives us some impressive testimony about his "social" self—his disciples and at least some of his enemies recognized him as a teacher of righteousness; as the herald and inaugurator of God's kingdom; as God's Suffering Servant; as a prophet of justice and mercy; as one who went about doing good, seeking not his own salvation, but that of others. They were aware of him as a man deeply at one with himself and with his heavenly Father; a man who was genuinely free and open; a man capable of mature love, who could affirm and uplift others without ignoring their defects and shortcomings. In this sense he was a whole man, living and moving and having his being in God—and this came through to those who knew him best.

But he was more—and herein lies the mystery of his divinity. We begin to understand this when we realize that *all* God's creatures, in their inmost depths, are accessible to him, since he has invested us with our inner secret identities. God's presence in a human being does not curtail or abrogate his human identity. Paul could say in all sincerity, "I live and yet not I—Christ lives in me!" (Gal. 2:20). All that we are, all that we have, all that is most uniquely our own—our identity, our freedom, and our capacity for love—all these are gifts from God, and all are perfected more truly in his presence than in his absence.

There is, therefore, nothing absurd in the notion that God, of his own free counsel and love, elected to create a particular human being to be the revealer of his reconciling love, the herald of his humanizing kingdom. In the very act of becoming a human being, Jesus was the Word of God—and that Word was the infinite axis of his finite human self. This was a unique event—and yet it was universally relevant to the whole human enterprise, everywhere and for all time.

This assumption of humanity occurred at the very junction point of time and eternity, finite and infinite. Never was there a time when Jesus Christ was not, for the Word is eternal. And yet there *was* a time when his historical identity first became known and his human character as a prophet and moral exemplar made its first impact on his first disciples. He who is our Lord and Savior is also our Brother. He who is God is also the God-*man*, "our only mediator and advocate"!

As we come to Jesus and seek to learn from him, we discover some strange effects he has upon us. He will not "stay put," at arm's length. We may try to hold him "out there" and speculate about him—then, suddenly and somehow, the relationship changes, and *he* becomes the inspector and judge and assessor of *our* existence. From the one whom *we* appraise, he becomes *our* appraiser! We inquire of him about his opinions and teachings, reserving the right to decide for ourselves whether they are acceptable or true—then, suddenly and somehow, this relationship of inquiry is turned about and he becomes "the way, the truth and the life" for *us.* We look to him as exemplar—then discover that he is pointing us past himself to God, with the demand that we put God's kingdom and his righteousness above all else in life or death. We acknowledge *his* perfection—then discover that he is confronting us with God's demand for *our* perfection—yet also offering himself as the means of grace whereby we may seek and expect that perfection in this life! We find our hearts moved with compassion in the presence of his passion and death—then discover he is redirecting our compassion toward the sufferings and needs of others, *here* and *now*. In Christ's presence, we cannot remain neutral—he has a way of drawing us to the point of decision: for him or against him, for faith or against faith, for discipleship or for alienation. This is the way he challenges us with God's sovereign righteousness and reveals to us our own freedom to share in, or to resist, God's wisdom and power and love. Baron von Hügel put it better than I can:

> For a Person came, and lived and loved, and taught, and died and rose again, and lives on by His Power and His Spirit forever within us and amongst us, so unspeakably rich and yet so simple, so sublime and yet so homely, so divinely above us precisely in being so divinely near . . . that His character and teaching require, for an ever fuller yet never complete understanding, the varying study, and different experiments and applications, embodiments and unrollings of all the races and civilizations, of all the individual and corporate, the simultaneous and successive experiences of the human race to the end of time. (*not cited*)

# 7

# *Christ in You, the Hope of Glory*

## *An Introductory Comment*

This is another of The Francis Sermons, preached on October 7, 1969. It deals with the mystery of God's selfhood as revealed in Jesus Christ, and with the mystery of human selfhood, also revealed in Jesus Christ.

Outler says, "When we try to probe more deeply, we run into infinite regress: Where, what, and who is the self that is appraising the self, and who appraises *that* self, and so on and on? All these selves are *one* self (if we are at all healthy and whole)—and the inmost secret of that one self is never really intelligible until we recognize the whole as a specific creation and project of God."

In a special way, this sermon helps us see Albert Outler as graceful while he preaches *God's* grace.

That quality accounts for the manner in which he helped break the barriers of racial segregation in Dallas in the 1950s. He did not threaten, twist arms, or harangue the community to accept social change. His way was not coercion, but persuasive graciousness.

## *The Sermon*

*Christ in you, the hope of glory (Col. 1:27).*

Everywhere we turn in the New Testament, the question that preoccupies the writers is the meaning of Jesus of Nazareth—for the human situation and for their own self-understanding. They all agree that this is the heart of the Christian message, and so they tell their stories and spin their theories with a common intention—to show that Jesus is the supreme clue to the divine mystery, and to the human mystery as well.

One of the most interesting of these theories shows up in Colossians. Here Paul, or whoever wrote the epistle, is talking about his own ministry and mission in the world—"to disclose God's secret, which he had withheld for long ages and through many generations, and now had disclosed to the world in Jesus. The secret is this," he says. "Christ in you, the hope of glory" (Col. 1:26-27).

This does not mean God had been playing it coy, but rather that he had preferred to let history unfold until there came a favorable time for both Jew and Gentile to receive the special news of God's personal love, come to life in Jesus. It is this special, personal love that the author speaks of as God's *mysterion,* "secret," "mystery," "unfathomable reality." The premise is that God, in his inmost being, is unknown and unknowable. "No man has ever *seen* God." He is not available as an object of knowledge or sense experience; he cannot be handled or harnessed by anyone. This truth about God helps us realize that *all* our material images of him are symbolic and nonliteral. It reminds us that such images and symbols are all too readily turned into false theologies about Zeus or Jupiter or "the Man Upstairs," the heavenly Spook who is a composite of our own wishful thinking. And so the mystics, in all religions and in all ages, have devoted themselves and called others to the search for pathways that lead beyond the boundaries of sight and sense, into the depths of God's hiddenness. They have told us that God is truly present in our lives, but never accessible for our manipulation. Their aim has been to uncover God's secret, to achieve real and abiding union with him.

Over against the mystics, but with similar motives, the

philosophers also have been concerned to probe into God's secret—his inner nature, his purpose and will. Most of these, until recently at least, have acknowledged the reality of the divine, the absolute, the ground of being, or whatever. But rational analysis, however skillfully or stubbornly pursued, never has gained access to God's *personal* reality.

As far as God's personal character and purpose are concerned, therefore, the philosophic quest has proved less fruitful than its devotees have hoped or promised. Our wisdom, however profound, is forever falling short of the hopes and hungers of our vision and intuitions. The energy of the philosophic quest comes from the eternal restlessness in the human heart, but it never quite succeeds in bringing that heart to the rest in God, which, Augustine taught us, it was made for. The reason for this is simple and basic. Philosophy is an enterprise of reason without the benefit of revelation—the venture of autonomous seekers on their own, using their rational powers to stalk God as if he were fair game for the human intellect.

Besides mysticism and philosophy, there are still other forms of piety and religiosity that seek God's secret—often with the claim that they have found it. God is thought by all too many to be accessible to magic formulas, to ritual and rune and religious observance. Churchgoing, church tending, generous support of religious causes—all these and so many others are the different ways by which they hope to harness God to their human wagon, to exploit his grace for their own selfish ends.

Against the subtle tactics of the mystics and the philosophers and the not-so-subtle movers of the superstitious, God's real secret has been "hidden"—from "the ages and the generations" and from the religious quests of humankind. In this sense, our *self*-directed spiritual quest is always tragic, because it is always unavailing. Our unredeemed religious imagination dreams up many versions of God's secret: that he is terrifying, implacable, jealous, cruel, and so is to be appeased; or else greedy and vain, open to bribes and wheedling; or else impersonal, aloof, indifferent, leaving us in desperate loneliness.

Many so-called modern observers have taken note of the problems and doubts of popular religion, of mysticism and philosophy. They also have been unfavorably impressed by the savage rancor with which *religious* debates are generally conducted (and as we know too well, these often are more uncharitable than those of politics). Many of our modern skeptics have drawn two correlative conclusions from the doubts and bad manners of Christians: (1) that the truth about God is that he just simply isn't there, after all; and (2) that in any case, what really matters is our self-concern and what we can do on our own. As for God, forget him—instead, concentrate on ourselves, on the *human* "secret."

And so we have a spate of studies about human nature and the inner secrets of personal existence—from psychology, sociology, anthropology, and so on. There are many interesting new books and articles on the topic of what makes us distinctive; what sets us off from apes, on the one hand, or computers, on the other (Mortimer Adler, Arthur Koestler, Gordon Allport, et al.). New ideas are abroad about the correlation of personality with the biochemical reactions in the human bloodstream.

Freud dismissed the quest for God's secret as "wishful thinking" and then failed to solve the *human* secret. His theory about the human unconscious and its inner dominance of our personal lives has proved illuminating and fruitful in many ways in modern psychology and medicine. And yet, quite clearly, this is not the whole story, and certainly not its vital core. As time has passed, the Freudian account of the human secret has come to be less certain and satisfactory.

Consequently, other efforts have been, and are being, made to decipher the coded secrets of human existence. What does it *really* mean to be truly *human?* And the blunt truth becomes plainer every day: The more we have learned about ourselves—our biopsycho-sociopolitical processes, our motivations and goals, our quests for identity—the less we really know about our inmost personal character.

Sooner or later it may dawn upon us that the human secret also has been hidden from the ages and generations, that it is very closely correlated with God's secret. More and more we are coming to realize that we cannot *locate* the human self; there just isn't any *where* inside the body that the self can be located as a thing—and obviously, no place outside the body, either. But this implies that if the human self exists at all, it does not exist in space, or in time, or in the causal order—and this is a very strange and awkward conclusion. Something obviously is wrong here. But we rarely notice that this same logic is often used to deny God's existence, since he does not exist in space, or time, or the causal order, either. And so one wonders why people who believe in their own existence (as deeply mysterious as *that* is) have such trouble acknowledging God's existence; the arguments are analogous in both cases.

My point here is that we are beginning to realize, more forcibly than ever, the genuinely mysterious character of the reality in which we exist and participate. In other words, we can recognize that God has a "secret" and that it affects our own "secret"—the quality and meaning of our own lives in *thei*r inmost depths. This mysterious reality in which we live and move and have our being is utterly opaque to mere curiosity and reason. If we are to know what God is like, in himself and in his personal character, it has to be by his action (which is to say, by revelation). Our knowledge of God comes to us, if at all, through insights we can receive and appropriate, but never control or command.

This is why the claim in Colossians that God's secret is "out"—in Jesus Christ—is so extraordinary and yet so decisive. It does not mean God has been playing games with his human children and finally has let a selected group of them win at the game of blind-man's-bluff—or that, before Christ, or apart from Christ, we have been deprived of real and saving knowledge of God. The claim of Christianity is not that Christ is God's *sole* revelation, but that he is God's *supreme* revelation—the manifestation in a human life of the mystery of divine love. Christ is the revelation that reveals the truth and import of all other divine revelations, whenever and wherever. The tremendous truth about Christ is that he is God's *open* secret, God's *self*-disclosure of his special love for humankind, the unique revelation of God's purpose to lift us from our preoccupation with self and existence into actual and authentic communion. Christ is *in* us—God's personal quality of truth and love is actually the inmost reality of our lives. Rightly and properly, therefore, Jesus Christ is the clue to our own identities. He is our real hope of glory—in this world and in the world to come. God's love in us, sustaining and suffusing our lives and our power to love and to live graciously—this is God's open secret; this is our newly revived hope.

All religions are concerned with human communion with God and the meaning of that communion for the quality of human life. This is, in fact, a definition of religion—the human concern for quality of life in light of our relationship to God, and vice versa. Some religions conceive this communion to be coexistent and coextensive—the human spirit is simply the visible surface of the infinite divine Spirit, in which all individual spirits subsist. This is the worldview of pantheism—and it turns inward to discover the Eternal, the Absolute, the Buddha, as the actual *ground* of personal existence. This is the essence of Buddhism and of Hindu mysticism—the sort of thing the Maharishi Mahesh made popular in this country a year or so back. But the fatal defect in all such identifications of the human and the divine is that they tend to humanize the divine more decisively than they succeed in divinizing the human.

There are other religions that think of communion with God in animistic terms—a little spook inside the human skin, a spark of the Great Spook in the sky. Halloween is more pagan than Christian, and Linus' Great Pumpkin still fascinates more people than will admit it. I know a psychiatrist, for example, who says he believes in witches and warlocks—and it is not at all clear that he is merely spoofing! But *this* sort of religion has two mortal faults: (1) It is essentially terrifying, and thus incurably harmful to any possibility of its devotees ever becoming fully human and humane—the human heart never flowers in an atmosphere of terror; and (2) it is now psychologically incredible—we moderns are haunted by mystery, but no longer by spooks and ghosts, and no doctrine of God as the Great Spook can possibly raise and nourish human hope, in our time or tomorrow.

The two other great monotheistic religions, Judaism and Islam, also stress communion between God and the human being as the heart and soul of true spirituality. And their great contribution to our religious understanding is their passionate aversion to any mislabeling of the human or the creaturely as "divine." Both have an innate dread of idolatry—the worship or absolutizing of *any* creature or created thing—and both have much to teach us Christians, who consciously reject idolatry but are, nevertheless, more readily tempted to fall victim to it. Judaism knows God's secret in its ethical and communal concerns. It knows that God is living and loving, present and provident—but the mystery of his *personal* self-disclosure in human history is more inferred than incarnate.

Thus we come back finally to Paul's fascinating notion that God's real secret is *"Christ in us"*—the very essence of our own personal identity. Both God's secret and the human secret are disclosed, together, in Jesus Christ. This means that Christians' communion with God is so complex and inward and continuous that the human condition itself is two-natured—with the divine Spirit truly present in our personal experience, without confusion or identification but also without separation or division. To those who open their hearts to Christ's Lordship and spiritual presence, he becomes an actual "second nature"—an energy-system that focuses and sustains their own human identity in all its projects, as these are directed toward their proper ends.

Who *am* I? This vogueish and introspective question has, nevertheless, a real meaning and urgency for men and women who live now in massed populations, with faces and numbers and names, but no clear identities. Who *am* I? There are all sorts of preliminary answers—the data on my birth certificate, passport, and, eventually, my obituary. There are biological factors to be included, too, and psychological and sociological. There are the accidents of birth and rearing—when and where and with whom I have been associated, and under what circumstances. All these are factors that help identify me to you—or you to me, and so on. And always there is more: There is something deeper, more elusive, impossible to define yet equally impossible to ignore. The self does not exist as a separate entity, but as the integral whole of several correlated focuses of personal activity.

There is, first of all, the physical organism (the body), and it has a decisive role in affecting a person's identity. There is also the *social* self—the self as I am seen by others, the self according to my reputation among those who know me. But that, as we all know, is not the whole story about the *real* self. Reputation and reality are never quite identical.

But when we try to probe more deeply, we run into an infinite regress: Where, what, and who is the self that is appraising the self, and who appraises *that* self, and so on and on? All these selves are *one* self (if we are at all healthy and whole)—and the inmost secret of that one self is never really intelligible until we recognize the whole as a specific creation and project of God. This is why I believe that, at bottom and in the depths of self-consciousness, our identity is not the product of biological and psychological processes after all. Each of us is, rather, a specific creation (or creative act) of God. Each inner self is God's own special project, the unique individual one is and was meant to be. This relationship to God is what really sets us off in decisive contrast to all other animals and all other machines. And this reality of God's love in us is truly our "hope of glory."

The word *glory* here may need a comment. In ordinary English it means "an exalted status or distinction bestowed by common consent"—and it has something of the connotation of the heroic or the supernatural. Sometimes it refers to heaven (as in the phrase "gone to glory"). Many people have supposed that our hope of glory must mean our hope of heaven bye and bye. But the Greek word *doxa* is far more mundane and commonplace: It means something that has achieved its proper and full realization; something at its best. This what we mean when we speak of a glorious day or the glory of spring—when nature is at her finest. When a person says, "It was a glorious experience," we understand that what happened was just as it should have been. And so, in terms of our own existence and destiny, our hope of glory is the hope of being, for any given time, place, and experience, as fully human and intelligible and helpful and loving as possible. And this extends to the whole of life—our hope that in the end it will have been true that, on balance, our lives have been more glorious than shoddy. "Christ in you, your hope of glory" means that any such hope depends—not upon our luck or efforts, our talents or our powers—but on Christ-in-us.

Christ in us is our hope of maturing into beings that are fully human men and women, at whatever age, here or hereafter. What this maturity means is that our human struggle may be endured and enjoyed even as we engage in it, if we are aided and sustained by the vitality of Christ's love, which cooperates with all our human energies. Nothing in this cancels or compromises the human struggle. Life continues to be a struggle to the end—for the venture of being human is the venture of using all our powers and talents, and of having them used up in meaningful service. That, too, is where our glory lies, and this is what glorious living amounts to.

Here, then, is our highest human hope. And we actually have seen it at least partially realized in the best people we have known. I think of my own select company of heroes and heroines, mentors, and exemplars, friends and colleagues, and some of my students. There were and are men and women who are undeniably human, undeniably individual and personal, and whose lives are radiant with a power and a disposition to love and to work, to suffer and to endure, to share and to enjoy life. And this unpompous, unself-conscious disposition to live graciously from an inner grace is surely their very own, but also, just as surely, not merely their very own. They live by grace, by God's gift of love and blessing; they live by the Christ within them, their hope of glory.

Thus we, too, can come to recognize and celebrate God's open secret: the indwelling Christ in human hearts. This is God's secret: the power to live in love, in joy, in hope!—and all this to the end that our lives may be whole and actually human and helpful and glorious. This is the foretaste of the fullness and glory of life eternal. This is his offer and his promise. This is our hope of glory. And the constant and final purpose of it all is, as Paul says,

> that our hearts may be strengthened and our lives may be knit together in love—all this in order that we may share with others the riches of a full understanding of the *mysterion* of God, revealed in Christ, in whom all the treasures of life's wisdom and knowledge are both hidden and yet also made manifest. —Colossians 2:2-3

Thanks be to God!

# 8

# *John Wesley—Then and Now*

## *An Introductory Comment*

At First United Methodist Church in Dallas, on November 8, 1970, Albert Outler brought John Wesley out of the past. What Wesley believed and taught can best be learned through his sermons.

Outler says: "It is important to realize that he chose *sermons* rather than any *creed* or *confession* as his standard or pattern for doctrinal teaching. Sermons have a very different form and function from creeds, or confessions, or tomes, or systematic theology. And if we study Wesley's sermons, we will discover a clear concept of Christian truth and life, in spite of their deliberately unsystematic style."

What Outler discovered about Wesley's sermons can be applied also to Outler's sermons—we learn about the man through what he preaches.

A farmer in a rural church, after hearing Outler preach, said, "Brother Outler, you don't have to teach. You've got the makin's of a durn good preacher!"

## *The Sermon*

Two hundred years ago today, John Wesley was writing his memorial sermon for the funeral of George Whitefield, to be held in Whitefield's "temple" on Tottenham Court Road in London. The temple is up the way, a couple of hundred yards or so, from Oxford Circus. Wesley and Whitefield had known each other since their student days at Oxford. John had been in Christ Church; Whitefield, across the street in Pembroke College. Both were charter members of the Holy Club—the original "Methodists" with their program of daily prayer and Bible study, rigorous self-discipline, and unselfish service to the sick and outcasts of society.

Then forty years later, Whitefield was dead and John Wesley, sixty-seven, was at the height of his career as leader of the Methodist Societies—the fair harvest of a revival that had begun thirty years before in Bristol and London.

It was altogether fitting for Wesley to preach at Whitefield's funeral, for Whitefield had, in a curious way, shoved John Wesley into his belated career as evangelist. It is not always remembered that if John Wesley had died before April 1, 1739, he scarcely would have rated a footnote in the history books, and the Methodist movement never would have survived the episodes of evangelical zeal on the part of the handful of exciting preachers such as Whitefield. Whitefield had, in fact, launched the revival in England while Wesley was still languishing in a sort of underground church (a "religious society"—an "Anglican for Church Renewal" kind of thing!) in Fetter Lane in London—a cozy, ineffectual affair. Whitefield, however, was then involved in a much wider and more popular operation in Gloucester and Bristol, but had a return engagement in Georgia and invited Wesley to pinch-hit for him in Bristol. But John was horrified at the thought of going out into the streets and preaching to an unwashed mob of miners and day laborers—the eighteenth-century equivalent of hard-hats! But that is the way he really got his start.

Thereafter, their ways had parted over doctrine—specifically, the doctrine of predestination. George Whitefield believed that God's sovereignty required, as a corollary, the divine predetermination of the destiny of every soul. John Wesley believed in the sovereignty and freedom of God, but felt very strongly that this sovereign God had provided us with finite freedom and that there is a mysterious interaction between God's initiative in *grace* and our response in *freedom.* He was willing to tolerate the doctrine of predestination—barely!—as long as it was held and preached *as an opinion.* But Whitefield regarded it as an essential doctrine, and Wesley quickly turned against him in a fairly savage sermon entitled "Free Grace"—to which he added a long denunciation in verse, "The Horrible Decree," written by his brother Charles.

But by November 8, 1770, all that was "long ago and far away." Whitefield and the Wesleys had been reconciled after a fashion, but had continued on parallel courses rather than as partners. Whitefield was actually regarded as a more eloquent and compelling preacher, and he had a wider range of influence among the nobility and the wealthy middle-class. Yet Whitefield is barely remembered, while the work and legacy of John Wesley are still with us after all the changes and chances of the last two centuries. Why?

For three reasons, at least. First, of course, was John Wesley's genius (belatedly discovered and exploited) for organizing and directing a network of "societies" and "classes" for his converts all over England, Ireland, and Wales—thus providing a social and cultural context for their "personal religion." George Whitefield and the other revivalists of the time preached to excited crowds and had thousands of conversions, but when the excitements cooled, the effects wore off and not much remained by way of social and moral reform. John Wesley, on the other hand, bound his converts into close-knit groups, with local leadership and new opportunities for participatory democracy, and in an ongoing organization capable of self-directed mission even in his absence (and all of this despite the fact that John was a born martinet).

Allied with this was the peculiar sense in which John Wesley was a social revolutionary. And it *was* peculiar, by the terms of current liberal or left-wing rhetoric. For Wesley was a staunch conservative in politics, economics, and by personal temperament—a Tory, a royalist, a vigorous critic of the American Revolution—the whole conservative bag! And yet no man during that century, including Jefferson and our other founding fathers, contributed more to the image of truly free people, *under God.* In Wesley's preaching, common folks heard of God's sacrificial recognition of their human reality and potential for perfection; in Wesley's societies, they found status, dignity, and the healing experience of being regarded as truly significant in their own right.

And this was revolutionary in actual social fact. It was the Methodist lay people—and lay pastors—who, more than any other group in Britain, reversed the trend toward anarchy and corruption in eighteenth-century England—chiefly because of their newfound *dignity* (sense of worth), their assurance of God's gracious and concerned evaluation of them in Christ. They emerged as a new class in English society, and they provided the moral, economic, and political muscle needed for social reform in the nineteenth century (e.g., the general franchise, trades unions, the abolition of slavery, prison reform, civil rights, etc.)—social reforms that made nineteenth-century England *relatively* Christian and humane, as compared to any *previous* age, or any *since then,* for that matter.

Then in the third place, there was John Wesley's distinctive message about God and Christ and people, about the imperatives and possibilities of the Christian life. Actually, he opposed predestinarianism because of his fear that it would encourage Christians to be less strenuous morally and psychologically—and this he abhorred, along with his other pet peeves, antinomianism and formalism. We have lost sight of the General Rules—for instance, that vivid passage in Rule 2: that we are to trample "under foot that enthusiastic doctrine that 'we are not to do good unless *our hearts be free to it*' " (i.e., until we feel good and ready, emotionally and subjectively!).[4]

John Wesley summed up his distinctive doctrine of cooperation between God and man in sermons, and it is important to realize that he chose *sermons* rather than any *creed* or *confession* as his standard or pattern for doctrinal teaching. Sermons have a very different form and function from creeds, or confessions, or tomes, or systematic theology. And if we study Wesley's sermons, we will discover a clear concept of Christian truth and life, in spite of their deliberately unsystematic style. It might be worth *briefly* summarizing the forty-four standard sermons here.

In the beginning, *faith*—since faith is the threshold and

foundation of all else in the Christian life. Wesley speaks everywhere of the primacy of faith, of the terms and conditions of faith, of the prevailing misconceptions and corruptions of justifying faith, of the relation between justifying faith and actual righteousness. The first five "standard sermons" are devoted to *faith.*

But faith must strike root in the heart—and so Wesley follows his opening quintet on justifying faith with a second cluster of sermons that expound his novel doctrine of Christian *assurance:* "The Witness of the Spirit," "The Circumcision of the Heart," "The Marks of the New Birth." Here he defines this vivid, inward sense of God's accepting love as "Christian experience," a too-narrow concept that was to be qualified later on.

His next step is to link God's *accepting* love with *expecting* love, for faith must be fruit-bearing; one's desire for salvation must produce visible evidence if it is to be credited as sincere. So Wesley turns to an extended exposition of Christ's Sermon on the Mount (13 sermons in series), plus a three-part essay on "The Original, Nature, Property, and Use of the [moral] Law." This particular series (16 sermons in all) is the largest single block of integrated material in the entire sermonic corpus—witness to the fact that the question of Christian behavior in response to God's grace is utterly crucial in Wesley's understanding of authentic Christianity.

Having put faith and good works into vital balance, Wesley then raises the tricky question of the boundary lines between a Christian's proper zeal in gospel witness and the invalid extreme of "religious enthusiasm." Wesley and his Methodist people were regularly denounced as "enthusiasts"—a charge he just as regularly denied. For he defined *enthusiasm* in its literal root-sense of hypersubjectivity: "overvaluing feeling and inward impressions, mistaking the work of the imagination for the voice of the Spirit; expecting the end without the means, and undervaluing reason, knowledge and wisdom in general." All this he heartily deplored and discouraged.

With all these distinctions established, he could then proceed to distinguish between "bigotry" and "Catholic Spirit"—and this brought him to the capstone of the system as a whole: "Christian Perfection," "the fullness of faith and love." *Here* he was easily and inevitably misunderstood. In general, the term *perfection* had, and still has, a fixed pluperfect connotation: perfected perfection—a state over which nothing more exalted can be conceived: human existence that has transcended human ambivalence. Obviously, Wesley never meant *this*, and he was always baffled when others, including his own people, misunderstood his idea of "perfecting perfection." To deal with *these* misconceptions, he added two sermons as commentary on the "Christian Perfection" sermon: "Wandering Thoughts" and "Satan's Devices." In them, he marks off the moral difference between conscious, deliberate sin ("the violation of a known law of God") and the lapses that come from what we would now call unconscious impulses which generate "wandering thoughts" (not sinful if not cordially entertained!), which also make us susceptible to "Satan's devices" (the lure of temptations, smugness, despair, etc.).

Faith is the heart of it all—the threshold of the Christian life, its sustaining reality, its final triumph. And faith, for Wesley, is the primary bond between God and ourselves, and ourselves and God. His sharpest focus was on what God does to and for us, and in and through Jesus Christ, through the personal agency of the Holy Spirit and the corporate influences of the church and the sacraments.

The core of any such theology is, therefore, the gospel message of sin and salvation—of our own sinful alienation, of God's denying success to all alienated human efforts; of God's prevenient grace in nature and in our human conscience, of God's incarnate and redemptive love in Jesus Christ, of God's edifying and sanctifying power in and through the Spirit—the message of the life-style and worldviews that are the human consequences of God's grace and our faithful response. "Holiness of heart and a life conformable to the same"—this was the programmatic motto of Wesley's entire theological effort (positive and negative, hortative and controversial, evangelistic and pedagogic, emotional and rational, etc.). And it all comes out in the sermons—the gospel of God's pardoning love, the moral imperatives of faith toward love and justice, the rules and guidelines of the Christian life, the interpretation of all creation (and of the modern world in particular) in terms of the rise and progress of religion in personal experience, in society, in this world and in the world to come.

In this sense, then, Wesley's sermons are a scripted panorama of the Christian life—of God's sufficiency, our need, the history of salvation, and the Christian self-understanding of it all. Many of Wesley's notions and much of his rhetoric are no longer communicative to some of us—to many of us, perhaps. But the nerve of his concern—that faith's search for understanding reaches to every facet and dimension of our existence, and to our search for our full humanity—all this is still as vital and relevant as ever.

Why is it, then, that we of the Methodist tradition have so readily neglected such a resource? How were we persuaded that other voices (some from the past, some elsewhere in the present) seem to speak more clearly and truly to the human situation, for now and for tomorrow? And is it really true that they do so speak? Only we can decide such a question, but any responsible decision must be based upon evidence—and that means an honest reevaluation of our Wesleyan heritage, and a reassessment of the actual possibilities of its renewal and reapplication in our time and circumstance. My own confidence and hope is that if Wesley were restored to his old place as mentor to the Methodists—or at least as one of them—our own future would be brighter and our ecumenical contribution more significant. How many others, I wonder, share this confidence and hope? Let us pray:

O God, who didst give us John Wesley for our spiritual forefather, give us now the wisdom and openness to learn from him the ways of faith and hope and love in Christ, that we, too, may love and serve thee in our own time and way with equal devotion and joy.

O may it all be our powers engage
To do thy holy will.

In Christ's name and spirit, Amen.

# 9

# *The Human Prospect and the Christian Hope*

## *An Introductory Comment*

On November 3, 1974, Albert Outler told the congregation of First United Methodist Church in Bloomington, Indiana, that the human prospect for the future is bleak and foreboding—that doomsday is upon us—but there is hope:

"This is what eschatology means, and has meant from the beginning: that the justification and vindication of our lives—their meaning and value—is not in our hands but God's, not in good fortune or bad, but in God's kingdom of love and righteousness."

Outler says that hope and expectation are wrought into the fibers of our organic life and are as native and truly human as dread and anxiety. "Hope and faith—trust in God's Providence—bring with them the capacity to survive in circumstances that none would choose or accept as satisfactory."

"If you have any word of exhortation for the people, say it" (Acts 13:15 RSV). This is an interesting vignette of a crucial turning point in the history of the very early Christian church, when it was still a Jewish sect—like the Qumran or Zadokite covenanters. Paul and Barnabas apparently were welcome in the Antiochene synagogue and felt at home—for when the point in the sabbath service for a "sermon," or "exhortation," was reached, the elders invited the visitors to speak, and Paul did so without hesitation (in a speech that included his announcement of a radical change in the Christian future—its mission to the *Gentiles!).*

But notice what it was that those Antiochene elders *wanted* Paul to talk about—Did he have any word of real encouragement? (That's what *exhortation* means here.) The obvious inference is that the Jews of Antioch, and elsewhere, were discouraged, and with good reason. They were already aware that their favored-nation status in the Roman Empire was eroding; already the possible (maybe probable) fate of Jerusalem was looming on the horizon. What was *their* future, and, even more important, what was the future of their mission in the world (their witness to the righteous rule and Providence of the One God)? They were living in the gathering dusk of their national independence, and though they could not have foreseen the long and tragic road ahead for their children's children, their forebodings were not unfounded.

What, then, could bolster their courage to live their faith in God's Providence, no matter what; inspire their motivation to witness and service, even when the promise of earthly gain and success was fading? *If* you have any words of encouragement for the people, *now* is the time for it—the time for it in a service of worship, the time for it in our daily lives.

In a strange and ironic way, history has come full circle—and with it a dawning recognition that the human prospect is almost suddenly and unexpectedly grim, that we and our children are, at best, up against a difficult future. The chilling fears of an actual doomsday are seeping into the marrow of our bones. The graffiti on history's walls stretch out now to the very margins, and they all add up to the same refrain: The human prospect has been weighed in the balance and found wanting. Lincoln Steffens' old boast that he had seen the human future (in Moscow!) "and it was working" is now being reversed: We have seen the human future (technocracy, the passing of European and of white supremacy, the rise and spread of "liberty" of sorts, the waxing of secular self-dependence, etc.) and none of it is working very well, anywhere, anymore.

By now we all must be familiar with the various recipes for global disaster, and we must be aware that they are boiling away furiously on our current history's front burners. The energy crisis has certainly been mismanaged by the West and is now threatening an economic revolution (with London dependent on Yemen; Washington dependent on Teheran!) as drastic and ominous as the Russian Revolution.

But that is only the iceberg tip of the real problem: The petroleum and mineral resources of this planet are being depleted, without prospect of recovery, at a rate that ensures the collapse of technology within a finite time span that is terrifyingly imminent. This, of course, is the other side of the population explosion, which means, also inexorably, that the planet cannot sustain human life as we know it for any very long stretch into the future. We used to draw up geologic-calendar clocks which showed that humanity appeared only during the last ten minutes or so; now we can project the human future, on that same scale, in seconds rather than minutes.

But there's also the Damoclean sword of nuclear warfare hanging over us, *and twitching,* as nuclear capabilities spread and the possibilities of nuclear terrorism increase.

And now there's the talk that industrial emissions (including aerosol sprays for shaving and hair-setting!) are raising global temperatures, threatening to dissipate the ozone layer that protects us from solar radiation. This is offset, somewhat, by other "scientific" evidence that we are entering a new Little Ice Age. But then there's the "Jupiter effect," which threatens us with huge earthquakes when the other planets line up against us on an axis out from the sun.

There is still a lot of underdeveloped land in the world (and maybe more petroleum), and there are the oceans (and promises of unlimited energy from sea water)—and it is true that we are incredibly resourceful animals as well as wasteful and self-destructive!

But the necessary resource to produce unlimited energy is

nowhere available—and this means that developers and ecologists are on a collision course. Even in the short run, there is simply not enough to go around (globally speaking), even if we cut down consumption levels (as we ought to have done long ago), even if we accept a negative Gross National Product (which means depression), even if we could raise productivity rates in a society where the fraction of the underproductive (the very young and the very old) is going up. Thus we can have inflation and a sagging stock market at one and the same time—a fact that would have blown Adam Smith's mind!—and the specter of worldwide depression (in which civilization and culture will suffer most) has come to haunt all the knowledgeable futurists that I know or have read. If there are any words of encouragement in this picture, now is the time for them!

The other side of the picture—the human role in a diminished future—is equally foreboding. Psychiatrist Karl Menninger has written a thundering book titled with a quaint question, *Whatever Became of Sin?* The answer, as it turns out, is that sin has a new name and sponsorship—it is now identified as social dysfunction—but is still doing a flourishing business. What has happened is that *customary* morality—social control by means of social approval and disapproval—has either collapsed or metamorphosed into a new (and so far futile) business called behavior modification.

In any case, the older control patterns of authority, subordination, and an ethic of conscious self-denial have been largely shattered, sometimes in the name of freedom, sometimes in the name of moral relativism, sometimes (and most often) without a name—just plain old self-assertion and antinomianism! The older models of deference to the high and mighty of this world (or to parents, women, and clergy) are all passé—and most of us are either willing or glad to have it so.

But in their place, what?—a paranoid glee in attacking the high and mighty (Abe Fortas, Lyndon Johnson, Richard Nixon, and now Henry Kissinger, Nelson Rockefeller, et al.) and a widespread and rising disrespect for the forces of social control: the law and most lawmakers and enforcers, the media, and the schools.

Results? A crime rate that keeps rising with no sign of abatement; a prison system itself half-criminal; a system of unequal justice (despite all the mouthings about equal justice by journalists who regard themselves as a law unto themselves); a catastrophic breakdown in family life; a new sexuality that presses for homosexuality as normal (this is going to be the big flap in The United Methodist General Conference in Portland in 1976!); the radical failure in our systems of public education and the decline of private and independent systems; the repudiation of the so-called Puritan work ethic, and any other ethic of voluntary self-denial and sacrifice for the common good.

It would be easier to accept this ruinous prospect for ourselves (or for some of us) if, *anywhere else* in the world, in *any* sizable segment or entity of human society, we could see what we could recognize as the augury or dawning of a new age, a new order of peace and justice and human joyfulness. But where would we look? None of civilization's basic institutions is flourishing, really, anywhere in the world (unless we except the Arabian-Persian oil economy, but that clearly is on the slippery road to disaster). The global economy is in bad shape (with worse to come), and so are all the various experiments in democratic government. And so on and on.

That Arco TV ad, in which an entire metroplex comes at last to be one immense traffic jam, is much too realistic to be funny (and obviously is not meant to sell gas). And who believes that any society in the world will accept inflation, scarcity, and unemployment without sliding back into authoritarian government control? Where is there a society that will willingly share dwindling resources *equitably*—from each according to ability; to each according to need?

This composite picture of an unfavorable human prospect is beginning to affect our morale and our self-confidence in our infinite resources for serving our own chosen ends. This is what it means to belong to the first generation in two hundred years for whom the dogma of progress has become doubtful, if not incredible. And this strikes at the heart of our human hopes, our confidence in tomorrow, our faith in the human future (and our own, within that larger outlook).

The early Christians looked toward an imminent end of the world with real anticipation—it meant, to them, an instant rectification of all accumulated injustices in one monstrous leap: a new heaven and a new earth (a new Jerusalem, a new reign of righteousness, peace, and happiness). Their world was going to end with a bang—not a whimper (not from them, anyway). For us, the prospective ending of the human world-epoch we have known appears as yet another injustice, this time on a cosmic scale. And this bids fair to cut the heart out of our Christian faith—our faith in God's Providence, our faith in ourselves and our future, our faith in hope and love and the beloved community, in this world and the next. If anybody has a word of encouragement to speak, now *is* the time for it!

There are no glib words that will suffice, just as there are no easy solutions. But Christians have some things to say to one another and to the world that do not depend upon what the world calls optimism or pessimism. The Christian church has survived more than one dark age and has no basal fear (certainly not on principle) of the end of human existence—personal death or the end of human life on this plantet.

This is what eschatology means, and has meant from the beginning: that the justification and vindication of our lives—their meaning and value—are not in our hands, but God's; not in good fortune or bad, but in God's kingdom of love and righteousness. This is why great Christian realists like Augustine and Boethius (and the surviving Christians in Russia and Red China) have eyeballed doomsday close up and yet have lived and worked and died serenely: Augustine with the Vandals pounding on the gates of Hippo; Boethius after long imprisonment; the underground Chinese Christians in almost complete anonymity. The point is that the church has survived crisis after crisis—and none of them by the church's own merit or wisdom, but because of the life of the Spirit in the human soul and community.

There is another point—and it has to do with the status of hope and expectation as basic elements in human existence. Heidegger taught us about existential *anxiety* (August and Sorge) and that life is orientated to death. But just as deep and basic as any anxiety in the human organism is the positive force of *hope* and *expectation.* This is wrought into the fibers of our organic life: to hope, to expect, to anticipate, is as native and truly human as to dread and to be anxious. Long before it has any sense of time and causality, an infant hopes and expects; long after the fevers of life are over and the busy world is hushed, the healthy human spirit is still leaning into the wind, hoping, expecting—whatever?—because the death of hope and expectation is spiritual death, whenever it occurs. Hope and faith—trust in God's Providence—bring with them the capacity to survive in circumstances that none would choose or accept as satisfactory. And they keep us at work—as we must be working, with all the intelligence and all the self-discipline and self-denial we can muster, with all the moral dedication to the humane causes of human justice and liberation and peace we can enlist and devote. We must not cop out; we must not go quietly into the encircling gloom—and we must not settle for less than the utmost from our intelligence and courage and capacity for human cooperation.

And yet hope deferred, or denied, makes the heart sick. And human hope, at its best, is rooted not in our confidence in human capacity, but in a radical sense of dependence on *God;* a lively faith in God's goodwill toward us in Christ; a profound trust in God's Providence for his children—even when they have bolluxed up the earth he gave them to tend and to enjoy. In short, Christian hope, like faith and love, is rooted in the gospel—in God's word to his human creation that in *his* will is *their* peace and joy!

Any word about a hopeful future in the face of a doleful prospect must begin with some open acceptance of our responsibility and involvement in this situation that appalls us (i.e., our repentance); it must begin with our confession that we have offended the Holy One by our unhallowed living and with our acknowledgment that we can never be truly happy until we become more truly holy—that is, truly loving toward God and our neighbors (which is to say, all our brothers and sisters in Christ). We must, in trying to reconsecrate our lives, realize that the old salvation metaphors of the cosmic courtroom, the schoolrooms, or even the psychotherapeutic clinics, simply must be surpassed. Those old rhetorics and their ethical implications must be transformed. We moderns are no longer guilt-ridden (in the traditional sense), but we are still hopeless—hard pressed to find meaning and joy and courage for life and death, and whatever lies beyond. Christian hope now turns, for the first time since the early centuries—not on a rosy future, but on a burning flame inside: a gospel for the guiltless who are still hopeless, apart from a new assurance which they may never profoundly have had, that God loves them, that we all are safe in his hands, whatever else may betide us.

Beyond the courtroom, the clinic—or the Washington snakepit—the human hunger for happiness still reaches out toward some sovereign caring power that is more than our desperate desire to be spared the mockeries of senescence and death. What if it were really true that "God so loved the world that he gave of himself in and for that world so that it [and we] might not perish [in final meaninglessness], but have eternal life [full and real humanity, here and hereafter]"? What if it were a living faith, which we could communicate with lips and lives—that God's reconciling love in Christ changes the inner realities of human existence, so that those who are justified by faith, as Paul puts it, "are *in* Christ Jesus, by God's own act, whom God has made our wisdom and righteousness, and in whom we are consecrated and liberated" (I Cor. 1:27-30)?

Hundreds of gospel promises in the New Testament point beyond the heavenly courtroom, or the earthly classroom, or the shag-carpeted clinic. They all, however, focus on God's justification of the undeserving, on God's sheer unmerited grace freely given to the hopeless. This is the first premise of any Christian message pretending to be authentic and biblical.

But any word about justification must be a word about Jesus Christ, the divine agent of God's gracious actions in redemption (pardon and liberation), whose sacramental life and death has hallowed and can hallow all of life, here and hereafter. Human life *can* be lived *graciously*, in and through the grace of our Lord Jesus Christ, who is God's love mediated in each human spirit by the Holy Spirit. But without such grace as the ambiance of our very existence, we are foredoomed to hollow triumphs that wreak havoc on their victims and leave us vulnerable to the frustration of human success, and even more to the indignities of death. The gospel is God's enacted promise in Christ that we can live intentionally in any human circumstance, following the leadings of the Holy Spirit, obedient to the highest and best we know of God's will for *all* his children, growing into a more genuine serenity than we can ever know otherwise, in and for and by ourselves. And this is by the power of Christ, shared with us in his victory over sin and death—that is, over their power to corrupt our faith and hope and love. It is in Christ that we can claim God's enacted promise that, as *his* children, our future surpasses any present human calculation, however grim, however cheerful. This is Christian serenity—the sustaining faith that through pain, deprivation, grief, and the dwindling sands in life's hourglass—"that when he shall appear, we shall be like him and shall see him [and ourselves] as he really is [and ourselves as he means us to be]."

The gospel message to "the guiltless" is rather less that Christ has appeased the Father's wrath than that he is the effectual agent of the Father's moral compassion. Our salvation comes, not by some sort of plea bargaining, but by our actual daily *participation in Christ*—in God's love, redemptive in Christ, sanctifying through the Spirit. Our eternal hope is where it always has been: in God's gracious purpose, to restore such overreachers as we to that happiness which lies within the reach of all authentic human aspiration—the only kind of happiness we can ever truly enjoy forever!

The Christian evangel is that human life in God's love is ultimately secured, and even now can be serene and joyful, since all final meanings are in the hands of God, "whose mercy is over *all* His works." It is, in its simplest form, the good news that God is on our side—a message to which our proper response is not pride or satisfaction or self-righteousness, but rather faith and gratitude.

And precisely from this faith and gratitude come the imperatives to Christian social action—"those good works following *after* justification," as its evidence and harvest. "For by grace you have been saved through faith; and this is not your own doing, it is the gift of God—not because of works, lest any man should boast. For we are his workmanship [and workers], created in Christ Jesus for good works, which God prepared beforehand, that we should walk in them" (Eph. 2:8-10 RSV). Evangelism is the *charter* for Christian social action—but the order is absolutely crucial. "Conversion" without enlistment in the Christian revolution is simply self-deluding. But good works apart from conversion and regeneration are neither better nor worse than any of the other self-defeating forms of works-righteousness still foredoomed to the despair of Romans 7.

And herein lies our *hope* and expectation, even now—our

confidence in both the grim short future and the doubtful long future beyond *that,* but most of all in *God's* future in any case. It is in the reality and the at-handness of God's kingdom, his love and Providence, his covenant and promises, his nearness and transcendence, his demands, his share in our agonies, that we must look for *our* inspiration and enablement to grapple, intelligently and humanely, with our problems now and forever.

Existence is always turned outward toward tomorrow. We recognize no limit. We live for the ultimate—in and with the inexorable certainties of death and history's eclipse. Death is served up to us piecemeal by life itself. A bitter disappointment, loneliness, sickness, the brittleness of the body—all these are presages, like the cobwebs of July, an early sign of autumn. Our hope here is less that we shall die and go to heaven than that we already have died (to all false optimisms) and that the new creation *already* has begun to bear fruit in our lives (love, joy, patience, devotion), in the face of pain and indignity and death. For the meaning of life—the only meaning that is finally tolerable—is that all of it is from God; that *all* of it is in his care and keeping; and that *our* part is to help God in the realization of the possibilities he has created for us and created us for. God is bound up with our existence in the depths of our being (creation), but he is wholly free of the world and of us, and is therefore our future. God has made us for himself—not only that our hearts may find their stability in him, but that his love in our love should never be lost; that it should live and spread and bear fruit in the tasks of life—through suffering into glory, through death into life.

Any church, with any power to receive and communicate some such vision of being and remaining fully human, will find men and women and youth to whom this Word of life is also a word of hope and encouragement—the truth as it is in Christ Jesus. Any church with its memories and hopes rooted in this gospel is a church with a past *and* a future. Any church that dies in this faith will be raised to a new mission in a world rebelling against God, but a world that cannot weary of his unresting search for ways to bring us to the hearing of his true Word in Christ:

> That word above all earthly powers [good or bad],
> No thanks to *them,* abideth;
> The Spirit and [God's] gifts are ours

Through him who with us sideth:
Let goods and kindred go,
This mortal life also;
The body they may kill:
God's truth [and our hope] abideth still;
*His* kingdom is *forever.*

—Martin Luther

# 10

## *The Hallowing of Life*

### *An Introductory Comment*

Western civilization was never Christianized, but was sacralized in a manner that exalted some "divine" emperors and divinely appointed kings, for example. But secularization did a thorough job of breaking the shackles of fake sacralization. Albert Outler says that what we need, more than anything else, if our newfound liberations are not to lead us into new strangulations, is a *resacralization* of life, a new sense of the pervasiveness of God's grace at work in moral action.

In this sermon, delivered at Kirkwood United Methodist Church in St. Louis, Missouri, on January 12, 1975, Outler talks about the place of humor in this tragic existence.

Albert Outler, a Yale Ph.D., in his boyhood days roamed the Georgia Appalachians; today his public thinks of him as sophisticated and cosmopolitan. Quite naturally, then, throughout his sermons, he evokes laughter when he uses such phrases as "chewing their cuds," "to boot," or "sacred cows."

He chuckles as he describes his sermons as "plain truth for plain people by an egghead." This laugh is the healthiest of all and makes for a kind of reverence people enjoy.

There is a biblical vision back of what I shall be saying here today. It is in Ephesians 1:17-2:10. I read it, a long passage, as you will realize, in a homemade translation. You can read it in any standard translation and still get a soaring sense of what the Christian hallowing of life really would be like.

Western civilization was never fully Christianized, but during the six centuries of its heyday, it did come close to being sacralized—with a strange mixture of biblical motifs along with heavy residues of paganism and superstitions. From the thirteenth through the nineteenth century, with the Renaissance and the Enlightenment as countercultures, the vast majority of Christendom (especially in Europe, America, and their cultural spin-offs around the globe) professed a common belief in the Holy, acknowledging a transcendent Mystery that encompassed and suffused their world and their existence.

Most Christians, in their more serious moments, had something that passed for encounters with the divine, the numinous, the supernatural. Even the jauntiest souls were jolted now and then by radical experiences of authentic reverence and solemnity. The generality of Christians took the supernatural and its active presence for granted; the neurotics (whose name was literally Legion, for they probably outnumbered all the others) lived in syndromes of anxiety that ranged from demon possession to holy terror.

The world was full of the sacred: sacred places, sacred people, sacred books, sacred objects—all set apart and sanctified for sacred rites and ceremonies. "The heavens declared the glory of God; and the firmament displayed his handiwork" (Psalm 91:1)—and all this seemed self-evident! It was a time and a climate in which reverence and awe came easily to the generality, when even aliens and mavericks (including unbelievers) found it credible to profess some sort of belief in the supernatural.

To be sure, they quarreled over competing views of the proper way to behave in a sacralized world, and they differed in their notions as to how the Holy was to be discerned, celebrated, and obeyed. This was the crucial issue between the Protestants and

Roman Catholics in their bitter bloody strife for two and a half centuries after 1517. The Catholics were committed to an ecclesial view of the world and human existence, in which the Holy was mediated to humankind by the Holy Church and Holy Sacraments, proffered or withheld by holy men—a sacerdotal view of the Holy and its interface with the human.

Protestants, generally, were no less sensitive to the immanent reality of the Holy. Indeed, by rejecting the notion of sacerdotal and ecclesial mediation of sacral grace, they brought humans into even starker intimacy with the divine, using Scripture, preaching, and the pastoral ministry as mediations in what was, at bottom—in terms of dread or trust, defiance or reconciliation, anguish or blessed assurance—an individual's encounter with God. But the fact remained that it was a rarity to find a man or woman, on either side, without a latent (or maybe lively) sense of the sacred, a knee-jerk reverence toward whatever appeared as numinous. People prayed (in the familiar phrase from the Book of Common Prayer) to be enabled by God's grace to live, work, and die "in reverence and godly fear." "The fear of the Lord is the beginning of wisdom," and from this minimum to the dizzying heights of mystic ecstasy, there was a spectrum of sacralized sensibility. Thus it was as natural as a mockingbird's song for Gerald Manley Hopkins to celebrate the Holy in his earthly experience:

> The world is charged with the grandeur of God.
> It will flame out, like shining from shook foil;
>
> . . . . . . . . . . . . . . . . . . . . . . . . .
>
> And for all this, nature is never spent;
> There lives the dearest freshness deep down things;
>
> . . . . . . . . . . . . . . . . . . . . . . . . .
>
> Because the Holy Ghost over the bent
> World broods with warm breast and with ah! bright wings.
>
> —"God's Grandeur"

One has only to look into the vast panoply of Western art, architecture, literature, and folkways to see how immense and yet also immanent this pervasive sense of existence as sacral really was. There is no other accounting for the great cathedrals and lovely parish churches, the ancient universities, the plays of Shakespeare, the poems of Milton, not to mention the more ordinary ventures of the human spirit. Christians lived and died in a climate dominated in many and diverse ways; conscious, as Temple once put it, of "the immanence of the transcendent."

The trouble with this view of world-and-life (as we can see now) was its prime connotation and correlation of the Holy with coercive *power.* Sacred places and persons and objects were all discerned as being surcharged with physical force—power that was dangerous, power that could be manipulated by those who were properly initiated into its mysteries and properly ordained to control its banes and blessings. Religious dread, in its primal form, is a *moral* sense: of unworthiness, of guilt and shame, of fascination and awe (or a mix of all these). But this primacy of the moral could be changed, all too readily, into a political concept: the dread of God's arbitrary *power,* and thence into an almost equal dread of those who mediated that power—those who blessed or cursed in a trade-off for deference, obedience, or radical dependence. Thus, sacred institutions and sacred persons came to stand between humans and God—and the hallowing of life came to mean, all too simply, the subjection of the less holy to the more holy, and a consequent bartering of human freedom for divine favor as dispensed by priests, preachers, and other wielders of supernatural power. Faith and fear were mingled, as were belief and superstition. Life in this world was subordinated to a pervasive and credible otherworldliness.

Even this might have been bearable (for the sacralization of human institutions had profits as well as debits) if sacralization had not proceeded to such a bold and ruthless alliance between altars and thrones, between ministers and ministries of grace and wielders of coercive power in secular society—so that those possessed of and accustomed to political and economic domination also were invested with auras, crowns, and sacralized scepters and swords.

This identification of sacralization with coercive power runs a long way beyond our recorded history—to tribal chieftains who claimed and were accorded divine ordination (or even birth), and to kings and emperors who thought themselves divine. The genius of the Roman emperors was divinity itself here on earth, and their European successors insisted on retaining the title *Holy* Roman

Emperor. "I rule by God's appointment, not yours," said Queen Elizabeth I to her Royal Council, on whom she depended so heavily—and there were earnest souls who remained devoted to the Stuart cause long after it had brought three kingdoms to the brink of ruin.

The main function of this sacralization of secular power was to act as a prop to oppression. It lent sanctity to a deferential social system in which inequalities and elites could be maintained and reinforced by appeals to God's sovereignty: his manifest purpose and pattern in the secular sphere. Pecking orders not only were natural; they were also supernaturally ordained—and thus rebellion came to involve sacrilege as well. "One's station in life and its duties" was an accepted and well-understood cliché in both church and civil state. To know one's place and to accept it with grace, good humor, *and diligence* amounted to the crown of civic virtue. The pyramid became a paradigm for human society—divinely ordained and supported. When we denounce oppression nowadays, our normal concern is with the selective oppression of minorities or women or other social groupings that have discovered their lot in life to be intolerable. What we keep forgetting is that far more ruthless inequalities and inequities were built into the deferential societies that preceded ours, when the oppression of the vast *majority* in any given society was more nearly the rule than the exception. This, of course, was the point of Marx's outrage over the observable fact that a tiny fraction of humanity actually was oppressing all the rest.

The tragic irony of it was that these models of deference and oppression themselves had become sacralized and sanctified by religion, by eager priests and clerics whose power came from their alliance with secular power. In pagan culture (Greek, Roman, Gothonic) members of the priesthood were civil functionaries—servants to the secular order, technologists of supernatural energy, whose services, practically speaking, were at the disposal of the divinely ordained powers that be. Treason was more than a civil offense; it was impiety, to boot. Christians had been taught otherwise from their beginnings:

> In this world [*saeculum*], kings lord it over their subjects; and those in authority are showered with titles and compliments. But it must

> not be so among you: on the contrary, the highest among you must bear himself like the youngest, the chief of you like a servant. . . . I am here among you as a servant . . . and now I vest in you the kingship which my Father vested in me. —Luke 22:25-30

"For the Son of man [a sacred image if ever there was one] came not to be ministered unto, but to minister and to give His life."

In the Fourth Gospel, in place of the eucharistic narratives in the Synoptics, there is the story of the Last Supper, in which Jesus washes his disciples' feet—to Peter's consternation—and the conclusion is a divine ordinance as clear and explicit as the eucharistic "Do this in remembrance of me"! Said Jesus, "If I, your Lord and Master, have washed *your* feet, you also ought to wash *one another's* feet. I have set you an example: You are to do this as I have done it for you" (John 13:14-15). Here was One whose office and ministry were hallowed and hallowing, through and through—but whose definition of the hallowed and hallowing life recapitulated the prophetic motif of the Holy as loving, the sacral as grace-filled. He made it incarnate and redemptive.

The story of the alliance of Christianity with civil power, and of the adoption by Christ's disciples of the signs and weapons of coercive power is, or ought to be, embarrassing. It is one that most of us deplore nowadays, especially in others who still hang in there with their old trappings of pomp and circumstance, their sense of innate ministerial privilege. And yet, with all our new-minted egalitarian dogmas, we still talk about seeking and wielding power (coercive power, at that), as if the wielding of such power were moral, or likely to be—if, of course, it were used to good ends (i.e., the way we *think* we would use it!).

The truth, as we all know, is that Western civilization's patterns of oppression and exploitation, of caste and class, of imperialism, nationalism, colonialism, and so on, were all supported by Christian rationalizations. The alliances between throne and altar were uneasy and ambivalent—so it was not always clear who was exploiting whom more. But it was the principle of the alliance—with the church supporting the secular power and the secular power supporting the church (with coercive power as the crucial bonus on either side)—that finally came to be the hated target of the philosophers, the apostles of Enlightenment, in the Western societies. We can always except the marginal figures like the Protestant radicals—save when *they* come into political power!

Moreover, the sacralizing enterprise of traditional Christianity had formed another alliance along the way—this one, with superstition. Biblical faith was, and is, supernaturalistic in *some* sense or other (it is not just about nature and the natural order, any way you want to define *natural*). And a fair amount of superstition exists in many of its levels and layers. But there is a radical difference—180 degrees!—between the biblical faith in transcendent Mystery, which always is oriented toward works and mercy, and the pagan secular faiths that seek to exploit Divine Mystery for some ulterior goal or gain. This was the point at issue very early on, when Simon Magus realized that the apostles were on to something pretty good, and he, too, wanted a piece of the action—as he thought, at a decent price. When Peter turned on him to denounce his greed, no one was more surprised by the outburst than poor old Simon! (Acts 8:9-24).

Thereafter Christianity's track record of blurring the radical distinction between supernaturalism (trust in the Holy as friendly!) and superstition (the Holy as technology!) actually has been downright disreputable, if the truth must be told without reserve. Luther denounced relics, but also came close to treating the Bible as a fetish, even as he eagerly placed his new religion under the protection and at the mercy of secular control. The Puritans denounced the papal pretensions to a sacralized politics (and they also cut the nerve of divine-right monarchy, for which we owe them many an unpaid debt), but they came up with a theocratic politics that all too readily supported secular injustice and oppression—including slavery, child labor, and the subjugation of women.

All of which is by way of explaining why, in the seventeenth, eighteenth, and nineteenth centuries, "modernity" turned away from a sacralized world and society toward what confidently was believed would be a splendid humanization—a self-conscious desacralization of the political order and, finally, of the church itself. To self-styled enlightened moderns it had come to seem self-evident that the sacral (and, of course, its agents and their trappings) was an essential prop to secular oppressions and that superstitition was an opiate for human powerlessness. Thus, modernity turned against Christendom and sacralization as such—against any and all religion that aided or even acquiesced in inequality or "unfreedom."

"Mankind will be free and happy," shrilled Diderot, "when the last king is throttled with a noose made from the entrails of the last priest." Voltaire cried, *"Ecrasez l'infame!"*—and that "infamy" was Christianity's record of professing to hallow life while it also sanctified tyranny (over minds as well as bodies). Desacralization, as a conscious program, came to rank high on the agenda, in much the same way as enlightenment and progress. And this is why we cannot *now*, in easy or good conscience, talk easily of returning to *those* good old days (which actually were terrible).

Thus it came about—to elide a couple or three long chapters of modern intellectual history—that we finally have arrived at as thoroughgoing a desacralization of the world as the earlier apostles of secularism ever expected in their furthest vision—further even than many would have supported or approved. Secular humanism has succeeded beyond the secularizers' wildest dreams. Everywhere liberation remains unachieved; but no one dast any longer deny it as a valid prime human right. Elitism has lost its principled defenders; theology has largely been reduced to anthropology; and supernaturalism has become a dirty word among the sophisticated, save for the "new" supernaturalists, whose weird powers are plainly as utilitarian (i.e., magical) as those of Simon Magus ever were. Recently on television, Katherine Kuhlmann was explaining that she now has reached the stage where those seeking her healing touch may or may not believe in God—only in *her* and in *themselves.*

This desacralization of modern life is very nearly full-scale. What is sacred anymore, and to whom? Obviously not the older sacred cows: family, motherhood, children, the unborn or the senescent, the church or the ministry, sex, property, privacy. One by one, all old tabus have been defied and erased—and yet, I'm told by those closer to where it's at than I've even been, many of the new freedoms are beginning to pall on those who first scaled the old barricades with such elan not so awfully long ago. One by one, the older hippie heavens have turned sour, and few new ones are turning up; the generation of American youth that committed mayhem on its universities is now out in the world, increasingly aware of its inadequate training for life in that society it sought to scuttle. Our mass media—having "stopped" the Vietnam war (or forced us to walk away from it), having hounded one Supreme Court Justice and two Presidents out of office, having pilloried the Rockefeller clan for the titillation of the rest of us—are currently reduced to grumbling about President Ford's mediocrities, even while the greatest shift in global power since Britannia first ruled the waves is going swiftly forward in the Middle East, where new successors to Saladin, Suleiman, and Persia's Shah are already emergent. And where is this being reported and assessed "the way it really is"?

We ought honestly to admit, however ruefully, that the negative aim of secularism was valid: to liberate humanity from intolerable oppressions supported by religion, tyranny, and superstition, intertwined and interdependent. We are well rid of all that—and of flat-earth theology, of false enchantments, of deferential societies in which God got the credit (or blame) for the pecking order, and so on. This was why Tillich's banishment of the supernatural (as it had been understood) was so persuasive; why a book as bad as Harvey Cox's *Secular City* was an instant success; why theology as shabby as that of the Death-of-God boys—Altizer, Hamilton, Van Buren, et al.—created such a stir. It all was part of the terminal stage in the desacralization project running back to Hume, Voltaire, Rousseau, and Feuerbach. It was the desacralization of the regimes, and the divinization of humanity, in a world we can envision in our reveries (which is what most current "theologies of the future" amount to).

The result is that, for the moment at least, the world we live in seems, more and more obviously, to be unhallowed; life for many seems more and more disenchanting. That the world is in parlous shape—with human affairs on every part of the planet in an unprecedented mess—is not to be denied; and I'm not quite willing to explain it all as my forefathers in the faith would have—by saying that, having sown the wind, we are now reaping the whirlwind (though it is plain as a pikestaff that we are gathering a bitter harvest which we at least helped to cultivate!).

Deeper than our daily woes is the starkest human tragedy of all: the prospect of living an unhallowed life in an unhallowed world, and of dying an unhallowed death with really nothing to redeem it. We could conceivably solve our other problems and still find it all meaningless—unless life itself has found a meaning over and beyond the limits of this *saeculum.* We could, on the other hand, conceivably find ourselves in worse and worse shape (planet-wise) and still do a lot better than mere survival, if only we could find our way *forward* to an *authentic* resacralization of life and death—a new awareness, individual and corporate, of the hallowed life; a new experience of the hallowing of life as humanity's chief business, our crowning joy and glory!

But what, conceivably, does this mean? Is it more than a revival of those older discredited notions of baptizing the status quo, of sanctifying once again the powers that be? If so, then forget it—and count me in on that oblivion, as well.

And yet, we must by now have begun to notice that humanity on its own is tragically inhumane and inhuman; that the unhallowed life is no more worth living than the unexamined life, or the fettered life, or the wasted life. There *is* more in heaven and earth than has been dreamed of—by our secular philosophers or even the dreamers and the utopians.

There *is* such a reality as the Holy. There is an encompassing Mystery that grasps us and suffuses our existence and calls us into harmony with reality; that thwarts our unholy ventures (sooner or later); that haunts us, inspires us, reminds us of our mortality, snaps open shuttered glimpses of a reality that transcends what we know as nature, without decrying or negating any of nature's values or final goals.

What we need more than anything else, if our newfound liberations are not to lead us into new strangulations, is a resacralization of life, a freshly vivid, pervasive sense of the Holy—its mystery and its intimacy—a new awareness of it, a new responsiveness to a participation in its radiance, glory, and illumination of our human capacities and potential. But, remembering the pits into which we fall whenever we meld the Holy with coercive power, we must not seek this new sacralization as a means of achieving our ends, but rather as the expression of our gratitude toward God and of a truly sacrificial love toward our neighbor and the new humanity—the normal fruitage from any *honest* gratitude. Life must be hallowed again—not so much as a way to redistribute power as to transform human existence by the revolutionary power of love, God's grace at work in moral action.

Our clue to all this has already been given us in the Lord's Prayer, once we rectify its woefully misbegotten traditional exegesis. For most of us it runs in chunks: (1) hallowed be thy name; (2) thy kingdom come; (3) thy will be done (comma) on earth as it is in heaven. Actually, these three petitions are focused in the single phrase *on earth*—which, of course, is the only place such petitions are as yet unrealized (since in heaven, they are and always have been mere commonplaces). Try praying the prayer like *this* and see what happens to our sense of the Holy in its impingement on our heart, conscience, and moral obligations: Hallowed be thy name on earth (by me and by us all); thy kingdom come on earth (to me and to us all); thy will be done on earth (by me and by all who love thee) so that what is routine in heaven may become revolutionary on earth, here and now! *This* is Christ's program for the hallowing of life—and any real success in such a venture would mean a radical transformation in the quality and glory of our lives; in the climate in which modern Christians could live and work and serve and die in a confident faith, knowing that none of our works of love and mercy is ever in vain, *in the Lord!*

Whenever I try to think practically about this new hallowing of life, this recovery of the sacred in the daily round and in Christian communion and service, I seem to come down to what I have come to call the four Rs of spiritual reality: reflection, radiance, rapture, and reverence. We can ignore the question of their priorities—in the Christian life, they come in a kaleidoscopic mixture, but always together in every authentic peak experience of any life that "is hid with God in Christ."

*Reflection* is the human capacity to be a participant observer of the world and of our involvements in it—the power to understand and adapt behavior and insight in accordance with reality. If the genus homo is sapiens, this is what makes us so—and God has not given us minds to let them be stampeded by passion or blinkered by logic. To think that we can park our rational functions on the threshold of some holy moment is to mistake what holiness and humanity mean, in their interaction.

*Radiance* is the outward and visible sign of an inward and invisible glory. This is a tricky notion, for it teeters on the edge between exhilaration and vanity. It has its pompous side (fame, acclaim, praise), and all this is tragically transient (literally, *vainglorious*).

The boast of heraldry, the pomp of power,
  And all that beauty, all that wealth e'er gave,
Awaits alike the inevitable hour:
  The paths of glory lead but to the grave.[5]
—Thomas Gray

Thus when a new pope is consecrated, a humble Franciscan friar thrice lights a yarn thread of oakum wool and, after having passed it under the papal nose, snuffs it out with this salutary reminder (oft forgot): *Sic, Sancte Pater, transit gloria mundi* (Thus, Holy Father, passes the glory of the world).

But there's another side to *glory*—a more truly human, healthier side—that can and should be hallowed. It comes clear as soon as we stop and ask what we mean when we report a sight or sound as being "really glorious." The obvious answer is something radiant, vivid, thrilling: a sign-event of the Spirit's presence and our recognition of it. I asked myself, when writing this paragraph, What are my first associations with the term *glorious?* Three popped out unbidden: a sunset in the Chisos Basin in the Big Bend; the discovery of the holograph of John Wesley's first sermon; and the apse window in St. Peter's when the sunlight hits it full force. This is a weird mixture, I realize, but all three have traits in common: a radiant flush of the Spirit; a sudden sense of being hallowed; an experience of being spellbound, almost literally, for a moment at least. All of us must have our own lists of such holy moments, and they would be instructive to reflect on and learn from.

What matters is that human life is, from time to time, *spontaneously* visited by these gifts of radiance and delight, and they are always earthly analogues to God's own glory—reflected in our *imago Dei,* however besmirched. I've known people (and so must you) whose faces were often radiant, whose eyes would shine, who lived in a sort of poised excitement, whose aura was manifest whenever they smiled, or wept, or offered a helping hand. Somehow, they already have tasted God's glory and have responded; they are already praising God, not only with their lips but in their lives—and in their love of his children. This, of course, is why the symbol of sainthood has been a nimbus—and however gullible it may sound, I myself have seen halos around at least a few people I have known, who were, of course, oblivious to the way they looked because they were so fully absorbed in significant activity. My list includes a Quaker saint, a Catholic cardinal, a midwestern anthropologist, and a student or two along the way.

This is at least in part what the Bible means by being human. All creation is finite, but only the human is *inspirited* and therefore capable of being inspired. Yahweh breathed the breath of life—personal identity—into the prefabricated human clod—"and he became a living soul." And it is this inner awareness of being a living soul among living souls—all needing love, service, and glory—that helps define the moral and spiritual dimensions of our tasks of sacralizing the world and hallowing all its heights and depths.

*Rapture* also belongs to those heights and depths, and we have spoken of the problem of to what extent they may be induced and to what extent they come as God's unmerited gifts—of vision, of joy, of transfiguration. The Christian experience, by and large, reports that the faithful and hopeful and loving are more often *overtaken* by raptures than they ever manage to *induce* them—and this confirms all else we know about grace and our radical dependence upon the divine initiative. The main point to raptures, and to charismatic phenomena of all sorts, is that they are not the Holy in themselves (and even less do they justify any holier-than-thou reaction). They are, instead, sign-events *of* the Holy, intimations of that Holy Mystery which is life's constant environment and atmosphere.

*Reverence,* in many ways, is what the religious life is all about. Reverence is our habituation to the Holy, our reflex response to its manifestations, our sense of awe in its presence—that is neither terror-stricken nor ecstatic. Ecstasies, raptures, and "trips" come and go. Reverence is the steady disposition of a holy life, the disposition of the human spirit at its best. It may be a sense of awe in the most ordinary experience, properly noticed and identified; it may be an awareness of mystery in some great occasion; it may be a stillness at the center of our busy and distracted lives. But always it is love: love of God and love of God's creatures. Reverence has little to do with solemnity and nothing at all to do with humorlessness. It can be jaunty or serious, lighthearted or earnest, indignant or serene. But always it is loving, always hallowing, and therefore it always enriches life's events with their true meanings, interests, and final values.

"But if you are led by the Spirit [and this is what St. Paul means by charismatic experience, in *any* of its contexts], you are not under the law." This is because the fruits of the Spirit are "love, joy, peace, patience, kindness, goodness, fidelity, gentleness, and self-control. . . . If the Spirit is the source of our life, let the Spirit also direct our course" (Gal. 5:18, 22-25 NEB).

This is the only way *I* can think of—or have ever seen verified in human life and history—to get beyond a desacralization and a secularism that have degraded human life, beyond the various moralisms and mysticisms that shackle or negate it, to *a true Christian humanism,* in which our participation in the Holy and our dedication to the hallowing of life are also our joy and peace, and happiness.

# 11

# *A Gospel for the Guiltless*

## *An Introductory Comment*

This sermon, preached at Kirkwood United Methodist Church in St. Louis on January 13, 1975, puts Albert Outler at the head of the vanguard that introduces the "new" soteriology—an experience of salvation that speaks to a "guiltless" society. Generally speaking, those of us in the West feel not guilt, but hopelessness. Secularism has shattered the forensic metaphor—God as Judge, the individual as defendant, Jesus as defender.

Some preachers talk about salvation as if they were judges in heaven's courtroom. But such preaching does not speak to the needs of all.

To both the guilty and the guiltless Albert Outler says: "The essential contract in this new gospel—that is, conversion from self-stultifying life to the life of grace in the Spirit—is the same as the old one: repentance and faith."

Outler preaches repentance and faith—a person's response to God regardless of the human condition, whether it be guilt, hopelessness, loneliness, discouragement.

In this sermon he does what he does best: He makes us think new thoughts, using the same "old" gospel.

## *The Sermon*

*If we claim to be sinners, we are self-deceived and strangers to the truth (I John 1:8-10 NEB).*

All of us who have any acquaintance with traditional Christianity are familiar with the notion of a gospel for the *guilty*—the wiping away of the guilt of sin, the appeasement of God's wrathful judgment by means of Christ's atoning death, the offer (in Christ) of God's unmerited mercy, and its acceptance (by faith) by those who were, in point of fact, wholly unacceptable, as far as anything like moral perfection might be concerned. Salvation was, first and last, a forensic, juridical transaction; its ruling metaphor was the heavenly lawcourt. Its inner verification was supplied by the fact that all of us were (and most of us *felt* we were) guilty before God and deserving of damnation, if strict justice were all we could expect or hope for.

This forensic perspective (this gospel for the guilty) has a long history and seemed to many as if it contained the essence of the gospel itself. There are echoes of it in St. Paul and in succeeding ages. Christian doctrines of salvation, especially in the West, have mirrored contemporary models of civil law: Roman law, feudal law, regal and imperial law, and (more recently) what we fondly call a government by laws, not people. This gave the general idea of salvation its typical scene (the heavenly court), its typical style (an adversarial proceeding), and a typical format (all its actors were ex officio—that is, their roles and authority were invested in their office or status). If you've never heard an old-fashioned evangelist preach on "The Last Judgment"—with God the Father as Judge, guilty sinners as the accused, the Holy Spirit as prosecutor (with an open and shut case), the Devil as executioner, and Jesus Christ as defense attorney, who finally must take his client's penalty on himself—then you've never really understood the classical Protestant soteriology; nor have you understood the massive, prolonged, bitter controversies that agitated Protestantism from the seventeenth through the nineteenth centuries, as to how much the human response to God's initiatives in our salvation had to do with the efficacy and effects of God's saving grace.

This was one of John Wesley's most urgent concerns and the

issue on which his sermon "On Working Out Our Own Salvation" was focused. To be justified (or saved), in this classical tradition, meant to be *pardoned*, to be acquitted as in a civil court (whatever the actual case may have been). A verdict of not guilty had been rendered; the defendant went scot-free. And this was a *just* "justification" because the Judge had the authority to render this merciful judgment without corrupting the law (i.e., given Christ's substitutionary atonement and the sinner's sincere repentance). Such justice was thought by some to be selective (i.e., predestination), but all agreed that the unrepentant or unbelieving had no grounds for protesting their damnation, since in the course of ordinary justice, "*none* of us should see salvation."

It is important to understand how basic this forensic lawcourt metaphor has been, and how generally it has affected both Jewish and Christian ideas of soteriology and justice. The notion of God as Judge, of his will as law, of human violations of God's Law as rebellion, and of guilt as the natural result of dread of consequences—all this is the taproot of the old linkage between anxiety and guilt. Misery or dread begets anxiety, and anxiety begets wishful thinking in an almost precise ratio. Within a forensic worldview there is always dread, which begets anxiety, which in turn begets guilt—and the wish for some magical sort of rescue or relief. Whenever I see a police car in my rearview mirror, my glance at the speedometer is reflex. Every time I run a yellow light and hear no siren, my sigh of relief is reflex. Every time there is a letter on my desk from the IRS, or from some court, or even an attorney, my shudder is reflex. I know, in my mind, that our system of justice is meant to serve justice; moreover, by intention and comparatively speaking, I have been a law-abiding citizen for more than six decades (I've *no* criminal record and only three moving violations on my traffic record).

But I belong to the generation—the last one, I think—that also knew we were already guilty of something or other and that, if any court chose to do so, it could condemn and sentence us on some ground or other that would be partially just, at least. *A fortiori*, since I can remember, there never has been any doubt in my mind that I was guilty before *God* of something less than true faith and perfect obedience and that he knew this better than I ("unto whom all hearts are open, all desires known, and from whom no secrets are hid"—a terrifying notion if you ever stop to *think* of it). There was no question, either, but that God's judgment was just and right—and that if I remained unrepentant and unconverted, his condemnation of me would be just and unappealable! This was the realization that tortured Augustine in the Milanese garden, Luther in the Erfurt monastery, Wesley at Aldersgate. Guilt is the dread of a *just* condemnation by One who is authorized to pass such a just judgment and to enforce it. Now, it is precisely this forensic, lawcourt metaphor that has faded from modern self-consciousness as the framework of our thinking about justice and righteousness.

If we want to locate the watershed between *our* "permissive" society and those that preceded it, never mind Dr. Spock (despite the distortions of moral discipline that he and his kind have foisted on a generation of parents and children). Look, rather, for those people who first conceived the notion that justice, law, and law enforcement are nothing more than human conventions—for *this* is the first premise of the prevailing view nowadays: that laws and the judiciary have no authority other than a political, cultural, social consensus (usually within the ruling group or establishment). And, with the collapse of the old notions of the divine origin and ground of the majesty of the law went all those *guilt* complexes that had stemmed from *transcendental* notions of justice, injustice, and incrimination. Once upon a time "law and order" had a metaphysical reference. Now it is only a tainted euphemism for the coercive power of those who have the police and taxing powers on their side. This domestication of the law and its agents is the real solvent that has washed out the moral cement that held Western society together, however tenuously. And with it went all the traditional notions about *guilt*—guilt before God and divine justice and right.

The practical consequence of all this is now a psychotherapeutic commonplace. Any effort to exacerbate an anxious person's guilt feelings is either futile or counterproductive. Guilty by whose standards? Condemnation by whose right and authority? We all know how haphazard and unjust our system of justice is—the court system, that is—and that it operates at different levels of equity for the powerful and the powerless. Nowadays, cases are tried in the papers and on TV, with the courts clearly responsive to public opinion. Grand jury testimony is often leaked; trial jurors are often influenced by publicity; the old presumption of innocence applies only to the obscure or to public favorites. There are some of us who doubt the infallible wisdom and justice of the Supreme Court; we only know it as the court of last resort. The blindfold has long since slipped from the eyes of Justice, and the law can be exploited by those who know how or can afford it. Is it any wonder that the organizing, balancing metaphors of the lawcourt (forensic views of right and wrong) have lost their organizing, controlling force, have left us with a mounting crime rate and with "ripping off " as an optional life-style for an increasing number of people?

Time was when the gospel to the guilt-ridden was: "You are *pardoned* and reconciled to God—through Christ's atoning passion, his appeasement of God's deserved wrath against your richly merited damnation.—Accept God's acceptance.—Sin bravely; repent sincerely.—Walk freely in the assurance of your sins forgiven.—I was sinking deep in sin.—Can my God his wrath forbear; and me, the chief of sinners, spare?—Would he devote his sacred head for such a worm as I?"

If we knew all the old gospel songs, we could carry this on indefinitely. The gospel was the certified truth that your sentence of death (just and merited as it was) had been erased. God was in Christ reconciling *himself to the world!* "There is therefore now no *condemnation* to them that are in Christ Jesus, who walk not after the flesh but after the Spirit."

This was good news indeed—and still contains the very essence of the gospel message. A person thus fully persuaded of election and perseverance in God's grace could live and die rejoicing—beyond the reach of human intimidation and despair, even in the full quota of life's trials and in the face of death. This made for a very sturdy faith.

But what if there is no such sense of guilt, no such dread of nonacceptance, no such expectation and hope in Jesus Christ? What if, after singing that "Jesus paid it all" or that "the burden of my sins was rolled away," there is no life-changing sense of God's favor and love and assured salvation? Obviously, one's first surmise is that the best alternative is to go with one or another version of modern religious humanism in which Jesus, among others, functions as a moral example of humanity at its best. In practical terms, this means *self*-salvation: the effort to become as human as we can.

This, then, is the triumph of humanism: salvation as *self*-achievement. Paradoxically, though, it is also the triumph of amoralism; for if there is no final negative judgment to be levied against us, then all we have left are the pragmatic sanctions in a world where the right and the good are value judgments about social, economic, and political power. And *this* is where we've finally arrived—or many of us, especially the young and the liberated. This is what Hobbes had in mind with his gospel of self-interest (although he would not have approved its actualities). This was the message of the deists and the philosophers, the gospel of Voltaire, Marx, Freud, Fromm—and now of our new supernaturalists as well—those who are interested mainly in what people can make of their supernatural powers and how they can be applied to human goals and values. This is what secularism has been aiming at all along: a radical rejection of the forensic metaphor of divine justice! This was the real concern at the heart of the Death-of-God hurrah: the elimination of God as moral *Judge.* And this, as far as I can see, is the conclusion toward which the *theoretical* implications of transactional analysis and similar life-views are pointed.

It has been part of Christianity's genius eagerly to accept all possible secular wisdoms, even as it also tried to avoid any essential compromise in its distinctive mission in the world (which is to form the human conscience in accordance with God's self-revelation in Christ, to bind and to loose these consciences in accordance with the divine imperatives of revolutionary love implied in that revelation). And now comes *our* crunch: What are *we* to do in the face of these new humanisms that have become a part of our own human self-consciousness? Where are we to draw the line between human self-sufficiency and divine grace—and on what principles, if any?

For those of us in the liberal Christian tradition, the problem is further complicated, of course, by the visible, powerful resurgence of new versions of older stereotypes: fundamentalism, authoritarianism, pentecostalism, the Jesus People, the rise and spread of mysticisms of various sorts. And all this is stirring both the surface and the depths of the Christian mind and heart—even though it can scarcely be the wave of the future, at least not in its present form. It is worth noticing, however, that even in these new revivals of the old gospel traditions, the older forensic images are generally subdominant—in some, virtually absent.

This suggests, to me at least, the basic transaction by which an open-minded, modern Christian might appropriate the secular *wisdoms* of modern humanism, even while rejecting their *gospel* of *self*-salvation. We can begin by abandoning our reliance on the *forensic* image of divine justice as our *basic* soteriological metaphor—and still reassert the primacy and truth of *divine justice* as the only valid ground of human freedom and all other human aspirations. The essence of the gospel—that our true joy and happiness is to be sought and found in God—does not require a forensic model or paradigm, not even in the interest of God's sovereignty. What *is* crucial, however, is the acknowledgment of God as just, and an understanding of what that justice implies: that his human children shall live and die in accordance with their actual human potential (i.e., God's original intention in creating and sustaining them, *de nihilo*). For human beings to live and die without achieving their created potential, and with no such prospect of achieving that created potential—here or hereafter—is the essence of injustice, as far as human existence is concerned. Nor does this need to be construed in juridical terms. First and last, justice is an ethical issue. A gospel for the guilty is a true gospel for men and women who feel themselves guilt-ridden—and I do not wish to be misunderstood as disparaging the truth, relevance, and power of this version of the gospel for those to whom it is *gospel!* But we need also a gospel for the guiltless—for those whose consciences do *not* condemn them in forensic terms, for those whose self-image is, on the whole, self-justifying and self-excusing.

And we might very well begin, I suggest, with the bold denial that any and all the gospels of humanism are anything more than self-deluding, and this for a very simple but profound reason. Humanism would be true if, and only if, human beings were without a radical flaw; if, and only if, we were self-perfectible. But both these ifs are plainly contrary to every observable fact—in human history and in the current human scene. The most obvious human reality we know—and can verify existentially—is the actuality of self-stultification and social injustice (in their various mixes). Human happiness, at its best, is evanescent and episodic, bracketed by a pitiless natural environment which provides for our lives and deaths but couldn't care less for our personal hopes and fears—in life or death. There is much talk these days about hope, about futurology, about political transformations yet possible. Inevitably, they have generated their matching brands of futuristic theology—of God working away on his own project of self-fulfillment—with us as his partners in becoming what we can become and in helping him toward *his* potential. But the fact is that the promises of any such humanistic life-view are cruelly self-deceiving. The fact is that the *humanum*, on its own and left to its own resources, still is (as it always has been) a tragic failure. Who is there—amongst us or any of our acquaintances—who has not fallen short of what *any* of us can clearly conceive (or wish for) as our human potential? Who disbelieves, really, that the human potential *is* achievable, or would be, if only . . . ? But this means we are being suckered, for even when we succeed, our highest achievements are already being slyly mocked by transience and death:

> Time, like an ever-rolling stream,
> Bears all its sons away;
> They fly, forgotten, as a dream
> Dies at the opening day.
> —Isaac Watts

Thus even if it be true that the guiltless no longer need a gospel of forensic acquittal, it is also true that the *hopeless* need a gospel that promises them something better than an epitaph like that of Willie Loman in *Death of Salesman:* "He dreamed the wrong dreams and never found out who he really was." Moreover, for those of us who never find out who we really are and what we really want, the tragedy deepens and the threat of *final* meaninglessness becomes as terrifying for us as those fumes of sulphur and brimstone that frightened our forebears.

For the human flaw—and the human tragedy—still remain. Our condition is still as ironic as it ever was. The best this world can give is not enough for what we can, and must, aspire to. Those who feel no guilt are still trapped in the toils of blind, uncaring fate—unless there is more to life than nature and society can offer us. What kind of gospel is it, then, to talk about human happiness in terms of partial, evanescent, death-bracketed values? This is to downgrade (or maybe even never to *know*) what *human* happiness really is; it is to compromise, with partial substitutes, for our deepest, irrepressible hungers. I may not be guilty of any crime that would deserve a loving God's rejection. But what is there to hope for if my most authentic outreaches are never to come to their final goal? Is life's agony and ecstasy finally worth it all? Who will deliver me from *this* death of thwarted hopes?

Suppose, then, we let the forensic, courtroom metaphor go and turn, as so many have, to therapeutic and clinical metaphors—what then? This is a clear advance, in many ways, and is much to be welcomed and incorporated into our pastoral theory and practice. But there is no avoiding the fact that *therapy,* in any and all its images, means nothing more than amelioration—not complete and real fulfillment. Therapy is the reduction of this symptom or that, the curing of this malady or that. It does not and cannot mean the resolution of our ultimate concerns. It cannot fend off death. Its best good news is never better than a comparative judgment that our frustrations are not as dreadful as they might have been.

Thus, beyond the courtroom and the clinic, the human hunger for happiness still reaches out in an intuition that there is and must be some sovereign power of caring that is neither a bloodless category nor a wishful dream. The good news we really need to hear is that "God so loved the world that he gave of himself that the world [we!] might not perish [in some void of thwarted dreams] but have *life,* in *all* its human potential." There's nothing forensic in that old text; it reaches above and beyond any sort of clinical model. This is real gospel (*good* news)—for those who may be guiltless but are nonetheless hopeless (or would be hopeless if they *really* expected ever to be *fully* human).

There is, therefore, real *gospel* in the message of God's love in Christ—"the power of God and the wisdom of God." "You," said St. Paul, "are *in* Christ Jesus by God's act, for God has made him *our* wisdom; he is our righteousness; in him we are consecrated and set free" (I Cor. 1:24, 30 NEB). There's nothing forensic here —and yet it is great good news to anyone who has canvassed the other options. "God was in Christ reconciling the world to himself [which is the exact opposite of the classical substitutionary theory of atonement!]. . . . For our sake [for the sake of true humanity] God made Christ one with us in our sinfulness so that we might be made one with God in his goodness" (II Cor. 5:19, 21). Here again, there is no forensic metaphor. Jesus Christ

> is the image [the *eikon*] of the invisible God; his is the primacy over all created things. In him everything in heaven and on earth was created, not only things visible but also the invisible orders of thrones, sovereignties, authorities, and powers: the whole universe has been created through him and for him. And he exists before everything, and all things are held together in him. He is, moreover, the head of the body, the church. He is its origin, the first to return from the dead, to be in all things alone supreme. For in him the complete being of God, by God's own choice, came to dwell. Through him God chose to reconcile the whole universe to himself, making peace through the shedding of his blood upon the cross—to reconcile all things, whether on earth or in heaven, through him alone.
>
> —Colossians 1:15-20 NEB

This is *gospel,* indeed—good news for the guiltless, who are nonetheless aware of their radical need for grace and love and peace. "Even here and now, beloved, we are God's children. What we shall be has not yet been disclosed, but we know that when it is [disclosed] we shall be like him" (I John 3:2).

Here then, are the great gospel promises, and they all point to the mystery of salvation, more hopeful and truly human than anything we might expect from any heavenly courtroom or earthly clinic. They all focus on a *theonomous* transaction of reconciliation which, on its human side, calls for two basic responses: repentance and faith. And the crucial agent in every transaction is Jesus Christ, without whose revealing and redeeming love we could never grasp this new level of meaning and value which transvalues all of life.

The *gospel* (not forensic but ethical) is the promise that we *can* live intentionally, following the inner leadings of the Holy Spirit, accepting what we are given to know of God's will—working, suffering, and hoping in the atmosphere of God's love, which also means the forgiveness of our sins by the same love that thwarts those sins from ever making us happy. Jesus Christ is the guarantor and agent of this promise, not only in his revelation of God's love but also in his sharing in our human lot and opening a way for us to share in his power and wisdom. His *power* is his victory over the power of sin and death. His *wisdom* is that God is all in all, that we can become all we ever can be in *him.*

The Christian gospel for the guiltless is not that Jesus Christ has appeased the Father's wrath, but that he is, for all of us, the Revealer and Agent of the Father's unmerited and yet unfaltering compassion. This is not to reject or even diminish the living truth in the grand articles of justification, pardon, regeneration, reconciliation, and so on. It is only to stress, more than our traditions usually have done, the fact that our Christian hope rests in God's calling us to participate in his goodness which is the primordial and ultimate ground of our true happiness—to participate both in the human *potential* and in the divine *actuality.* The human potential is for happiness (not just "peak experiences," but settled and suffusing joy). The divine actuality is holy love, accepting and justifying even such over-reachers as we are. Happiness and holiness are correlates, and Jesus Christ is their link: happiness, the fruit of our love of God; holiness, our love of God and neighbor (love of God for his goodness and love of neighbor out of gratitude to God).

The essential contract in this new gospel—that is, conversion from self-stultifying life to the life of grace in the Spirit—is the same as the old one: repentance and faith. "Repent and believe the gospel"—believe the good news that God is indeed the giver of life's meanings and joys and hopes, that life in his love is ultimately secure and, even now, can be serene, since its meanings *beyond* life and death are secured by his love.

What is repentance? The best answer is still the literal one: *metanoia,* a genuine, basic change of *nous*—that is, one's inner intentions. What do we know about ourselves really—what are our real intentions? Are they self-interested, self-centered, self-righteous? Are we willing to discover the unvarnished, honest truth about our self-deceptions? Are we willing to undergo an actual change to something more authentic? If so, this is *metanoia,* a qualitative change of intention, heart, and hope. Its inner impulse comes from God's prevenient grace; its sustenance and final guarantee comes from God's unfailing and invincible love (what John Wesley called converting and perfecting grace).

Notice that I have not referred to the old forensic images—and also have been trying to honor the good essence of modern psychotherapy and religious psychology. But the best of God's good news lies *beyond* all these, in the heartening word that "God is on our side" (Rom. 8:31). And if that be so, what then can separate us from the love of Christ—save unfaith or self-righteousness? (Rom. 8:35-39).

Nothing that I know about psychotherapy's contributions to our liberation from our unhealthy guilt complexes and self-defeats cancels or even limits this theonomous view of the human potential and its achievement, in Christ and in the Body of Christ. In *these* terms, or something like them, the Christian gospel is still alive and well—and never was more desperately needed by guiltless people, people whose very guiltlessness has added to their desperate need for a truly hopeful word. And this is its challenge: Let the Spirit change our self-awareness, accept our radical dependence upon God's grace and gifts, freely given in love. Let the Spirit make our lives offertories of love and service to humanity—and so let us enter into the *joys* (and the tasks) of our Lord!

# 12

## *The First Pentecost*

### *An Introductory Comment*

This is the first of six sermons on the doctrine of the Holy Spirit preached at First United Methodist Church in Longview, Texas, on November 23, 24, and 25, 1975 (and also in May 1975, at the New Mexico Annual Conference).

Vatican II was an exciting Pentecostal experience. Not all such experiences are; for instance, Albert Outler often despairs of the condition of the church in the world. In the mid-to-late 1970s and into the 1980s, he felt that some of the bishops of The United Methodist Church were not attending to their superintending—not "bishing." They had opted, in too many instances, to let the boards and agencies speak and act for the whole church.

Out of this despair came the 1978 Outler document on the general superintendency, which called for the bishops to be and to act in the manner set forth in the constitution of The United Methodist Church.

Some bishops have gotten the message, and that particular Outler despair has waned (but not vanished), only to be replaced by another—the doctrinal crises in The United Methodist Church.

Outler has had many Pentecostal experiences which have more than matched the despair of the times, and he knows he will have them until he finally comes into the one that lasts eternally.

## *The Sermon*

*And when the day of Pentecost was fully come . . . (Acts 2:2 KJV).*

I want to talk to you about the Holy Spirit—as God present in our hearts and lives, God immanent in the church, God in history—seeking to lead the church and the world into the fullness of the truth of his self-revelation in Jesus Christ. These are difficult times for the church and the world, and the surest ground of hope I can see anywhere is in the resurgence of interest in the Holy Spirit and the Spirit's power to renew and sustain us, no matter what the daily news may be. The signs of this resurgence are everywhere. The United Methodist Church is still comparatively calm. But in our Wesleyan heritage, the center of the Christian life is Christ, and its Active Agent is always the Holy Spirit.

And so I invite you to six meditations on the Holy Spirit in the Christian life—in all its dimensions:

1. The First Pentecost
2. The Spirit in the Heart
3. The Spirit in the Church
4. The Spirit in the World
5. The Harvest of the Spirit
6. A New Pentecost?

I realize I should begin with the crucial disclaimer that I am not indifferent to the great social and practical issues of these tragic times. If you want yet another rehearsal of doomsday and the gloomy prospects for humankind, just let me know! If you want to canvass the requirements for a new American Revolution, the updating of the Spirit of '76 in 1975 and 1976, let me know! If *you* see any really cheerful light on the human horizon, by all means, let *me* know!

But as a church historian, I'm interested in the way the church has survived the hard times and grave crises before this present one, and I'm convinced that it has been the work of the Holy Spirit in every case—always a revival of faith (sometimes from unexpected quarters), a reawakening in the hearts and minds of the Christian faithful—that gave them fortitude and hope.

Eighteenth-century England was in a bad way, as we all know.

The Methodist revival was not a *direct* reform of the political and economic ills of the time. What it did was to bring new life and dignity to the disinherited—liberation (*Christian* liberty) to the oppressed, new hope (Christian hope) for the hopeless. And what followed was not only a tremendous *spiritual* renewal, but eventually a basic reform in the nation and the world (what Bernard Semmel has aptly described as *The Methodist Revolution*).

But long before Methodism, Christianity itself had been born in hard times and had grown up with the end of the world staring it in the face. This is why the first *Christian* Pentecost is a sort of model for Christians in crisis in any age—and certainly for our own, plus whatever future looms ahead.

That first Pentecost began with a shattered dream, recounted by the disciples on the road to Emmaus: "We had hoped that [Jesus] was the one who was going to redeem Israel" (Luke 24:21). The Gospels give us quite candid accounts of the general muddle amongst Jesus' disciples in their days and nights in the Cenacle after Calvary and Easter and the Ascension. There was the inevitable impulse to cop out—to go fishing (with Peter), to despair (with Judas), or the more typical reaction of the majority: to ease back into the obscurity from which they had been snatched for those brief months.

But they also had their memories of having been with Jesus and his express command for them to hang in there: "He charged them not to *depart* from Jerusalem, but to wait for the promise of the Father." And there was the promise: "You shall receive *power* when the Holy Spirit has come upon you; and [then] you shall be my witnesses" (Acts 1:4,8 RSV).

Then came that groping interim of forty days—in the Cenacle, in the Temple. For want of anything more earthshaking, they even held an episcopal election (the first jurisdictional conference in history!). It was no big deal either; Matthias appears and, after this single mention in Acts 1:26, disappears.

And then finally, Pentecost morning—not at all expected, and without a program (not even a steering committee). It may even have been unconstitutional! And this is the first main point in any understanding of the Holy Spirit: We cannot organize the Spirit. The Spirit cannot be programmed, cannot be turned on or off like a switch, cannot be manipulated. Pentecost surprised the disciples as much as it surprised the other people in town. "The wind bloweth where it listeth"—revivals come when they come. God sends by whom he will send, and more often than not, uprushings of the Spirit are upsetting to the comfortable in Christ. One of the predictable signs of the Spirit's visitations is that they overturn our routines—although it is a mistake to identify just any old upset or hurrah as a visitation of the *Holy* Spirit!

There is a clue tucked away in all this confusion: "These [the Apostles] *tarried* . . . and continued with one accord in prayer and supplication, with the women" [the first United Methodist Women!] (Acts 1:14). And this suggests a second thesis. When in dismay, *tarry* (not in idleness, mind you, but genuine, mutual searching for light, and faith, and the new horizon!) and continue, *with one accord*, in prayer and supplication—with the women as well as the men (i.e., the *entire* Christian community!). In times of the church's prosperity (membership, attendance, finance, program activities on the rise, etc.), it may be the Spirit's motion to stir up internal criticism and dissension or to thaw out the frozen pews, or to shake the complacent and pry them from their lees: to discomfort the comfortable.

But in times of demoralization and confusion—such as we are in now—dissension and hassling are counterproductive or, indeed, self-destructive. Our cherished majority rule in The United Methodist Church—valid enough in a strong, healthy church with strong opposing factions—means that 50 percent plus 1 can impose its ideas on 50 percent minus 1 (and then claim to speak for the church as a whole).

Those people in the Cenacle were not up there squabbling—and one of the sorest needs of our times in the Christian community (and in The United Methodist Church in particular) is to realize once more that being *in one accord*, with prayer and supplication, may be the condition for our survival, in any sense that survival is worthwhile. This does not mean servile abandonment of anybody's informed, scripturally based convictions. But it does mean a profound and self-denying concern for a deeper unity and concord in the Spirit than we have now (or have had in living memory)—a subordination of our power struggles in the interest of a more vital experience of true communion. If Methodism goes down (or continues in its current slump), it will not be from any flaws in our heritage, but because of ideological and power struggles over stakes in church politics (local and denominational) which simply are *not* worth the consequences they will bring. "With one accord, in prayer and supplication, with the women"—this in itself would be a new Pentecost!

Spirit of God, descend upon our squabbling church, our empire-building priests, prophets, and bureaucrats. Wean us from the earthly notion that power is worth more than concord, that ideologies are worth spiritual schism. And as thou dost teach us to love *thee* as we ought to love—teach us to love *one another in thee*, that we may be saved from those more enamored of their causes (even good causes) than of their precondition: true koinonia in Christ. Teach us that true love "seeketh not her own," but rather *thy* will to unity and the concord of all the faithful!

But concord, prayer, and supplication are means to other ends: witness, service, and outreach. And that's what happened on Pentecost. I freely confess that I do not understand the details as they are recounted by Luke in Acts 2. I don't understand about those tongues of flame—except as metaphors for a sudden newfound eloquence, new uprushing insights that tumbled over one another as the full import of what their experiences with Jesus really meant, for them and for their people and for the world. I've seen people in the flush of vivid insight, and the metaphor "tongues of flame" has been brought home more times than once. What mattered is that the Apostles were filled with the Holy Spirit and began to speak as the Spirit gave them utterance; and that this not only drew a crowd, but communicated their newly understood gospel to a veritable mulitude—of tourists yet!

Now, let's take this tongue speaking bit seriously, and let us keep our cool about it, too. For my part, I want to keep open the question as to what tongue speaking communicates, and how. I've heard a fair amount of it, and I've yet to hear anything that had grammatical-syntactical linguistic structures I could recognize or guess at. What is more, the only interpretations that made sense to me were all echoes of commonplace biblical truths. The others were weird excursions that left me unedified. What I have found edifying is the joyous exaltation of spirit that I've seen in the typical charismatic groups I've visited. So far, no gifts of glossolalia have been vouchsafed to me, though I've been accused often enough of speaking in unknown tongues! (With my accent, even when I speak in known tongues, I've had people crack up!) So far, I've yet to hear, or hear of, any new doctrinal insight proposed by the tongue speakers that wasn't a variation on already familiar themes in Christian history—except some really new notions that ignored both Scripture and tradition, and which I felt entirely free to disregard.

I am, therefore, inclined to agree with Cardinal Suenens that tongue speaking is not the badge of a new spiritual elite, holier-than-the-rest-of-us, whom we must accept as miraculous or reject as pathological. Cardinal Suenens describes tongue speaking as a form of "non-discursive prayer—a preconceptual expression of spontaneous prayer . . . a verbal expression independent of any specific linguistic structures."[6] The gift of tongues is not unlike the gift of tears—open to abuse, but expressive of feelings too high or too deep for flat prose. It is a way for the overfilled to try to express the inexpressible.

What is crucial is that we take tongue speaking as nondiscursive *prayer*—neither more nor less—and that we ask of the tongue-speakers, and of ourselves, that everybody keep their heads clear as to the difference between glossolalia as a claim of a higher spirituality and glossolalia as a symptom of hysteria. The extraordinary gifts of the Spirit certainly include tongues, but they do not include spiritual pride. Thus, wherever spiritual pride is very evident, even "sanctified" pride, we can safely say, "Sorry, but there's something phony here." The other crucial distinction to be made is that the baptism of the Spirit is not to be thought of as superceding water baptism or conversion. There are divers gifts and fruits of the Spirit, but none that allows the eye to say to the hand, "I have no need of *you.*"

It helps to remember, though, that although the tongue speaking got the Pentecost crowd's attention, the centerpiece of the whole affair was Peter's sermon. It is the earliest evangelistic sermon on record—and a model for this tradition ever since.

Unity in spiritual concord and prayer, tongues of flame, glossolalia—all are aiming at a still further end: Christians reaching out in love to others, with their words and lives as their placards and billboards. They were known as Followers of the Way because they had become witnesses to Christ and servants to his brothers and sisters.

Peter's sermon itself has more in it than we can analyze. Three things, though, are worth noting:

1. "I speak," says Peter, "of Jesus of Nazareth. . . . Accept as certain that God has made this Jesus, whom you [and we] crucified, to be both Lord and Messiah."

2. "Repent and be baptized—in the name of Jesus, the Messiah, for the *forgiveness of our sins* [justification by repentance and faith]."

3. In the days afterward, "They met together to hear the apostles teach, to share the common life, to break bread together and to pray. . . . They kept their daily attendance at the temple. . . . They shared their meals with unaffected joy, as they praised God and attracted the favor of the people."

This is the agenda of evangelism in a nutshell: the primacy and centrality of Jesus of Nazareth, Lord and Messiah; salvation by faith; the outreach of love to all who are moved to accept this salvation by repentance and faith; and the unaffected joy of their new life together, in nurture, service, and true communion.

I began by saying we've got problems—in ourselves, in our church, in the world, or wherever, and none of these problems will go away while we are *talking* about Pentecost (old or new). But all these problems would appear in a vastly different light if we could see them in this Pentecostal perspective, if we could accept and respond to the Spirit as it draws us into more concord and fellowship than we're accustomed to, if once more we put Christ at the center of our hopes, underlined and accented our stress on salvation by faith, and allowed ourselves really to *enjoy* our life and work together, in Christ and the Spirit—in Christian witness, Christian nurture, Christian service, Christian communion.

It's either this or something like it, or else a future that is too dismal to contemplate, too tragic to bear.

> Spirit of God, descend upon my heart;
> Wean it from earth; through all its pulses move;
> Stoop to my weakness, mighty as thou art,
> And make me love thee as I ought to love.
>
> —George Croly

# 13

# *The Spirit in the Heart*

## *An Introductory Comment*

In this sermon on prayer, preached at Longview First United Methodist Church in November 1975 (and also at the New Mexico Annual Conference on May 28, 1975), Albert Outler says: "Wesley was a praying man; his daily rhythm was different from mine, for he woke early and bright and immediately began to pray. I come to in a fog and have to reassemble my world and reorient myself in it by stages."

But those who get up later and groggier can have a prayer life as genuine as that of those who bolt up early and clear-headed. To begin the day, punctuate the day, and end the day with prayer is the discipline we all should follow.

Outler also punctuates his days with short naps. Many who enter his office probably think his couch, which resembles a psychotherapist's, is for his "patients." In fact, however, it is for, in his words, a "short rest stop that gets me on the road again."

# *The Sermon*

*Continue to pray in the power of the Holy Spirit (Jude 20 NEB).*

"Every time I feel the Spirit, moving in my heart, I will pray." This sounds pious enough and reassuring, until we ask how often we—and the generality of Christians—*feel* the Spirit in our hearts so that we are moved to pray: to *stop* to pray, to pray consciously on the move, to pray with and for our families, to pray for the world, to pray with others, to open our hearts and wills and lives to God and lay our concerns and commitments (personal and collective) before him?

The third General Rule in The United Methodist Church—the oldest remnant of our Wesleyan heritage in the *Discipline*—reads as follows:

> It is expected of all who desire to continue in these [Methodist] societies that they should continue to evidence their desire of salvation. . . .
>
> *Thirdly:* By attending upon all the ordinances of God; such are:
>
> The public worship of God.
> The ministry of the Word, either read or expounded.
> The Supper of the Lord.
> Family and private prayer.
> Searching the Scriptures.
> Fasting or abstinence [i.e., self-denial of all needless self-indulgence].[7]

Here, more than almost anywhere else, lay the secret of the ongoing vitality of the Methodist societies, for these "ordinances," taken together and broadly, amount to "the life of prayer," since prayer is not just what one does in moments of formal ritual. It is, rather, the whole round of God-consciousness, and what we feel and think and do in those moments (or hours) of actual and real *God*-consciousness. Wesley was a praying man. His daily rhythm was different from mine, for he woke early and bright and immediately began to pray. I come to in a fog and have to reassemble my world and reorient myself in it by stages. But the same principle applies in both cases; to begin the day with a time of prayer that looks ahead, to punctuate the day with moments of intentional awareness of God's abiding grace, to close the day with a retrospective review that seeks and accepts God's appraisal of the day's work and life's ongoing business; or to wake in the assurance that we resume our tasks in and for God (which is what it means really to live), and to drift into sleep, secure in God's providence (which is a prototype of "dying" in faith and peace). The early Methodists were praying people: Their class meetings were prayer meetings; their conversations spoke of God without self-consciousness (embarrassment *or* pomp!); they taught their children to pray, not least of all by praying with them. Incidentally, we used to use such phrases as "he drank in this or that conviction with his mother's milk" or "she learned this or that at her mother's knee"—and everybody understood them. Phrases like that sound quaint now, don't they—like "prayer meeting"?

I've no statistics, and I mistrust so-called or pseudoscientific studies of deeply personal affairs, but it is my overwhelming impression that *prayer* as a means of grace or a constant discipline in Christian living is at a low ebb amongst mainline Christians and in their churches today. Many of the ministers I know well enough to ask about this can talk freely enough about Transactional Analysis or ESP or psi-phenomona or biofeedback, but not, I find, about prayer. They speak about their private prayer life not only with reticence (that's O.K.!) but without enthusiasm (which seems ominous). Seminary students are having marvelous experiences of liturgical prayer (traditional and newfangled), but their private prayer life as such (at least the ones who come in to talk about it) seems meager and stylized. Lay folk may be more ardent and disciplined in prayer—I don't know—but if one can judge by their public prayers, one would not think so.

The secret of United Methodist spirituality, evangelism, outreach, nurture, and spiritual growth is prayer—and always has been. But it would follow from this that the secret of Methodist shortfallings in spirituality, and such, is the low level of our prayer life: its neglect, its formalization, its ancillary or decorative role in our spiritual habits and disciplines—namely, the demise of the prayer meeting and the rise and spread of encounter groups of various kinds.

What is more, there are basic stereotypes in much of what passes for public prayer. Invariably, such prayers begin with thanks to God for this and that—which is a sound instinct but presupposes a steady state of God-consciousness that may not really be there. Moreover, there often is at least a tinge of complacency—thanks to God for bounties that somehow belong to the partnership we've struck up with him. Then, usually, comes what passes for repentance—a rehearsal of our sins and moral failures which, at least every now and then, sounds more like remorse than contrition, more like denunciation of currrent social dysfunctions than deep soul searching, and covers the territory of general transgressions more than focusing clearly on where we really live and on our actual sins. Here is an example of a prayer that at least had a concrete focus: At a Southern Methodist University Convocation, someone prayed that our beer should be warm and our wives cold until we shook ourselves out of our apathy about Vietnam. Dubious taste and arguable politics—and yet. . . . Incidentally, however, I've heard very few such prayer-concerns lately about the massive cruelties in conquered Cambodia—and I don't mean the Mayaguez incident, either. Finally we come to our petitions, which are usually eloquent enough and far-visioned enough, but often sound more like exhortations to ourselves than wrestlings with the Spirit for help and blessings.

Genuine prayer simply does not seem like the "in" thing these days. For instance, Brooks Jones said to the Dean before he (the Dean) went into a trustees meeting, "I'll be thinking of you." The Dean paused, then commented, "You know, that's what people say nowadays when they're too embarrassed to say 'I'll be *praying* for you!' "

I don't mean to sound critical, and certainly not self-righteous. My own prayer life is more and more difficult to sustain, more and more stylized and episodic, more and more preoccupied with the mounting cares and problems that cluster around my own concerns and family and school—or related too vaguely to the world crisis, and without many decisive and tangible results that I can see and feel. I am a minister, a theologian, a modern man: What would it do to my image, nowadays, if I were regarded as being pious, devout, given to sizable chunks of prayer time during my days and nights! Besides, how would I get my *work* done—since, as it is, I'm always playing catch-up?

Even so, we might as well forget our slogans about "renewal" and "evangelism" and "The United Methodist Church Aflame for Christ"—or even our obsessions with structures and church politics as means of grace—unless and until Methodists become a praying people, a people to whom prayer comes naturally and is a constant activity in our daily rounds; until our communion becomes the *conscious* context of our concerns for and contributions to our human community.

I realize, of course, that a good deal of this decline in our prayer life and spiritual self-discipline is a reaction against an older, gross supernaturalism which we have outgrown, and rightly so—hot-lines to heaven, prayer as supernatural leverage, prayer as spiritual exhibitionism, and the like. That was a heresy—the notion of prayer as human manipulation of the Spirit. And we are well shed of all notions of prayer as giving us a special handhold on deity or the possession of special powers that make *us* special. This, of course, is the problem about spiritual healing. I've never doubted that "more things are wrought by prayer than this world dreams of." It's only that I don't read as Ms. Kuhlmann or Dr. Roberts seem to: "More things are wrought by pray-ers (like me) than this world dreams of." And now that we are in a flood tide of a new supernaturalism—with newfangled forms of sorcery, psychiatric magic, Transactional Analysis, transcendental meditation, and so on, it becomes more and more important that we rethink and renew our understandings of prayer—most of all, of prayer in the Spirit, invoking the power of the Spirit not only to teach and guide us in prayer, but actually to pray in and through us, to divinize our prayer and lift it above and beyond the easy reach of self-interest and magic.

The clues for this are everywhere in the Bible—which means that *one* of the prime preconditions of any authentic prayer life is a new immersion in the Scriptures, a new listening to the Word in Scripture, a new eagerness for the hearing of faith. The two most familiar examples will serve our purpose: Isaiah's vision and our Lord's model prayer.

In Isaiah 6, it all begins with (1) a specially significant uprush of God-consciousness, followed by (2) a reflex experience of self-knowledge (repentance), followed by (3) purification and pardon by God—*at his initiative* and without merit—followed by (4) a divine call and a human commitment. And there it is in a nutshell—the human experience of God (of God's glory, etc.), of our human situation, of pardon and commitment—in a specific crisis situation. Here one sees how the Spirit bestirs a new awareness of the human situation *before* God, a new awareness that this God of *glory* is also the God of *grace,* a new awareness of God's callings and causes in the world—and then, a new awareness of *our* role in this mystery of God's agonizing in the world: the God of *glory* is also the God who continues to seek *the world's redemption* and who needs *our help.* There is nothing here about thanks, and even less of petition: This is the human before God; this is God's gift of grace to the end of human repentance: God's call and human response.

The Lord's Prayer is not as commonplace as it has come to sound to us. It begins not with thanksgiving or repentance, but with acknowledgment—acknowledgment of the hallowing of life as a mirror of God's holiness. The first petition is not for ourselves, but for God's righteous rule on earth—as of course it is already regnant in heaven. The next petition is for a sufficiency of life's needs, no more. And the next is a swap-off: our sins pardoned as we pardon others—which is to say, God's *grace* carries with it his expectation that we be gracious. The last two petitions are unflattering: (1) Don't put us under pressures that might buckle us under; and (2) deliver us from the plausible concept of the dominion of evil and those plausible persuasions that evil has the last word in our existence.

And yet, we cannot pray on command, by imitation, by model or rote and have it come out right. We cannot make prayer our quid pro quo for God's grace—for that is still manipulation, albeit a subtler form than some others.

But we *can* truly pray *in the Spirit, by* the Spirit and *with* the Spirit. It is not as if we occasionally reminded ourselves of an absent God—and tried to summon him up for a brief conference. It is, rather, our growing accustomed to the living presence of God in our inmost hearts—prevenient grace, as John Wesley used to say. What we need, if we are truly aware of what faith and grace mean, is not to get the Spirit to do our praying for us, or even to teach *us* to pray so that an otherwise inattentive Father will somehow get the message. Our petition, rather, is to the Spirit, that he "take the dimness of our souls away."

"I ask no dream"—although we could do with grander, nobler dreams than we usually have dreamed for the Christian mission in the world, and for our own roles in that mission. "No prophet ecstasies"—no spiritual highs, no pious crystal gazing. "No sudden rending of the veil of clay"—bad psychology, this, because of its body-soul dualism, but still a valid insight that neither ecstasy nor psychedelic experiences get us out of the real world for long and that the essence of authentic experience is its relevance to our actual living in the real world. "No angel visitant"—odd, isn't it, that we've ceased, generally, to believe in angels at about the same time our parapsychological friends have come to believe in psychokinesis and such stuff. "No opening skies"—no advance dope on the New Jersusalem, even with all these secular utopians running around. "But take the dimness of my soul away"—now *there's* our *real* problem. Dim, dull, perfunctory, halfhearted, self-pitying, lackluster—how many of these adjectives apply to how many of us who call and profess ourselves Christians, who even speak of evangelism and mission, who have a cross and flame on our stationery, who repeat good slogans such as Methodism Aflame for Christ, but only as *slogans*? And do we really expect *the world* to listen to what we say—or do we realize that the world has to see something *shining* in our eyes and faces and lives before they will listen as we preach the gospel of liberation and joy or sing "true-hearted, whole-hearted, faithful and loyal" without a suppressed yawn. Do you remember that oldie, "Peal out the watchword, silence it never / Song of our spirits, rejoicing and free!"? And have you ever heard it sung dragged out and limping?

Now, the power of prayer and of the buoyancy of the Christian spirit is always the power of the Spirit, moving in our hearts to pray. And it is the Spirit that takes the dimness of our souls away by the shining of his love and peace and joy.

The old boys had a word for this outward expression of the inner light of the Spirit-filled life—and I'm inclined to suggest it to you as important to effective Christian witness and service, as sound doctrine, and as one's quota of scars and bruises from one's struggles for social justice. The word is *radiance*, and most of us know it when we see it, except in ourselves (and it's not very healthy to keep peering into our spiritual mirrors). It's not a halo I'm talking about, or a nimbus—but radiance: the outward and visible sign of an inward and almost unconscious light and joy and buoyancy!

Now, a certain amount of intensity can be cultivated, and turned off and on—and one suspects this in the case with some hyperpituitary evangelists, salesmen, politicians on the make. But real radiance cannot be turned on, except as a by-product of authentic Spirit-given love, joy, peace, patience, and the like. What they call charisma nowadays can be *cultivated;* what the public relations people call public image can be furbished and sold. But Spirit-given serenity, joy, and fortitude come from a basic spiritual relationship that results from the habit of God-consciousness in the Spirit; from many experiences of God's trustworthiness and grace, in grief and joy, pain and health, defeat and victory. I've known radiant souls like this, and so have you.

We can't be radiant by deciding to be radiant, or by smiling, or by putting our best foot forward for this or that occasion. Radiance is a by-product we never really know we have—and we had best not inhale any praise to the effect that we are radiant, either! It will give us spiritual emphysema. It comes, when and if, from the Spirit in the heart—from a heart weaned from earth, a heart moved by the Spirit, a heart attentive to what the Spirit is saying and doing and prompting. And all faithful Christians have the Spirit in their hearts—this is what sanctifying grace really means. Indeed, every child of God has the Spirit in his or her heart—this is what prevenient grace really means. And this makes evangelism possible; just as the gospel makes it imperative; just as love makes it joyous even in difficulties.

"If you are led by the Spirit in your heart," Paul explained to the Galatians long ago, "you are not under law but under love. . . . For the fruits of the Spirit are love, joy, peace, patience, kindness, goodness, fidelity, gentleness,and self-control. There is no law that deals with such things as these"—they come from the *inner* resources of the spiritual life, which is to say, the Holy Spirit in the heart. "And if the Spirit is thus the source of our lives in Christ, then let the Spirit also direct our course" (Gal. 5:18, 22-23, 25).

This is the great and precious privilege of all God's children who live in faith, hope, and love in the Spirit. Who, then, should ever be willing to settle for less?

# 14

# *The Spirit in the Church*

## *An Introductory Comment*

This sermon was preached at Longview First United Methodist Church in November 1975 (and also at the North Texas Annual Conference, May 1972; the New Mexico Annual Conference, May 1975; and the Northern New Jersey Annual Conference, June 1976).

Albert Outler is not mystical in the conventional sense of looking toward "absorption" into the Godhead. But mysticism, as a keen awareness of the numinous and the presence of God, accounts for the awe and reverence he knows and experiences in worship, in the Eucharist, and in his daily life.

This sermon reflects the spirit of Origen, Gregory of Nyssa, and Clement of Alexandria—three church Fathers who have shaped Outler's thinking as much as, or more than, any others. His language here is experiential; it sounds like moanings of the Spirit too deep for words. It sounds like prayer!

## *The Sermon*

The history in the Acts of the Apostles describes the birth of the Church and its first shaky struggles to survive and get moving—a sectarian movement within the Great Synagogue of Israel, its members distinguished from all other Jews by their peculiar conviction that the hoped-for Messiah had *come.* It records the shock waves sent out by the Pauline mission to the Gentiles, and the problems that loomed up as their apocalyptic expectations began to falter—and finally had to be altered. Luke goes to some pains to clarify his conviction that what made the crucial difference, in the very beginning and thereafter, was the dynamic action in the church of the Holy Spirit, who now had come to *abide* in human history, in and through the Christian koinonia.

This is why, in Peter's sermon on that first Pentecost, we have the prophecy of Joel quoted, and declared as finally fulfilled in the new movement:

> This will happen in the last days: I will pour out upon everyone a portion of my spirit; and your sons and daughters shall prophesy; your young men shall see visions, and your old men shall dream dreams. Yes, I will endue even my slaves, both men and women, with a portion of my spirit, and they shall prophesy. And I will show portents in the sky above, and signs on the earth below—blood and fire and drifting smoke. The sun shall be turned to darkness, and the moon to blood, before that great, resplendent day, the day of the Lord, shall come. And then, everyone who invokes the name of the Lord shall be saved.
> —Acts 2:17-21 NEB

Up until then, and in the Old Testament generally, the work of the Holy Spirit had been understood as episodic, as the divine intervention in special events, or as special outpourings of divine light or power—in short, as something discontinuous and extraordinary. Peter's claim is, therefore, all the more remarkable: that this pentecostal birthday of the church was the final fulfillment of Joel's prophecy; that *now* the Paraclete had come to reside and preside in the earthly koinonia of Christ's discipleship, constantly and permanently. The immanence of the transcendent had come to have a new and special reality in and through the church. The flaming-tongues bit had been an episode, as in the Old Testament, but now the old Covenant of Emanu-el (God with us) and the new age, ushered in by Jesus Christ (God for us), had finally converged. The Risen Lord, whose memory was at the mercy of the oral traditions of the disciples and the varying interpretations of the historians, had provided his people with an abiding, vital presence *in their midst.* The age of the promised Paraclete had dawned and would never end until the fullness of the Parousia. Its historical point of reference was the Incarnation—but its present inexhaustible font of life, light, and power was the Spirit of God-with-us, Christ-with-us, "even to the end of the *saeculum* [age, or world]."

Now, it is mildly embarrassing but literally true that after all these years of studying church history and sharing in the joys and failures of the churches in my own time, the marvel of the church's survival still strikes me as inexplicable on any conceivable human basis I have been able to think of—or have ever heard proposed. The apostles (with the exception of Paul and, maybe, Peter) were ordinary men by human standards. The books of the New Testament are not great literature in the traditional sense of literary genius (e.g., as compared to Homer or Virgil). They are, as you know, written in *koine* Greek—the everyday language of the common people. The leadership of the church has had less than its share of towering eminences—we've beefed up many a reputation in retrospect for people who didn't loom very large on the horizon in *their* time. The church has staggered or swaggered down through history, depending on its worldly fortunes, good or bad—and always has been involved in history's ambiguities and ambivalences. It never has achieved its own ideals; it has fought a constant (and often losing) battle with culture-religion—and it has had its critics, despisers, and persecutors in almost every age.

But it *has* survived. It has moved and changed with moving and changing times; its light at times has sunk low, down to a firefly's glowing, and then at other times blazed up in surprising and splendid ways. Sometimes it has seemed a threat to the secular establishment; sometimes it has been no better than establishment's religious arm and agency. Much of the time it has been marginal to, or subdominant in, society at large. And yet, in its survival, it also has made an enormous difference in world history. Stop and try to think of what the Graeco-Roman world would have been like without the church—or the middle ages, or the global expansions of Western civilization (which itself is unthinkable without its Christian ingredients), or even our own parlous times. Where would the impulses have come from to dignify women, to liberate slaves, to conceive of a human community in which all persons, equal in sin and separation from God, are also equal in and through his redeeming grace? Where would the ideal of *love* as power ever have displaced the notion of *coercion* as power—to the extent that it ever has? Outside the Judaeo-Christian tradition, there is no social ethic in any human tradition where the rights of the weak and defenseless were construed as moral imperatives to the strong and self-sufficient; where it is understood that God is on the side of the oppressed and is and always will be the incorruptible Judge of the high and the mighty, and of all oppressors of Christ's poor!

As a historian, I have no credible explanation for this story, even as I know it. As a churchman, I do have an explanation, but it sounds a mite weird in some ears: The church has survived in and by the power of the Holy Spirit as he has struggled to discipline the Christian conscience, to fortify the Christian will, to unleash the Christian laity in mission, to inspire and inspirit all Christians to greater courage and more resilient hope. The Spirit in the Church—leading the repentant into the truth of Jesus Christ's revelation of the Father's kingdom of justice and peace, leading the faithful into the truth that can free and unshackle men and women who have been bound by self-will or falsehoods about existence! The Holy Spirit in the church, inspiring the writing of Scripture and its valid interpretation and the "hearing of faith"! The Holy Spirit in the church, consecrating each sacrament and stimulating all our sacramental insights—that is, our burst of vision of the outward and visible signs of inward and invisible grace (the grace of our Lord and Savior, Jesus Christ)! This understanding of the Spirit in the sacraments redeems them from all suspicion of hocus-pocus and yet also makes them much more than audiovisual aids. In the heart and mind of the preacher, the Spirit is active, even as he also is, and already has been, in the hearts and minds of the hearers—this is the precondition of good preaching. The Holy Spirit is the inner spring of joy in Christian faith, even in times of stress and grief.

Joy is a flag flown high from the castle of your heart
When the King is in residence there!
So let it fly in the sky that the world may know
That the King is in residence there!
[a favorite chorus in "charismatic worship" services]

*All* this is either consciously communal, or else it quickly becomes private, withdrawn—socially irrelevant, actually selfish. This is why private piety, or even small encounter-group piety is never enough, in and of itself. "The *visible* Church"—as defined by our Articles—is the company of faithful persons amongst whom the Word (Christ) is rightly preached and heard (and it takes the Holy Spirit to bring this off, truly) "and the Sacraments duly administered [but with the Spirit, who applies his seal in baptism, and who consecrates the bread and wine into effectual symbols of Christ's broken body and shed blood, thus making rituals into sacraments]."[8]

It is the Spirit, then, who makes the church, who keeps the church, and who offers up the church (sinful and fallible as it is in all its human aspects) to the Father through Christ: *from* the Father, *through* the Son, *in* the Spirit—*to* the Father, *through* the Son, *by* the Spirit. And this is what the Apostolic Benediction is really trying to say to the people on the eve of their exit, so that no matter what else has been said or left unsaid, God's people go out of the "holy place" with a summary of what was intended and meant by having met together.

The church is, therefore, a unique phenomenon (however closely it resembles all other human associations). It is a community defined by its faith in Christ and by its function as the Holy Spirit's agency within Christ's koinonia and the world. It is, first and last, a community in communion and in mission—communion in the Body of Christ through the Spirit's ongoing guidance; mission to all the world through the Spirit's continuing stimulus and power. Its concern always begins with the individual believer—repentant, reconciled, a new creature in Christ—and it always reaches out toward the Spirit's manifest goal: all human lives and destinies, understood as every life and destiny is understood in Gospel terms—*from* God, *through* Christ, *in* the Holy Spirit.

There are hundreds of different patterns of human comradeship in modern society: some of them helpful, some harmful, some trivial. All of us belong to various special-interest groups or peer groups (the current "in" word for these just now is *caucuses*!)—with various business, political, social concerns (all of them self-interested!). Some are for fun, some are intensely involving and demanding. Who, in our time, has no cause or caucus to promote, or else some cause or caucus to defend oneself *against?*

Time was when the church served many of these various interests *directly*—social, economic, political, cultural, humanitarian—all at once for many of its people. Time was when the church was the chief bastion, in many communities, of public morality, social stability, and good fellowship (all this and heaven, too). But "the old order changeth, giving place to new—and God fulfills himself in many ways, lest one good custom should corrupt the world." And one thing this has come to mean for sure: that as a rival, or substitute for, other meaningful group relations in the modern world that are dedicated to popular standards of human interest and value, *the church is facing social and functional obsolescence*—even when its popular interests are the same as those of our secular counterparts. The blunt truth is that the church is far less effective as a political force than we have supposed or pretended, far less powerful as an economic factor, far less influential as a pacesetter for moral standards and human life-styles. On the whole, the churches have contributed more to the current tragedies of the permissive society than they have to the conservation of personal and social disciplines of unselfish service to the common good. I've been fascinated by the glimpses we've had recently of Maoist Chinese society—the moral climate of their educational system, their open and unabashed devotion to the public good, *beyond* self-interest. It sounds strangely like an old-fashioned Methodist Sunday school—with a different Bible but with much the same "Puritan work ethic" which we Americans have now been taught to scorn.

Sooner or later, we had better face it: In secular terms, the church is no longer a decisive force in the secular city—if indeed it ever was—and this disenchantment has finally spread to include Harvey Cox himself, the great high priest of the "secular city." Moreover, the notion that the church has only to become still *more* secular, *more* utopian, more preoccupied with human values—so nobly phrased in our incessant and inflated pronouncements

—is as surefire a recipe for obsolescence as any the church has already flirted with in *other* ages when she was losing her grip on her environing society.

But the panic that pushed us into the futility of trying to compete with secular institutions on their terms has finally brought us all to new disappointments. The world some of us once knew—Western hegemony, Renaissance and Enlightenment cultures, faith in technology, trust in the holy dogma of human progress—that world is beginning to fall apart, beyond any hope of recovery. The bases of a secular human hope—anywhere for *any* real future—have turned shaky everywhere you look. Take Britain, for example. Even the secularizers are now turning away from their earlier hopes for political solutions to human problems, to a splatter of new supernaturalisms—from ESP and psi-phenomena to seances and dreams and witches' cradles, to biofeedback and transcendental meditation. What we have discovered, in the tragic (predictable) failures of the utopianism of the 1960s, the shame of Watergate, the horrors of Indochina, the abdication of American leadership in a leaderless world, is that secularism leaves a deep, disturbing vacuum in the very depths of the human spirit. Our desacralization of the world (our banishment of the Holy Spirit or, alternatively, our futile efforts to domesticate the Spirit) has resulted in the dehumanization of modern society, and no amount of success in the human-potential movement will be able to do more than ameliorate this disaster—and even then for no more than a small fraction of distraught humanity.

All of which is to say that the church now has a new and pressing opportunity to recover and renew its essential and unique emphasis upon the sacred; upon the divine mystery of God as transcendent, as our ultimate ground and end; upon God's self-revelation in Christ; upon his vital personal presence in his Holy Spirit; upon the mystery of salvation; and upon the perfection of human existence in love. This cannot be done just by repeating our old language; it must be done by renewing our old experience in new contexts and on new occasions. For the church is, and always has been, the community of the sacred and the saving, where the solemn and joyful reality of *God* (as transcendent, sovereign, and gracious) becomes the focus and identifying mark of our unity. The church is the community of the Spirit, where the mystery of God in Christ is re-presented, renewed, revived. This is our first and final business—and we have neglected it or taken it for granted (now for a full generation), with the result that the church itself is in mortal jeopardy. "Drink this cup, all of you, in memory of me"—and be made one in Christ, one in fellowship with the living and the dead, one in our ultimate concerns and commitments. Something like this must happen *every time* and in every place the church is called and gathered—or else it is not *the church* that has happened, whatever else may have.

This is, therefore, a frank and earnest plea for a revival of personal religion, and for renewed devotion to the Christian sacraments as the very life's blood of the church's existence and vitality. But, if we then suppose that this is all there is to the gospel, it shows how readily we have been misled into the false dichotomy between "personal religion" or "Christian social concerns." For as often as we rightly revive our sense of the sacred and saving, the holy, the mystery of God in Christ ("as oft as you eat this loaf and drink this cup") the obvious imperative consequence is that we must seek out practical, effective ways to convert and transform the *whole* of life in terms of its ultimate meanings (all of which exceed the secular and the merely human). We must show forth the Lord's *death* (and its implications) until he comes again (until his kingdom triumphs in this world). This is the charter for a permanent Christian revolution in and for *this* world—the only valid and hopeful revolution I know about. For the fatal flaw in typical secular revolutions is not their professed goals (which usually are admirable, often even noble), but their radical self-interest, their blind self-righteousness—and hence, their inbuilt tendency toward the corruption of their own best goals. The essential meaning of Christ's death, by contrast, is suffering love for *others*, love that seeks justice—not for oneself, but for *all* God's children, because they are *his*.

If a life is to be a living demonstration of Christ's death, then it also is an undertaking to change the world—the total environment of human existence—in the name and spirit of Christ, by the norms of Christ's love. This means "peace on earth," *for Christ's sake.* It means an end to racism, sexism, poverty, blighted personalities, corrupted human relationships—*for Christ's sake and on his terms.* It means the full recognition of human sin and enmity—not just our inhumanity to our fellow humans, but our rebellion against God himself!—and this means the full awareness that *suffering love* is an inescapable part of any authentic *Christian revolution.* The way of holiness leads through the world, to be sure, but up the sin-scarred slopes of Sinai and Calvary as well.

"Until he comes"! How glibly we pray "thy Kingdom come; thy will be done on earth"—and this means not merely our prayer for God's righteous rule on earth and in human life, but also our willingness to help bring it to pass, here and now, in all the places we live and work and have our influence. The Christian revolution is always ad interim—"until he comes," until the final triumph of righteousness on earth!—but it is also a radical and unselfish commitment to humanly meaningful change.

Without the Spirit in the church, it not only would not be the church; it would be (and all too often is) an idolatrous, self-serving association of deceived and deceiving pietists or moralists. Without the Spirit in the church, our sermons would become editorials, our sacraments hocus-pocus, our social-action pretensions just another lobby in a political process where clashing interests compete, all in the name of public welfare and the common good. Without our reliance on the Spirit in the church, we must fall back upon our own human resources, which (however impressive in some ways and for short runs) are finally self-defeating.

The great privilege of the Christian is to live *in* the Spirit, to learn to pray, and work, and risk, and die in the Spirit. The great mystery of the church is that it lives or dies by the Spirit. "Spirit-filled church" is not just a cant phrase of the pentecostals; it is an exact description of the New Testament ideal. Here is the Wesleyan understanding of the dynamics of the church, our first and last hope that stands a chance to bring about *renewal* in the church, instead of those dreary and sterile *restructurings* we keep advertising under the rubrics of "renewal."

A hymn written by one of my oldest and dearest friends, Henry Hallam Tweedy—first a teacher and then a cherished colleague at Yale—caught this vision of the Spirit in the church. It says many of the things I've been trying to say:

> O Spirit of the living God,
> Thou light and fire divine;

Descend upon thy Church once more,
And make it truly thine!
Fill it with love and joy and power,
With righteousness and peace,
Till Christ shall dwell in human hearts,
And sin and sorrow cease.

# 15

# *The Spirit in the World*

## *An Introductory Comment*

In this fourth Newnham Lecture (also preached at the New Mexico Annual Conference, May 1975), the thesis is set in the first paragraph: "Christianity, turned inward, has lost its apostolic impulse. Preoccupied with self-maintenance, with housekeeping, or minding the store, it has lost its sense of mission—just as does any organization, board, agency, or whatever that is preoccupied with self-maintenance and housekeeping." The motivation of the apostolic impulse comes from and in the Spirit.

Albert Outler used another old friend's hymn to end this sermon—Harry Emerson Fosdick's "God of Grace and God of Glory." In many instances, he concluded his sermons with poems, and drifting from plain utterances to prayerful, if not mystical speech, he reveals an awareness that no matter how definitive his thoughts about God, the mysteries are greater still. Ultimately, the language of the poet expresses the inexpressible.

Christianity, turned inward, has lost its apostolic impulse. Preoccupied with self-maintenance, with housekeeping, or minding the store, it has lost its sense of mission—just as does any organization, board, agency, or whatever that is preoccupied with self-maintenance and housekeeping. John Wesley said, "The Bible knows nothing about solitary religion." It knows nothing about effective social reform from merely humanitarian motivation, either.

It is doubly confirmed by Luke-Acts and by Matthew that the early Christians' clearest memory of Jesus' last command to them was that they take the *world* for their parish, their mission field, as their endlessly receding horizon:

> You shall receive *power* when the Holy Spirit has come to dwell in your hearts and *koinonia* [not before—witness their 50-day numbness between Easter and Pentecost]. *Then,* you shall be enabled to be my martyrs [witnesses] first in Jerusalem [where you are now] and Judea [the surrounding territory] and Samaria [the people you like least] and thence to the uttermost parts of the earth.
>
> —Acts 1:8

Considering their resources and talents, this program and timetable must have sounded pretty silly to any sensible Roman bystander (or Jew, either, for that matter).

"Go ye, therefore, into all the world and disciple all the world's peoples"—a universal mission as a definition of the business of the church. The goal: a Christianized world which also, thereby, would be a humanized world. Since that first age, we have somehow managed to separate these two conjoint visions: (1) a Christianized world not fully humanized; or (2) a secular vision of a humanized world with a secular religion—that is, communism!

In the original mission, it was and always would be the Spirit that would do the leading and guiding and advance planning. The Spirit would deal patiently and redemptively with the incredible ineptitudes and malfeasances of the church in its missionary and evangelistic outreaches. From Jerusalem to Antioch and Asia Minor, thence to Greece and Rome and Spain and afterwards to Europe—and the western reaches of Asia Minor; from Jerusalem to Pella and Edessa and Persia and India. The history of the Spirit in the world and the Christian mission is one of those thrilling epics we know too little about—and about which we have become increasingly unenthusiastic as we have seen the missionary enterprise falter in our time (in its European and American outreaches at least), and as we have discovered that what we know about ourselves (that we are *in* the world, and also too much *of* it), was true of most of the other epochs of missionary history as well.

One thing is clear: that, except for a few spiritual giants on the earth from time to time, Christianity has spread over the world and has made its impact on the world by means of martyrs and servants who were, for the most part, as ordinary as you and I—with our admixture of gospel and culture-religion which has done a fair amount of unintended harm along with much well-intentioned good. The Latin missionaries spread the gospel and the remnants of Roman culture (chiefly preoccupied with law and government). The Greek missionaries spread the gospel and the Byzantine tradition (chiefly preoccupied with mystic communion and stately ceremonials). Western Christianity spread the gospel and Western culture (chiefly preoccupied with science, technology, and "progress"). And now, in the Third and Fourth worlds, Christianity is metamorphosing again into something native—the gospel and the survival of their own culture-religion (e.g., Christianity's prospects in Africa). But always it is the *world* that is the Christian horizon. Always it is the fully human community that is our goal. Always it is the Holy Spirit that makes this happen, insofar as the Spirit can work in and through our faltering hands.

For it has been the case from the beginning that Christian evangelists found that the Spirit was always "out there" ahead of them, that they never got a "hearing of faith" (a true hearing of the *Word*) apart from the Spirit's preparation for such a hearing—in both the evangelist and the hearer. This is the import of Paul's discovery that "God has not left himself without a witness anywhere in the world"—and that witness was, of course, the Holy Spirit. The Spirit is still our reliance, our only hope for any real or lasting effect from our own efforts. To speak *from* the Spirit in our hearts *to* the Spirit in the hearts of *others,* expecting them to hear and respond, less to *us* than to the Spirit, but in no case with any power of coercion or any impulse to proselyte (i.e., to bring them in under false pretenses on either side)—this, I take it, is the essence of evangelism, the reason the authentic evangelist intrudes as little as possible into the mysterious event when the Spirit speaks through one human spirit and is heard by another in the same Spirit.

John Wesley was very much impressed by the discovery (made in his time by the new explorers and world travelers) that, of the inhabitants of the globe in the eighteenth century, no more than 5 percent were Christians. This he took more as a challenge than a proof of Christianity's ineffectiveness. But he was equally impressed and even more emphatic that in those countries *accounted* Christian (France, England, etc.), the percentage of *real* Christians, as compared to nominal or almost Christians, was appallingly low. This, too, he took as a challenge.

But he had a vision of the whole world suffused with the knowledge of God as the waters cover the sea—of a human community centered in Christ and built up by love through the Spirit. There was, of course, an unconsciously imperial paradigm in this perspective: It bears the marks of the vision of a variegated world community of British Methodists (we all have these built-in cultural and racial biases, even those who call themselves ethnics, as if we weren't *all* "ethnics," literally). One sees their equivalences in the cultural biases that are so plain in some of our boards and agencies.

But in Wesley's brave new world, the main features would not be just piety and Christian conformity. It would be a different sort of human community—one that had realized all the political, economic, and social reforms implied in the gospel—and spelled out in the ethical imperatives of the Sermon on the Mount.

Wesley's "Tory socialism" has its political implications—divine-right monarchy, yes, but also *minimal state power* and *maximum local self-determination.* A class and caste society, yes, but one in which noblesse oblige is the true sign of real "class," and in which merit could and did open doors of escape (upward mobility) in almost any field. Wesley's doctrine of "surplus accumulation" as the devil's most successful weapon against unwary entrepreneurs was more assertive and more radical than anything Marx ever proposed in his redistribution of capital and the means of production. Wesley's own life, in which he sought and found his home (physical and spiritual) amongst Christ's poor, is still reflected in that quaint question we still ask our men and women coming into full connection: "Will you visit house to house?" and "Will you instruct the children in every place?"

Bernard Semmel has recently explained the distinctive features of *The Methodist Revolution*—which I wish were understood by our General Board of Church and Society, and more explicitly set forth in our disciplinary statement of Christian "Social Principles."

But Wesley was never a social reformer for the sake of social reform itself. He had been brought up with a vivid horror of violent revolution and radical constitutional change. And he had seen England systematically corrupted by Sir Robert Walpole with the avowed aim of damping out political instability. He therefore mistrusted governmental or civil competence as far as any building up of a truly righteous and humane society.

It is sometimes said that Wesley's revolution was one of converted hearts and changed lives, but this is far too simple. Actually, he set out to serve the human needs of the people (in the Methodist societies and the three kingdoms called Great Britain). He ministered to their souls and bodies; practiced medicine (of a sort) without a license; ran an employment agency; maintained a loan fund; and distributed very large sums of money to the poor and needy. But more, he created and administered small encounter-group structures and processes that taught people how to behave and function as responsible leaders—and this produced a new breed of citizens among England's poor and laboring and small merchant classes.

His prime stress was on conversion—but he saw, as one of the outcomes of conversion, a far-reaching reformation of *manners*—of public decency and civility, of social controls (conscience and social approval) over any and all sociopathology. Methodists loved God, confessed Christ, lived by the Holy Spirit; *but* they also honored family life and all its decencies and values. They practiced industry, thrift, and sobriety. They not only deplored crimes against persons and property—they were a powerful social force in the suppression of crime and mob violence. And so they became a decisive influence in British social, economic, and political life for a full century after Wesley's death.

Now, all this is by way of saying that Methodists, of all people, have the right and duty to seek to follow the Holy Spirit after Pentecost, *out* of the Cenacle and the Temple—out *into* the world (not the world as our "oyster" or domain, but as our "parish"), with a mission to serve it at every level of human need, and also with a mission to transform it—always with an eschatological "till the nations of the world are brought into the kingdom of our God and of His Christ" (cf. Rev. 11:15).

And what would such a world be like? Maybe something like this:

1. The human being as a child of nature and steward and trustee of *all* our natural resources. The buzz word *ecology* sounds newer and more modern than it is. God put Adam and Eve in the primeval paradise *to tend it*—neither to exploit it nor to let it lapse into untended wilderness.
2. Persons as social beings: children of society and culture but also trustees and bearers of human culture.
3. Persons as economic beings: to make all the goods of earth and human technology serve the optimum needs of all men, women, and children—without exploitation, waste, or self-indulgence. Gain all, save all, give all—have you ever stopped to think what a revolution that would work in the world and in society as we know it? Can you think of a better one, really?
4. Persons as political beings, with their earthly citizenship rooted first of all in the human community, but always as "colonists" of the kingdom of heaven while here on earth.

This, as some of you have recognized, is a replica of the outline in our disciplinary statement on Social Principles—and some of you also know that I regard the *outline* of that statement as the best thing about it. But what does this have to do with the Holy Spirit? Much more than we have been accustomed to think or to realize. For every one of these features of human social morality is an aspect of *human community*—and the Holy Spirit's main job in the world is the creation and upbuilding of persons in a spiritually oriented human *community*.

All young men and women see visions; all old men and women dream dreams—visions of what might be, dreams of what has been and might have been and still may be. But every vision and dream is illusory if based on nothing more than human power for its realization. This is why utopias are always fascinating, why wishful thinking comes so naturally, why it is so easy to confound our human prescriptions for happiness with God's design to make us happy and holy.

For it is the Holy Spirit: God-in-us, God-with-us, God-for-us—and God-against-us in every abuse of our God-given gifts, talents, and aspirations—who is the real ground of our effectual participation in the world's work and the world's weeping, the real source of our capacity to grow and to build and to enjoy. It is the Spirit who is the real enabler of human liberation and lasting human achievement—in personal growth and fulfillment, in social and communal attainment.

The Holy Spirit is the divine mystery within which the human mystery of selfhood emerges, matures, experiences the joys and sorrows of life, and enters the daunting mystery of death. The human potential is the gift and the project of the Holy Spirit, finite and creaturely in every respect save one—*aspiration.* This, like all other metaphors for *breathing,* is a special "leading of the Spirit."

The Holy Spirit is the divine mystery within which the human mystery of communion and community comes to whatever flower and fruition it ever does. For the truly human community is simply and literally one in which "love and joy and peace and patience and kindness and goodness and fidelity and gentleness and self-denial" control our interpersonal, social, economic, and political relationships—in their main overall perspectives, in their climate and atmosphere, in their development and stability. In any other basic mode of human interaction, we have *self*-indulgence and *self*-salvation: "idolatries, lusts, magic or magical thinking, contentiousness, selfish ambitions, party intrigues, jealousies, and the like" (Gal. 5:20-21). And it is this sort of world that is the inevitable fruit of any life-style other than life in the Spirit. "I warn you," said Paul, "as I warned you before, that those who behave in such defiances of the Spirit will never inherit the kingdom of God" (vs. 21)—on this earth or in heaven.

Are you even mildly interested in being a Christian revolutionary—in the biblical sense, in the Wesleyan spirit: a man or woman dedicated to real and urgent social change, governed always by a concern to conserve all the human good that has been achieved; to reform and renew the structures and processes that inhibit human fulfillment (personal and social); to reject all false forms of radical human self-reliance?

If so, then let the utopias instruct you without deceiving you; let the sordid actualities of radical revolutions warn you against the false hope that you can shatter to bits whatever you dislike in the world and then remold it to your heart's desire—however high-minded your ideals may have been. The cruelties of humankind are horrifying—and slavery and oppression (of any and all kinds) are amongst the worst of those cruelties. But the most horrid have come from tyrants who proclaimd they were acting in and for the public good: this is the essence of the evil of Marxism, Stalinism, Maoism, and the new dictatorships that justify themselves by pointing to (or promising) some slight gains in social welfare.

The Christian Revolution—revolution in and by the Holy Sjpirit—is something else again, and we had better start relearning it: from those first Christians of whom it was complained that they were turning the world upside down; from those medieval monks who gave the world a new culture and even a new technology; from John Wesley and the Methodist revolution; and from modern prophets like Walter Rauschenbush.

Indeed, it was this vision of the permanent, nonviolent, gracious Christian revolution that inspired this hymn by an old friend of mine, a hero of my early years, Harry Emerson Fosdick—a man for *his* season (if not for all seasons), and who still has something to teach us:

> God of grace and God of glory,
> On thy people pour thy power;
> Crown thine ancient Church's story;
> Bring her bud to glorious flower.
> Grant us wisdom, Grant us courage,
> For the facing of this hour.

# 16

## *The Harvest of the Spirit*

### *An Introductory Comment*

This fifth Newnham Lecture, grounded in Galatians 5, describes the "harvest of the Spirit" as the appropriate way in which faith, energized by love, may express itself. According to John Wesley, that method of expression falls somewhere between two extremes: the way of the Calvinists, who are prepared to compel people to be just; and the way of the antinomians, who say, "You can't compel people to be moral, so leave everybody free to do his or her own thing."

Albert Outler says that Wesley "sought a third alternative to these polarities, fixing on an earlier phrase in this same fifth chapter of Galatians: 'faith *working* by love.' "

This harvest of the Spirit expresses itself in the graciousness commented on by his granddaughter Melissa, who, as a child, lived in the Outler home. She calls him Gaffer and counts him her best friend in all the world.

# *The Sermon*

We have spoken of the Spirit in the heart, the Spirit in the Church, the Spirit in the world. Now we turn to a synoptic view of the Christian life itself—"life in the Spirit"—an analysis of "the harvest of the Spirit," the fruits of the Spirit in Christian living: their marks and measures. The outline and model for all there is to say on this subject is already laid out for us in one of the most remarkable passages in the New Testament: John Wesley's favorite amongst the Epistles of Paul—Galatians 5.

The basic issue here, for St. Paul and for us, is Christian *freedom*—freedom *from* the law (by which he meant freedom from self-conscious moralism) and freedom *in* Christ (by which he meant finding appropriate ways to "live in the Spirit").

> You, my friends, were called to be free men; only do not turn your freedom into license for your lower nature, but be servants to one another in love. For the whole law can be summed up in a single commandment: "Love your neighbour as yourself." But if you go on fighting one another, tooth and nail, all you can expect is mutual destruction.
> —Galatians 5:13-15 NEB

Next Paul turns to the radical antitheses in human existence between unbridled *appetite* and true *inspiration;* between the impulse of our "lower nature" and the exaltations of "life in the Spirit." His inventory of "appetite" covers, if only by title, almost all the *social* sins you can think of (for it implies even the mass obscenities of war and of social and economic injustice). The first trio of these anti-Spirit, antihuman impulses is the human sex syndrome, since it is so imperious in the human species and so unbridled by instinct. In our times, we have abandoned even the social mores that once inhibited sexual instinct, in part and up to a point. Thus we have open advocates, even in the church, of permissive sex and of deviant sex—including homosexuality. I find this incredible and disheartening, calling for resolute action. Next, for Paul, come idolatry and sorcery—which is to say a false supernaturalism: the effort to harness the supernatural under human management and dispensation. And, as we are all aware, this sort of pseudosupernaturalism is flourishing nowadays in what passes for very sophisticated circles. Then he points to a cluster of interpersonal distempers: quarreling, contentions, envy, outbursts of rage, selfish ambitions, dissensions, party intrigues, and jealousies—various features in a composite portrait of an unloving, self-centered, mean-spirited person who acts out a sociopathic disposition. St. Paul, at least, would not have been surprised by the antisocial behavior on the rise through the length and breadth of our society. The Apostle's concluding cluster of vices includes various forms of recklessness and irresponsibility—what appetite does, as it gets more and more out of control. It is clear that what he has in mind here is the unbridled life so brazen in the Gentile world (drinking bouts and drug orgies)—the world by which Christians, a despised enclave, were surrounded.

One is tempted to stop and reflect upon this catalogue of immorality replicated in our time as our society sinks deeper and deeper into a demoralization which may or may not be reversible: sex on the loose, literally; a frantic search for supernatural powers for our own purposes (pseudo-religions, including *some* forms of so-called faith healing); astrology and the occult, in consciousness-expanding exercises; Transactional Analysis and transcendental meditation; psychedelic and addictive drugs. Do your observations correspond with mine? Can you deny that the moral fiber and moral tone of society at large and our public life are sagging? What are we to make of all the signs of incivility so evident—in our schools, in business, in politics: contentions, outrage turned into violence, selfishness surpassing altruism? How did America become a society of reckless dissidents? This is a disturbing question to face in the upcoming Bicentennial Year—for if our Revolution was an act of dissent against imperial tyranny, still it was sustained and justified by a community of moral consensus. Ever since, our nation has been sustained by a decent measure of moral consensus, except for the tragic episode of our Civil War; but even that consensus has collapsed and this helps to make my point. Now, our dissidence has taken a different form: not of civil war, but of a disunited multitude, without a common vision or communal purpose.

St. Paul's conclusion is simple, stern, final: "I warn you again, as I warned you before, that those who behave in such self-serving ways will never inherit the kingdom of heaven!" As things stand now, one begins to suspect, they aren't even going to inherit the kingdom of *Earth.*

This is the shadow side of sin, of self-indulgence, self-centeredness—which is to say, life lived apart from, or against, the Spirit. Paul then proceeds to the bright side of his gospel: the harvest of the Spirit in Christian experience (see Gal. 5:22-25).

The crucial point here is that "life in the Spirit" is an orderly life, regulated by conscience and concern, but not by legal rules that can be legislated and enforced by threat of punishment. "There is no law dealing with such things as these [fruits of the Spirit]"—that is, you can't legislate at this level. This opens up the thorny issue as to whether or not a secular society can legislate morals and what sort of moral influence a secular government can wield. For remember, when you are talking about secular government at any level, you're talking about coercion, or the threat of coercion. The coercive power of government may be concealed, but it's always *there*—and where coercion is applied to invalid ends, it is doubly dangerous. Here a chasm yawns between the legalists, who say, on almost every issue, "There ought to be a *law!* " (to *compel* people to be just, humane, decent) and the antinomians, who say, again across the board, "You can't *compel* people to be moral, so leave everybody free to do his or her own thing, short of a clear and present danger to the public safety."

John Wesley found himself in the middle of a controversy like this—between moralists with an elaborate code of right and wrong (and ferocious penalties for wrongdoing) and "the German stillness" (i.e., Moravians who stressed spontaneity and waiting for the Spirit to move in their hearts). Wesley sought a third alternative to these polarities, fixing on an earlier phrase in this same fifth chapter of Galatians: "faith *working* by love." Indeed, so concerned was he about this pious permissiveness that his original General Rules contain the following passage, which some younger Methodists may never have heard in full:

> It is expected of all who continue in these societies that they should continue to evidence their desire of salvation.
>
> *Secondly:* By doing good; by being in every kind merciful after their power; as they have opportunity, doing good of every possible sort, and, as far as possible, to all men:
>
> To their bodies, of the ability which God giveth, by giving food

> to the hungry, by clothing the naked, by visiting or helping them that are sick or in prison.
>
> To their souls, by instructing, reproving, or exhorting all we have any intercourse with; trampling under foot that enthusiastic doctrine that "we are not to do good unless *our hearts be free to it.*"
>
> By doing good, especially to them that are of the household of faith or groaning so to be; employing them preferably to others; buying one of another, helping each other in business and so much the more because the world will love its own and them only.
>
> By all possible diligence and frugality, that the gospel be not blamed.
>
> By running with patience the race which is set before them, denying themselves, and taking up their cross daily; submitting to bear the reproach of Christ, to be as the filth and offscouring of the world; and looking that men should say all manner of evil of them *falsely*, for the Lord's sake.[9]

In other words, Wesley thought you *could* legislate morals—"doing good"—given two decisive conditions. One of those conditions is positive consensus: A voluntary society can legislate the moral atmosphere for its own members, or it can drop them from the group. This means that where there is real community, there can be a positive code of public morals. Where there is not, legislation comes to resemble the "resolutions" on church and society which we have in our church (and which others have). There is an elaborate statement of "Social Principles" in the *Discipline.* It is the law of the church; it is full of high-sounding phrases: *We* affirm . . . *we* reject . . . *we* demand . . . *we* condemn—all ten-million-plus of us Methodists (there used to be more of us!). What is presupposed here is that all Methodists, or even most Methodists, understand and approve that statement (which, of course, is not so); and that if a Methodist should defy the law of the church, he or she might be excommunicated (which is not so, either).

The other condition for legislating morals is negative. Laws can and ought to be passed *in restraint of* active evil, injustice, predatory or obnoxious behavior. Such prohibitions of harmful behavior are necessary for the public safety and any high level of civil tranquility. Even here, though, they are difficult to enforce—and this is the crux of our current national tragedy. We're heading into our

Bicentennial Year with all the hoopla of a political campaign and all the gimmickry of souvenir hawkers exploiting our present yen for nostalgia.

The miracle of America *was* that it was "*one* nation out of *many* nations, *under God.*" But who can say that we are *one* nation any more, a national community with a unifying moral consensus, or even a shared national consciousness? Between them, the Congress and the media managed to curb an imperial presidency—but they have neither the consensus nor the vision required to lead the nation (after Vietnam, after Watergate, before Armageddon). The judiciary has become a law unto itself; big business and big labor whipsaw Middle America between them in the weirdest economic crisis we've ever had. The races are pitted against each other—and our moral stature in the world has sunk to a dangerous low.

Life in the Spirit—the harvest of the Spirit— is *above* the law, in this sense. It cannot be *compelled;* it cannot be promoted by high-flown rhetoric—not even by General Conference resolutions. It is a *gift:* the gift of God's grace in Christ, God's gift of the Spirit, the gift of repentance and forgiveness of sins, the gift of a new heart—"if anyone is in Christ Jesus, he is a *new* creature" (lives in a new world).

Life in the Spirit is a gift of gratitude, gratefulness, graciousness—faith's response to God's love in Christ. It is faith's response to the love we have received and to the needs of those we can serve. *This* is above and beyond the coercion of any outside force, beyond the grasp of any self-centered desire or any selfish notion that we can somehow earn God's favor and reward.

The most striking feature of each of these fruits of the Spirit in Paul's list, and of all of them together, is that each one moves from inside to outside ourselves. Every one refers to a person who is focused on other persons. Life in the Spirit is a life of love—in which the love of God in Christ flows through the Holy Spirit, into our hearts, and out again: in works of mercy, piety, and altruism.

This is why love itself heads the list. For it is the comprehensive term for life, acknowledged as from God, given back to God in *worship,* and given out to neighbor—every human being we can reach—in *service* (see I Cor. 13:4-7).

Love, therefore, is the exact opposite of *appetite*—for appetite is a reaching out to take in, whereas love is a reaching out to benefit.

This is why love can include sex and sanctify it within the covenant of holy matrimony, whereas sexual appetite, as such, may not be truly loving at all. This is why even the bond of matrimony may become *unholy!* Love is *concern;* love is caring; love is the quest for what is truly good for God's other children, love is gratitude in action—since the Christian is debtor to all and servant of all. I sometimes think it a pity that the church ignored the "third ordinance" of Jesus Christ—in John 13—that Christians should wash one anothers' feet from time to time, in token of our chosen role as *servants* in Christ's name and Spirit: "Love one another as you have been loved: as I have loved you!"

After love comes *joy*—which means here the gladness of the heart assured of God's grace, the security that is trusting God's Providence rather than trying to plug into some supernatural outlet so as to run our own life's appliances. We oftentimes get mixed up about joy—confuse it with pleasant distractions, or fun and games, or false highs, or peak experiences that exalt us and then subside. The most truly joyful people I have known have not needed much distraction or "entertainment." They have had their own resources of self-confidence in God's care and keeping. "A Mighty Fortress" is a hymn of joy—not because it sees the Christian life as tranquil and serene (quite the contrary!), but because "God's truth abideth still" (and we in it), because "his kingdom is forever" (and we are heirs of that kingdom, joint heirs with Christ).

After joy comes *peace*—a strange and wonderful notion, not of the absence of stress and pressure, but the absence of *enmity* or bitterness or self-pity. *Peace* is Christian steadiness, the spiritual gyroscope inside the Christian heart, which pulls us back toward the vital balance between the polarities of futile excitement or resigned despair. The truly peaceful and peaceable Christians I have known—and have been blessed by—were not at all apathetic or blah. They were so fully reconciled to God that they were as steady as a balanced flywheel.

Peace is linked to *patience*—and here again we have a word that has had its biblical meaning corrupted. For all too many of us, it means waiting out some unwelcome episode ("this too shall pass"), or of putting up with nuisance, frustration, oppression. "The patience of Job" is a phrase we used to hear, to refer to some uncomplaining saint whose sufferings we ourselves could not have borne. As a phrase, it is misleading: The biblical Job complained long and loud, and it took a voice from a whirlwind to tell him to cool it. No, patience, for Paul and in Christian spirituality, is simply the willingness (born out of love and joy and peace) to pay the price—that is, to suffer whatever discomfort or discouragement may come with a given mission of love and service—and to go on "paying the price" till the job is done. Patience is the power not to let the so-and-sos of this world wear us down, to endure hardship like good soldiers, to continue in our commitments in joy and peace, because of God's love and our dedication to *his* good causes in *his* world.

Patience is linked to *fidelity*—which is simply the inner determination to do what love requires, whether one is being observed and monitored or not. Partners in a marriage may be "faithful" enough whenever they are being monitored—but what would they do *if* they could get away with it? If they know that God is their witness and their consciences are their Spirit-guided inner judge, they will be as faithful in secret as in public, because they are covenant-keepers and not merely law-abiding citizens. Partners in a business may be kept honest by mutual self-interest—but it is a better relationship if it is based on mutual loyalty. Partisans of good causes may *talk* a big game, but what do they do when the crunch comes, or when the good causes generate opposition or threaten loss? To act on and out of principle—in the Spirit and with none but the Spirit to bear you witness: that is fidelity.

To fidelity, Paul adds *gentleness*—which is not weakness at all, but strength reined and guided by love—and *self-control.* And *self*-control may seem to be an exception to my opening statement that all Christian virtues are turned *outward*—but not really. Self-control means that our love, joy, peace, and so on well up from within, from the Spirit within, and not from imitations of what we see in others. It comes from within the self; it is not dedicated to the self:

> I want a principle within
> Of watchful, godly fear,
> A sensibility of sin,
> A pain to feel it near.
>
> . . . . . . . .

O may the least omission pain
My reawakened soul,
And drive me to that grace again,
Which makes the wounded whole.
—Charles Wesley

*That* is Christian self-control!

Notice that there is not a single word here about ecstasy—which was quite deliberate, since Paul knew very well that, in the Gentile world in which these Christians lived, spirituality all too often was linked with ecstasy, emotional highs, orgies (as we can see it again today). He was not opposed to ecstasy as such; he himself was an ecstatic, and says so. But his ecstasies were not as important to him, at bottom, as these ethical fruits of the Spirit. "Life in the Spirit" is not ten feet off the ground or out of this world. It is, rather, that witness and service in and through life's tediums—in love, joy, and peace!

Here, then, is the Christian's plumb line for self-appraisal: If you profess to be in the Spirit, then how loving are *you*—how joyous, peaceful, patient, gentle, self-controlled? Or, even if you haven't thought much about these particular biblical terms—how loving, joyous, peaceful, patient, and so on are *you?* You might be more in the Spirit than you had realized—and if so, you ought to know it in order to become more self-consciously Christian, more truly *self*-controlled, more fully spiritual.

Galatians 5 is Paul's declaration of independence from legalism, his declaration of dependence upon grace, and his declaration of the interdependence of Christians in their life together in the Spirit.

> Brothers and sisters, you have been called to freedom; only do not turn your freedom into license for your lower nature, but be servants to one another in love. For the whole law can be summed up in a single commandment, "Love your neighbor as yourself"—as God in Christ loves *you*.
> —Galatians 5:13-14

There is room for more signatures to this declaration. Isn't this a good time for us to sign up too?

# 17

## *A New Pentecost?*

### *An Introductory Comment*

In this sermon, preached at Longview First United Methodist Church on November 25, 1975, Albert Outler talks about a new Pentecost that may be in the making. He hangs loose as he voices appreciation for the expressions of gifts of the Spirit bursting out in many areas of the universal church. He seeks to balance John Wesley's warm heart—his gift of the Spirit—with an appreciation of Wesley's richly stored knowledge and scholarly ability.

When in 1975, Ed Robb, then president of the Good News movement, leveled a blast at United Methodist seminaries, claiming that in none of them could an evangelical student hope for a decent exposure to the Wesleyan heritage, Albert Outler went into orbit. This was an especially low blow, since his life was dedicated to recovering and re-presenting Wesley, not only to Methodists but to other Christians as well.

Outler was surprised when Robb and some of his friends showed up at his study on day with an openhearted challenge to help them do something more constructive than cry havoc. Outler confesses: "I have always believed in the surprises of the Spirit; it's just that they continue to surprise me whenever they occur."

# *The Sermon*

One of the most damaging criticisms of Christian experience as too many of us know it—and many others suspect it—is that it is blah, ho-hum, Dullsville. This is an old complaint, for I remember the story (from my youth) of the little boy who confided to his grandmother that he had enjoyed the circus more than church. "If *you* ever went to a circus," he assured her, "you'd never want to go to prayer meeting again." We can't use *that* story with the younger generation any more, without having to explain about prayer meetings.

But there *is* still the problem about nominal Christianity being dull, isn't there? How many of us have been to worship services where our emotions were not deeply stirred, where our minds were left to spin along in neutral without being stretched, where good advice was ladled out but no decisions required of us, where the music was so-so and the liturgy either perfunctory or weird? How many of us have served on church committees, or boards and agencies that spent more time and/or money on input than their *output* ever seemed to justify? How long since you had a "peak experience" when you were in church, or when you were engaged in church work? If your answer is "Many a time—and recently, too!" then God be praised—for you are blessed beyond the average and should be deeply grateful.

Even so, look at the world outside the church and try to think how the church looks to outsiders—or even to our inactive members on our rolls, who are in the church but not of it. Where do they get *their* high moments, their occasions of inspiration, their bursts of joy and glory—their releases from drabness or boredom? What are their antidotes to loneliness, to alienation, to the dreadful anxieties of an economy in absurd imbalance, a society whose institutions (family, school, government, etc.) are not functioning very well anymore? None of the answers here is very edifying: mass-media entertainment, the pontifications of our media pundits (our society's new breed of preachers), the leisure-time use of fossil fuels when their depletion is now imminent, the false escape hatches of alcohol and other drugs, permissive sex, and other self-indulgences. The point is that fewer and fewer of what is an expanding population are turning to the church for the answers that some of us believe it has, or to Jesus Christ as the supreme source of liberation, joy, and hope. And all the while, the tides of unhappiness and meaninglessness wash up higher and higher on humanity's polluted beachhead on our fragile planet.

This is deeply ironic and tragic, since from time immemorial, religion (in all its vast variety) has had the common function of lifting existence out of its humdrum, providing symbols of significance and exaltation, heightening the sense of meaning, transmitting signals of transcendence. In other words, religion has served to make life exciting and provide a higher, mysterious vision of the human prospect (even if also a sometimes terrifying one). Religion has pointed us to the Holy—to the encompassing mysteries in which we live and move and have our being and face our death.

In nature religions, the basic reactions to the Holy are fear and appeasement: how to temper the wrath of the gods, how to curry their favor. In the great monisms (Hinduism, Buddhism) the basic reactions always have been adaptations to and incorporations into the infinite. In the three great monotheisms, the basic stance in Islam is submission (to God's will); in Judaism, obedience (to God's moral law); and in Christianity, *faith and trust* (in God's grace in Christ and the communion of the Holy Spirit). Thus we have expanding religious horizons, with the fullness of God's self-revelation in Jesus Christ. And yet in all its forms, religion has sought to *hallow life,* to remind men and women of its sanctity, to transform nature into spirit, to exalt human experience from routine to wonder and glory.

The first Pentecost, remember, was an exciting event—the hubbub in an overcrowded Jerusalem, the miracle of tongues, Peter's sermon, the conversion of a multitude—upsetting the establishment and drawing the charge that these new enthusiasts were trying to turn the world upside down, to which the Christians' reply was that they were only turning a topsy-turvy world right-side up again.

That first Pentecost subsided (enthusiasm is a trendy thing). The new community had to get organized and develop stable patterns of survival through a history that the early Christians never expected to have to cope with. The first crucial difficulty of any religion that lifts its people up and beyond the surrounding culture is its children—the upcoming generations in any given historical succession. Saints do not beget saints—and revivals do not last forever. Luther observed that their normal life cycle was a generation, and the influence of men or women or small groups upon successors seems at least to relapse. John Wesley was struck by this remark of Luther's (he mentions it 5 times in his *Works*) and always pointed out that the Methodist revival was different. *It* had already lasted two generations (he was proud to claim) and gave promise of outlasting Wesley's long life (as it did).

But if pentecostal events and religious excitements ebb and flow, notice the impressive record they have left across the centuries—often in out-of-the-way places, often amongst the poor and oppressed. If there is a tendency in church history for things to sag and for various movements to have their day and cease to be, there is also an opposite force at work. The Spirit is present in the ordinary life of the church—in its sacraments, its pastoral ministry, the witness and service of its faithful laity—the church visible in the world. And there are those uprushes of the Spirit in the churches—always disturbing to the establishment, but not necessarily disruptive. St. Francis of Assisi reminded medieval Rome of how simple, how joyous, how loving the Christian faith could be. The Brethren of the Common Life did as much in northern Europe. Until the Reformation became a life-and-death struggle for survival, there was a great deal of joy and gladness, of praise and exaltation in Protestant Christianity. Indeed, Luther was so upset by the "enthusiasts" (who went further than he in celebrating *their* Christian liberty) that he accused them of trying to "swallow the Holy Ghost [whose symbol was the descending dove], *feathers and all*" !

The Wesleyan revival was pentecostal in the crucial sense that its central theme was the inner witness of the Spirit—of God's justifying love and sanctifying grace. Dr. J. Edwin Orr, in *The Flaming Tongue,* tells the story of succeeding revivals in the nineteenth and early twentieth centuries in Britain and America—more of them than I had realized, and all of them exciting and significant.

In our time, revivals and camp meetings and brush arbors and tent meetings (in the old frontier tradition) have faded into mementos of a dimly remembered past—for most people. Nor am I about to suggest that they can be revived—not in their old forms at least. But I do lament the loss of intensity and the sense of urgency about the great issues of sin and salvation that they generated (even if only episodically—for it used to be said that you could tell if a man was a Methodist by checking on his pants: baggy in the knees from praying, shiny in the seat from backsliding!). In the place of the waning revival styles of pentecostalism (and by pentecostalism I mean neither more nor less than a conscious appeal to and experience of the Holy Spirit's presence in a Christian congregation—*not* any of the particular forms of that presence, like tongues, or faith-healing, or snake-handling, or whatever), our forebears in a previous generation turned to Christian education and the Sunday school as a way of stirring and maintaining interest and participation in Christian experience—and they tended to set "nurture" and "conversion" over against each other, as either/ors. *I* can remember when Sunday schools were exciting—and so was Epworth League. But that, too, seems to have lost its magic, and our church schools, youth fellowships, and Wesley Foundations are in process of serious slippage across the church.

Then came other innovations designed to liven up church life and heighten the spirit and morale of our people: Sunday night chautauquas, forums, family nights, dramatic productions, religious art, and so on. On another level, we've had a fearful and wonderful time with liturgical innovation: new forms of services and prayers, experiences of audience participation, banners, balloons, guitars, jazz masses. I recall an experience in that ugly old Victorian church in London called All Souls—Langham Place where John R. Stott is pastor. This robed Church of England priest led his evangelical congregation (intergenerational and interethnic) in the Anglican litany while allowing reports to be given on how the parish's missions were doing. He mixed evangelical preaching with social-gospel renewal—and then in the London papers the next morning there was the picture of Chaplain Evans of SMU, dancing down the aisle of Perkins Chapel, cassock and all!

After that, almost like a whisper in the 1960s and a louder rustling in the 1970s, comes the new pentecostalism—and a new crisis in the churches. In Dallas, for example, we have Dr. Criswell, denouncing tongue-speaking and baptisms of the Spirit as second blessings; and Dr. Connatser, whose congregation has had to move from its modest Beverly Hills building into the Bronco Bowl in order to accommodate the crowds. Methodists are only lightly touched here and there—since our denominational preoccupations just now are with our new structures and programs or with the battle between the Good News people and the liberals. But there *are* pentecostals in many places—for example, in Tyler Street Church in Dallas, Texas; and in First United Methodist Church in Wichita, Kansas (a high-steeple church that is much involved).

The most unexpected push in this movement has come from the Roman Catholics: for instance, the Southwestern Regional Conference for Charismatic Renewal in Dallas; Cardinal Suenens' Perkins Lectures in Wichita Falls, Texas; the Church of the Redeemer in Houston; the New Covenant community in Ann Arbor. Said Cardinal Suenens,

> Everything points to the fact that we are living at a turning point in the history of the Church, in which the Holy Spirit is revealing, to a degree unknown before, a mystery of death and resurrection. . . . He is inaugurating a spiritual renewal of exceptional richness.[10]

Now, I'm very far from clear in my own mind and heart as to what this all adds up to or portends. When Baptists, Methodists, and Roman Catholics make a common discovery of new life in the Spirit and from the Spirit, it really does seem that we *are* in a new age, a new climate where the old lines of cleavage no longer mark off boundaries and barriers. A new four-layered book was published last year called *A Charismatic Reader,* in which Episcopalians, Lutherans, Baptists, and others talk about their encounters in the Spirit, the Holy Spirit in the church, speaking in tongues, and so on. And this is only one of a hundred books churned up by this new awakening in the churches—and the best of the lot, in my judgment, is Cardinal Suenens' *A New Pentecost?*

Meanwhile, my Jesuit friend Joe Fichter has done a highly critical sociological study on the Jesus people and the charismatics. He concludes that there is more excitement than social impact in the movement, more talk about speaking in tongues than new insights and new horizons in what is being said. Father Andrew Greely has answered Father Fichter with opposing arguments and evidence, and so the debate goes on.

But where does all this leave *us?* For one, I find myself recalling both Gamaliel and St. Paul. Gamaliel, you recall, cautioned against persecuting the Christians on the eminently sensible ground that nobody could know *then* how the new movement would turn out: "If this new idea of theirs is of human origin, it will collapse; if it is from God . . . you risk finding yourselves at war with God." And Paul in prison, hearing that the gospel was being preached in terms not quite like his own, was able to rejoice that, even so, the gospel was being preached—and that was far better than nothing!

There's no use denying any longer that we desperately need refreshment of the Spirit in the Christian churches. There's also no denying that we *do not need* disruption, contentions, or schisms. And both St. Paul and John Wesley agreed on the constructive way to reemphasize the doctrine of the Spirit in the church, without disruption and schism.

Both start with the notion of the Spirit's gifts to Christians: wisdom, spiritual insight, healings, prophecy, discernment of spirits, ecstatic utterance, interpretation (I Cor. 12:1-11). All these gifts are quite varied; none is the special badge of spiritual superiority: They are given to promote *unity* in the Body of Christ—and they are cancelled or tainted whenever they breed self-righteousness. (If the eye says to the hand, "I don't need *you,* for I'm above you in spiritual vision," then the whole body is sick.)

Wesley makes the same point but in a different perspective. Baptism should be followed by justification and regeneration ("conversion") and they should lead to sanctification (being made perfect in love in *this* life). But—and this is the crucial point—conversion does not downgrade baptism; and the baptism of the Spirit (about which he was very chary) does not downgrade conversion. Beware of pride, and its offspring, self-righteousness; beware of schism and factionalism.

Back to St. Paul—everything about spiritual gifts in First Corinthians, chapter 12, is preparatory to what he specifically designates as "a better way." This is to say that charismatic renewal is, or may be, good—it may be what we need now—but always and in any case, there is *a better way*—not a different or contrary way—and that way is love. *That,* of course is what First Corinthians 13 is all about.

And this is the ever-old, ever-new horizon for this perennial problem in Christian experience—for the *new* Pentecost that we need would mean the recovery of *loving community,* a conversion of strangers or ecstatics to brothers and sisters in Christ. It means that those of us who do not speak in tongues should neither envy those who do nor be intimidated by them, but rather try to understand it, as Cardinal Suenens suggests, as nonverbal aspiration, given voice if not intelligible utterance. Those endowed with extraordinary gifts by the Spirit must devote them, without pride of self-righteousness, to the health of the Body of Christ.

Deeper than all questions of ecstasy and excitement and charismatic renewal is the question of spirit meeting Spirit, of burdened hearts finding self-knowledge and new freedom, joy and love, *in the Spirit*, whether in our gatherings for worship or study or in our routines of work and play. To become aware of, and to practice, the presence of God—in church and shop and office and home and classroom—there's where the mystery comes in, where the joy wells up and life is lifted from ho-hum to Right on! Christians, even in difficult and foreboding times like these, have power of hope, of challenge, and of joy within themselves, and in their common life and work together, which helps refresh a tired world and make each day a holy day, each Sunday a sabbath of praise and thanksgiving.

I for one—old and weary as I am, and as anxious as I am about the human prospect—am willing to say with Suenens:

> The long history of the Church is filled with the wonders of the Holy Spirit. Think of the prophets and saints who, in times of darkness, discovered springs of grace and shed beams of light along the human path. I believe in the surprises of the Spirit! Who would dare to say that God's imagination is exhausted? To hope is a duty, not a luxury. To hope is not to dream but to turn dreams into reality.
>
> Happy are those who dream dreams and are ready to pay the price to make them come true!
>
> And we *can*, you know, you and I—even *we* can find joy and power and confidence for living and dying, not in ourselves but in God's grace—for are we not persuaded that neither life nor death nor anything in all creation can separate us from the love of God which is in Christ Jesus, our Lord?
>
> And if we *are*, then are we not already more than conquerors through Him who loved us and gave Himself for us and to whom we have given ourselves?[11]

Peace, therefore, and blessings, joy, and glory!

# 18

## *Zion in the New Wilderness*

### *An Introductory Comment*

In this sermon, preached at First United Methodist Church in Dallas on March 14, 1976, Albert Outler describes the howling wilderness of our forebears as pretty much passé. But we have a new wilderness, in which physical discomforts and hardships are less ominous than our emotional, moral, spiritual discontents and deficiencies. Outler says, "America was—and still is—a covenant community, open to all who will contract into its conditions: to seek first the kingdom of God and *his* righteousness and to live gratefully and generously with all those things that may be added unto us."

Albert Outler is thankful for this nation—especially the southern half—but beyond that, he is thankful to God for the world. He feels at home, whether researching in a London library, conversing with an Australian aborigine, having lunch in Rome, or digging around the countryside in Israel. But in these "last days," he is more at home with his books. He studies and writes (and preaches) with one foot in heaven and one on earth. He walks two roads—one paved with grace and the other with things of this world. One day he will run out of things of this world—but grace? Never!

# *The Sermon*

Have you ever wondered how differently recent world history might have turned out if the moon (or even one of the planets) had been discovered to be humanly habitable—that is, what it would have meant to humankind for a new demographic frontier to be opened up? That really *would* have been "a giant step for mankind," wouldn't it? It would have meant a new set of options for at least some of our earthbound crises. Is it any wonder, then, that the discovery that we are stuck here on planet Earth, with most of its geographical frontiers closed and most of our life-support systems in swift depletion, has proved more depressing than even our previous ignorance or indifference. As the grim realities of the human prospect have slowly seeped into our consciousness, human behavior (all over the planet) has begun to resemble that of overcrowded animals.

It was different for people in the Old World in the sixteenth and seventeenth centuries. At first, it was *gold* that fascinated the Old World. But as the sixteenth century came and went, the imagination of many Europeans began to focus on the New World as an alternative to their intolerable situations at home. Remember, by the time the Pilgrims came to Plymouth and the Puritans to Massachusetts Bay, Europe had been wracked and ruined by wars and oppression for so long that even a howling wilderness had come to seem like a promised land.

This Promised-Land metaphor took on new reality when groups of people turned from their biblical memories of Exodus, the Sinai wilderness, and the conquest of Canaan, to actual decisions that involved taking their future into their own hands. Remember that they had been defeated in their attempt to remake *England* after an Old Testament model—the New Jerusalem in Westminster! Whereupon, they fled (as refugees, literally) to America as their *new* Zion in the wilderness. Odd, isn't it, that the Puritans' theology was a liberation theology; theirs was "the sacred cause of liberty." It was a theology of *politics* (i.e., the ruling idea of a covenant commonwealth), guided by a biblical ethic of mutual self-restraint, mutual commitment to the public good—that is, the kingdom of God on earth (and in the American wilderness).

It's hard to realize, nowadays, how vividly those biblical images and that biblical vision inspired and sustained those pioneers, first in New England and then as they moved farther westward. Long before any thought of revolution, Cotton Mather could speak, exaltedly, of God's mighty acts in this New World:

> I write the *Wonders* of the CHRISTIAN RELIGION, flying from the Depravations of *Europe,* to the *American Strand:* And, assisted by the Holy Author of that *Religion,* I do . . . Report the *Wonderful Displays* of His Infinite Power, Wisdom, Goodness, and Faithfulness, wherewith His Divine Providence hath *Irradiated* an *Indian Wilderness.* . . .
>
> 'Tis possible, That our Lord Jesus Christ carried some Thousands of *Reformers* into the Retirements of an *American Desert,* on purpose, that . . . He might there, *To* them first, and then *By* them, give a *Specimen* of many Good Things, which He would have His Churches elsewhere aspire and arise unto.[12]

A hundred years later, John Cushing would re-echo this ancient theme of Zion in the wilderness—in his July Fourth oration of 1796:

> We are met to celebrate the Fourth of July. . . . This day completes twenty years since these United States were declared free, sovereign and independent. . . . It is a day to be remembered throughout all generations. But since that memorable era a new generation has risen up . . . who ought to be told of the goodness of God to their fathers and to them.
>
> In the history of the United States [and there had been only twelve years of it since the Treaty of Paris!] there is as great a similarity in the conduct of His Providence for us to that of the Israelites as is to be found in the history of any people. Our fathers were few in number and feeble when they first landed in this howling wilderness. . . . And what brought them here? To enjoy *liberty,* civil and religious. . . .
>
> With a great sum we bought our liberty. Independence has cost much blood and immense treasure. . . . It is evident that we have much to remember with gratitude to God. . . . And we should tell of His Providence to our children and give it in charge to them to tell their children. . . . God's goodness in making us a free people ought to unite our hearts to fear before Him all the days of our lives.
>
> *(not cited)*

The central idea in all these celebrations of Providence in America—and it goes on for thousands and thousands of pages!—was that of *covenant,* a covenant entered into by God with his people, with "covenant mercies," "covenant duties," "covenant obedience." The essence of the covenant-idea is that of willing subordination of human wills to God's will, of willing obedience to God's righteous rule, of voluntary self-constraints in the interest of the public good, and of implacable resistance to all human tyrannies, all denials of due-process, all invasions of conscience by coercive power.

Even elsewhere, as among the deists of Virginia, where the Enlightenment idea of a "social contract" was preferred over the biblical notions of covenant, the same basic premise was affirmed: that liberation *from* tyranny meant liberation *for* responsible, self-disciplined citizenship. For all of them—Puritans and deists alike—the least government was the best government, and the prime function of any government was always defined as the restraint of evil and the redress of any and all injustice. The positive goods of human community were to be sought and achieved by men and women covenanted or contracted to self-denial and altruism, with compassion and equal opportunity for all.

Nor did this vision quickly fade, despite the fact that the original covenants and contracts had been drawn too narrowly and so did not include the native Americans, the enslaved blacks, the dispossessed Mexicans in our expanded territories. For example, it did not save us from a civil war—the English tragedy was reenacted two centuries later in America and it tore the nation apart. But what *never was* altered throughout this checkered history was the American confidence in God's Providence; that this was, by his design, "the land of the free and the home of the brave." Listen to this 1889 eulogy of America:

> This is a providential nation. How youthful and yet how great. How rich in glorious promise. . . . A hundred years ago the states hardly exceeded the third million in population, today they approach the sixty-fifth million. . . . The world's throngs are drawn to us. The country must grow and prosper. In the solution of social and political problems, no less than in the development of industry and commerce, the influence of America will be dominant among the nations. . . . The spirit of American liberty wafts its spell across seas and oceans, and prepares distant continents for the implanting of American ideas and institutions. The influence will grow with the

nation. . . . The center of human action . . . is rapidly shifting, and at no distant day America will lead the world. . . .

We cannot but believe that a singular mission is assigned to America, glorious for itself and beneficent to the whole race, the mission of . . . securing to the multitude of the people social happiness and equality of rights. With our hopes are bound up the hopes of millions of the earth. . . .

The chosen nation of the future! She is before my soul's vision. Giant in stature, comely in feature, buoyant in the freshness of morning youth, matronly in prudent stepping, the ethereal breezes of liberty caressing with loving touch her tresses, she is (no one seeing her can doubt it) the queen, the mistress, the teacher of coming ages. To her keeping the Creator has entrusted a mighty continent . . . which he had held in reserve for long centuries, awaiting the propitious moment in humanity's evolution to bestow it on men when men were worthy to possess it. . . . Of this nation it is the mission to give forth a new humanity. She embodies in her life and institutions the hopes, the ambitions, the dreamings of humanity's priests and prophets. . . . The nation of the future! Need I name it? . . . It is the United States of America.

*(not cited)*

I'll give a dollar to anyone who recognized that the author of this eulogy was a Roman Catholic, and an archbishop at that! Its hope and confidence are matched by a poem written not long after—by a daughter of oppression—proclaiming a new humanity for *all* the wretched on the earth.

Not like the brazen giant of Greek fame,
With conquering limbs astride from land to land;
Here at our sea-washed, sunset gates shall stand
A mighty woman with a torch, whose flame
Is the imprisoned lightning, and her name
Mother of Exiles. From her beacon-hand
Glows world-wide welcome; her mild eyes command
The air-bridged harbor that twin cities frame.
"Keep, ancient lands, your storied pomp!" cries she
With silent lips. "Give me your tired, your poor,
Your huddled masses yearning to breathe free,
The wretched refuse of your teeming shore,
Send these, the homeless, tempest-tost to me,
I lift my lamp beside the golden door."

—Emma Lazarus, "The New Colossus"

I wish I knew how such rhetoric sounds in your ears *now*, in these Bicentennial days—after two hundred years of the American experience. Were Mather and Cushing and Ireland and Lazarus talking about the America *we* know—an America that has lost its morale and morality, an America that cannot manage its technology to human benefit, that cannot solve its problems of ethnic pluralism? Already, many of us are sick of the Bicentennial because we were cynical to begin with about the motives and morality the public relations people are promoting. Henry Luce—he of the once-resplendent empire of *Time-Life-Fortune*—used to speak (in the 1950s and 1960s) of The American Century.

Now America is a blinded giant, in humiliating retreat around the world—a world itself in deep trouble and headed for worse—while here at home, we are in the throes of a national neurosis in which most of our foreseeable options are uninspiring. Even this would be tolerable if only the quality of life in the American community (family life; cultural life; life in our business, social, cultural spheres, etc.) were not itself tragically flawed (with every index of social pathology you can think of on a negative tilt).

Here we are, at the end of two hundred years of national existence, trying to find something *really* to celebrate, something really precious to claim from our heritage, trying to pull ourselves together for another century of national effort and achievement—and we are finding it all very hard and confusing!

What happened to that earlier dream of Zion in the wilderness? And what can we do now? These are questions that need pondering long and hard—in private and together—for unless we *understand* this present predicament of ours, we can scarcely grapple with the future it is opening up.

My essential thesis is that this Bicentennial is just precisely the right time for us to tackle the job of *reinventing* "America"—for reflecting on those basic ideas that really gave us what greatness we have had, as distinguished from the accidents and illusions which we mistook for greatness. America will still be alive on her 200th birthday, come July Fourth—and if she is not now well, she still has immense powers of recuperation. There *is* an American future that no one else can fashion for us, but that we, with God's grace and our obedience, can fashion for ourselves—or else "meanly lose the last, best hope of earth."

Let's begin by realizing that our idealized pictures of the America-that-was had more than a tinge of hokum in them; that those older heroes and heroines had their full share of faults; and that *their* Zion had more flaws than they recognized and confessed to. This would give our present *realism* a positive prospct, if only we can find out how to turn it into action. For example, we know now that America in 1876 was in a pluperfect mess—that Grant's presidency was worse than Watergate, that Custer's defeat was as shocking as our defeat in Vietnam, that business and labor were at each other's throats, and that the problems of racism and sexism had scarcely been acknowledged *even as problems.* But America pulled itself together and went on to expand and grow and, in its way, to prosper, with no thanks to our politicians or journalists (then or now).

We can go on to realize that the accidental parts of America's greatness were *room* (geographical space for expansion) and *resources* (which could be developed by developing technology that coincided with our expansion). Now we're running out of room and resources at the very same time—and we're going to have to live *together,* and on less, with more dependence on the rest of a hostile world than ever before. This will come hard, and it will mean that instead of waiting for our leaders to pull us together and ahead, we will have to tackle that job ourselves, on smaller and more humanlike scales. None of us can solve the whole problem; but each of us can begin to be more and more a part of the solution and less and less a part of the problem. The alternative: no Tricentennial.

Our forebears spoke, feelingly, of New England and other frontiers, as "howling wilderness"—by which they meant, in part, the harsh weather and physical hardships but also, in part, their emotional hardships and dangers. It rarely troubled their consciences that the Indians, the blacks and the browns whom they feared, regarded *them* as predators and oppressors. *Their* main point was to endure, to overcome, to conquer—to push out, and up and onward: Excelsior!

That particular brand of wilderness is pretty much passé. In its place, we have a *new* wilderness—a wilderness in which physical discomforts and hardships are less ominous than our emotional, moral, spiritual discontents and deficiencies. For the older pioneers, new horizons meant new land, unsettled territory. For us, new horizons must mean new levels of insight, new visions of community, new resilience under unfamiliar social and psychological stresses.

The clear and pressing dangers in this new wilderness are to our sanity, our morality, our spiritual hopes and expectations. These dangers come from an economic system that does not minister to the economic needs of humankind; from a political situation in which a neutered presidency, a reckless Congress, an opinionated judiciary, and an arrogant press (our self-appointed fourth branch of government) constitute a government that cannot "secure our domestic tranquility" or safeguard us in a hostile world. There is also the danger, ever more apparent, that our reliance upon government (which always finally means coercive power) is even more delusive than our older reliance on enlightened self-interest. And with this grows yet another danger—that if political, social, economic chaos continues to spread, we shall abandon our confidence in self-government (of, for, and by the people) and turn, in fatal despair, to some tinhorn demagogue or some white-plumed knight on horseback.

A new wilderness: a howling wilderness, yes; a wilderness with doomsayers, hucksters, and pontificating journalists, yes; a wilderness in which our social institutions—schools, churches, voluntary associations—are deteriorating, yes. But it's *our* wilderness, and it's up to us to carve a new Zion out of it, *if* we are still committed to that once luminous vision and its requisite conditions of a "new order of the ages" as it says, in Latin, on our dollar bill.

For Zion never was real estate; it never was technology; it never was nationalism—and it never was Utopia, either. Zion—the kingdom of God on earth, the new community that gives life meaning *despite hardships and frustrations* (which is, of course, what the metaphor of *wilderness* has always meant)—is an idea, a vision, a revelation. It points to a special quality of life, personal and social, in which faith and hope and love are the energizing forces of fellowship and dignity and joy. "Zion" is a religious idea: a covenanted community of people who consecrate themselves to a special life-style ("faith working by love"); people whose sense of dignity conferred on them by God impels them to recognize and respect the dignity of all others; people whose reigning thought is caring and sharing and sparing—who gain their satisfactions more from the public good than from their private advantage. This has to come from a religious commitment—to the love of God above all else and all else in God—because self-interested men and women simply will not keep their promises under stress if self-interest is their chief value.

God gives us some such vision as this—the biblical vision of covenant and apostolic simplicity; the Christian vision of "the body of Christ" whose members need not be equal in order to be equally important; the American vision of freedom under God, with liberty and justice for all. For then, guided by such visions, we *can* reinvent America. We *can* begin rebuilding the crumbled walls of Zion ("the beautiful city of God"), and we can do it in *our* lives and in *our* time and without waiting for some beneficent government to provide us with much more than liberation from the clogs of unequal opportunity. "We're Marching to Zion" *can* become something more than a half-remembered revival hymn, long since dropped from our hymnal—a drumbeat for new hope, an awakening trumpet to those who now are numbed by a sense of hopelessness.

America was—and still is—a covenant community, open to all who will contract into its conditions: to seek first the kingdom of God and *his* righteousness and to live gratefully and generously with all those things that may be added unto us. Such, then, would be our new Zion in this *new* Wilderness. Amen.

# 19

## *The New Jerusalem— Ross at Harwood*

### *An Introductory Comment*

Those present on March 15, 1976, at First United Methodist Church, located at Ross and Harwood Streets in Dallas, were challenged by Albert Outler to see there the New Jerusalem. (This sermon, with variations, was preached later at The Woodlands United Methodist Church in Houston on September 14, 1980, and in Canberra, Australia, on August 24, 1981. Obviously, its point is relevant anywhere.)

The century-old poem "The Kingdom of God" is a favorite of Albert Outler. In this sermon he describes how social-dropout Francis Thompson saw St. John's New Jerusalem, and then how he (Outler) thought both John and Thompson would describe that church at the corner of Ross and Harwood streets, or wherever.

He sees visions and dreams dreams. People driving by saw the concrete at that corner; Outler saw John's New Jerusalem. People on the street saw tall buildings and street lights; Outler saw the Heavenly City—the kingdom of God in the hearts of the people.

# *The Sermon*

Francis Thompson, a hundred years ago in London, was something of what nowadays we'd call a hippie—a gifted but nearly useless misfit, drifting out of theological seminary into medicine, and thence into drugs and poverty. But the spark of faith—and the soul of a poet—never died in him and, finally, in midlife, he found his way back up into the light, with the loving help of Wilfred and Alice Meynell. Maybe he was not a *great* poet (though better than anybody writing nowadays), but two of his poems continue as uncommonly relevant for our own time; and it's a pity they have fallen out of fashion with the people who "teach" English literature. One is called "The Hound of Heaven," a poignant mirroring of Thompson's own experience of God's grace, pursuing him down life's labyrinthine ways with a love that would not let him go. Most of us know *that* poem, if only by title. The other was found in his papers after his death, with a scribbled rubric, "The Kingdom of God"—and its point is the one that I'd like to try to make at this time: that God's business may *seem* remote and exotic, but actually is more local and domestic than we are apt to realize. God's provident presence is in *our own* lives and agonies, in our own backyards, here in Dallas as well as in Nashville or Canterbury, Geneva, Rome, or wherever. The Kingdom is *among* us—wherefore, let us discern it, rejoice in it, consecrate ourselves in its service.

O world invisible, we view thee,
O world intangible, we touch thee,
O world unknowable, we know thee,
Inapprehensible, we clutch thee!

Does the fish soar to find the ocean,
The eagle plunge to find the air—
Do we ask of the stars in motion
If they have rumour of thee there?

Not where the wheeling systems darken
And our benumbed conceiving soars!—
The drift of pinions, would we hearken,
Beats at our own clay-shuttered doors.

The angels keep their ancient places;—

Turn but a stone, and start a wing!
'Tis ye, 'tis your estrangéd faces,
That miss the many-splendoured thing.

Thus (when so sad thou canst not sadder)
Cry;—and upon thy so sore loss
Shall shine the traffic of Jacob's ladder
Pitched betwixt Heaven and Charing Cross.

Yea, in the night, my Soul, my daughter,
Cry,—clinging Heaven by the hems;
And lo, Christ walking on the water
Not of Gennesareth, but Thames!

Jacob's ladder "pitched betwixt Heaven and Charing Cross" will make more sense to those of you who realize that in Thompson's time, even more than now, Charing Cross was the transportation hub of London. It would translate now to the bustle and headaches of Dallas-Fort Worth Airport. There *are* gremlins at the airport—but are there angels? Answer: yes, more times than you might imagine. "Christ walking on the water not of Gennesareth [Galilee] but Thames" could be White Rock Lake for us, or Lake Grapevine or Lake Ray Hubbard—or even the Trinity River (odd how rarely we think of Dallas as ever having been dedicated to the Holy Trinity by some wandering Spaniard!).

But this was Thompson's vision, in that London swamp where he had drifted about as human flotsam. The kingdom of God is not somewhere *else,* in some distant space or time. It is, rather, God's gift to us *here and now* (and a gift is always given with a task)—in the Dallas that is, and in the Dallas that yet may be. Thus it becomes *our* task: to *live* in God's kingdom and to make it the pattern for our lives together.

Let's turn to the presumptuous task of reinventing Dallas! Here we are, by somebody's designation, an All-American City, a Bicentennial City—and yet we desperately need reinvention, a revival of morale and civic consciousness, a livelier sense of community, with refreshed hopes and enlarged horizons.

I rarely come into this church (or even pass by it) without noticing (or remembering) the lintel of the front door. For it stands out there as a mute witness of the older Dallas this church was built to serve.

A bit away from the heart of the old city, it stood just midway between where its first members lived and where they worked. It caught them, one could say, coming and going. This church—and its sister downtown churches—gave a special flavor to the burgeoning city. My father visited Dallas in 1928, worshiped in this building (when it was almost new), and then came back to Georgia to tell us that "Dallas was a strong church town." And Dallas, by common report, has had the image of a friendly town, a self-made town (it was in a seminar on urban sociology, at Emory, that Dallas was first cited to me as an example of that rare phenomenon, a city with relatively few "natural" advantages but with enough human leadership to make it a growing metropolis—more than 260,000 people, in 1930).

When Mrs. Outler and I came here to live and work in 1951, Dallas reminded me of nothing so much as what fifteenth-century Genoa or Venice, or even Florence would have been like, updated. I was fascinated by the coincidence that the president of the city's then biggest bank was *named* Fred Florence! It was a city where commerce was king, and culture and even religion were marginal values. But they were marginal values that every progressive city needed and hence Dallas had to have them too!

Yet even then, the city was beginning to change—the demographic revolution, which has altered the whole place out of all recognition (almost out of my memory), was already in early flood. Downtown was already farther and farther away from where more and more of the members of First Church were moving to. But never, in my wilder fantasies, did I imagine what now is an accomplished fact. In those early years, race relations in Dallas were in what seemed like good shape, since nobody on either side had calculated, really, what racial justice and liberation would cost (we don't yet know, but now must learn, *quickly* and *the hard way*). It was, therefore, almost easy to integrate Perkins School of Theology in 1951 (we had only a few rocky passages and at least one close brush with real disaster). But 1954 hit Dallas hard—I still remember my unbelieving dismay at hearing the superintendent of the Dallas Independent School District promising us, in a committee meeting, that he would prevent desegregation in Dallas by every lawful means. And now comes the crunch, in which, in a year, we are going to discover how much maturity and vision we have gained in the past twenty-five years.

In those same twenty-five years, Dallas has grown and grown—and is still growing—and this growth span has coincided exactly with a massive and baffling demographic shift with twin features: suburban flight and urban blight. Moreover, with all our struggles for and achievements of urban renewal, the inner-city church has seen its residential roles reduced and its service roles increased a hundredfold. This congregation has long since moved away from the crossroads—which means that First Church has become more of a metroplex church, more of a nerve center for Methodism in Dallas as a whole, than any other church in the region.

Meanwhile, the traditional American middle class—historically the secret weapon of America's achievements as an open society—is itself in the throes of unaccustomed recession. It is being whipsawed between increased taxes and living costs and reduced "surplus accumulation" (available money for voluntary donations). By middle class, one usually has meant, historically, the people in a given society who *pay more into* their governments (city, county, state, national) than they receive in services—people who are accustomed to "progress," to upward mobility, to rising above their social and economic origins (or of seeing their children do so). Historically, this segment of American society has been its backbone: Out of its surpluses came the base-line support for institutional religion, education, and community philanthropy. But what happens—rather, what is *going to happen*—as this middle class loses its dominant role in the American economy, in American culture, in American politics? Peter Schrag has written, exultantly, about *The Decline of the WASP.* As a declining WASP (White, Anglo-Saxon, Protestant), I could bear this cheerfully enough if any of the alternatives were even mildly heartening or hopeful. One of those is the liberal dream of a welfare state (in which it is believed that the government actually can create wealth, and can distribute it fairly). Another alternative is the sort of thing Robert Heilbroner foresees in *The Human Prospect:* an economic statism, mortgaged to multinational business and financial interests. And if you ask why some churches in America are declining, the answer is only partly due to doctrinal shifts (conservative versus liberal, or whatever).

The rest of the answer lies in economic, social, and political areas (none of which has a predictably rosy future).

Now, the point to this short and amateurish essay in demography is quite specific: First Church, Dallas, (along with its counterparts in this city and other cities) has a more difficult and yet a more challenging and heroic future than ever before. For we have come into a time when the burdens we are called upon to bear will balance off the bonuses we can expect to receive (at least in the terms by which such bonuses have been figured in the past). This is true of all large urban churches that make any effort to be inclusive, any effort to make a dent upon the body politic—but it is especially true of this church and its future. This is why the enterprise here is a great deal more important than the fate of a local congregation, why the tasks and opportunities outweigh the prestige and conveniences of such membership—why they concern all of the rest of us who know, deep in our hearts, that if the church in the inner city fails, the rest cannot be far behind. But also, if a church like this leads the way, the way is open!

This brings us back to our starting point, with Francis Thompson. For churches, which once paid their members bonuses of social prestige and community clout over and above the means of grace, must now decide whether to shirk these new and added burdens, whether to settle for some sort of survival-pattern—or really to try (with whatever faith, hope, and imagination they can muster) once again to pitch Jacob's ladder *here* ("betwixt Heaven and Charing Cross") betwixt heaven and *this* crossroads center? It is a good time to wonder aloud (even as we cling to heaven's hems) if we might expect to see Christ again, here, in *our* midst—neither on Gennesareth nor Thames, but here, at Ross and Harwood,

> Where cross the crowded ways of life,
> Where sound the cries of race and clan,
> Above the noise of selfish strife,
> We hear thy voice, O Son of man!
>
> Till sons of men shall learn thy love
> And follow where thy feet have trod;
> Till, glorious from thy heaven above,
> Shall come the city of our God!
>
> —Frank Mason North

It sounds corny and romantic—more than a mite incredible, too—to think of standing on the top of this church's tower and looking at the vast, intimidating collage of all the symbols of an exuberant materialism stretching in every direction as far as the eye can see, and still believe that what happens at the base of that tower (that is, *here*) makes much difference in this huge urban sprawl, whose heart has long belonged more to mammon than to God.

My answer is a faint affirmative ("Lord, I believe; help thou my unbelief!"). The Christian future in Dallas depends on many things that are yet in doubt. But the possibility is here, and I think I can point to *some* of the signs of hope. First—and again back to Thompson—wherever urban churches have recovered or renewed their primal dedication to the immanent Kingdom ("God is here—let us repent and rejoice and adore and go forth to serve"), it turns out that *there are* people who find in this both a gospel and a morale-building vision. If one thing is certain about the hidden hungers of us moderns, it is that we are *seeking God*—often unaware of our hunger, almost always without the right words or symbols. Vague, confused, inchoate—we are nonetheless stirred by recent rumors of angels:

> Not where the wheeling systems darken
> And our benumbed conceiving soars!—
> The drift of pinions, would we hearken,
> Beats at our own clay-shuttered doors.
>
> The angels keep their ancient places;—
> Turn but a stone, and start a wing!
> 'Tis ye, 'tis your estrangéd faces,
> That miss the many-splendoured thing.

Imagine a church where more often than not, people could say of their experiences: "*I* felt *God's* presence (comforting *or* disturbing); there *was* a ladder to heaven, and *I* saw farther than before into the mystery of God's grace and glory; Christ himself joined us at his Table—and made himself known to us—in the breaking of the bread, in the opened Bible, in the shared tasks of love." Suppose there were such a church! Where would it have to be? Anywhere! And if anywhere, why not *here*? And if *here*, is there any doubt that this would become a spiritual interface betwixt earth and heaven, betwixt heaven and Ross at Harwood?

There are interesting signs, even in Dallas, that the old order is changing—and that God may be fulfilling (and revealing) himself, even here, in ways that have yet to dawn upon us in their full effect. More and more people in "Big D"—long identified by their love affair with riches and power—are disenchanted with their chances either for affluence or for its normal fruitage in human happiness. The old days of oligarchy are gone; our current experience with competing party, class, and ethnic causes is disenchanting. The old system isn't working well—and its partisans are defaulting.

There is even a revival of the old Goals for Dallas project. We now have a new one, updated (and, more important, slightly reconceived). The old Goals program was self-consciously secular; it carefully excluded religion and questions of value-systems from all areas of city planning. In the new Goals program, there is an added task force bearing the clumsy rubric, The Quality of the Citizenry—and your pastor and I have been serving on it together for the past two months. I think he and I agree that it has been an odd experience, but still mildly heartening. It seems to have been organized in order to *prevent* creative discussions of value judgments. The majority of its members are moral relativists (they are also thin-skinned and defensive) so that probing analyses of our moral options have been unfruitful. It is, however, as typical a core-sample of the old Dallas and "new Dallas" struggles for hope as you could ask for.

In just two months, it has verified two hypotheses that are important, each in its own way: First, few people are *satisfied* with the "quality of human life" (private or social) in Dallas (insofar as it is a community and not a mere urban aggregate). No one on the task force professes to believe that our institutions (churches, schools, businesses, or city government) are functioning effectively in upgrading the overall quality of life. The second hypothesis generally accepted is that new value-systems (or the old ones transformed) are necessary for any significant enrichment of life—for life to have *quality, meaning,* or *value.*

Within the task force, we are committed to a secular, lowest-common-denominator level of moral and spiritual reference. Outside, however, I can speak my own conviction (as Dr.

Oliphint has and will and as the rest of us must, as we have occasion): that human life and culture are never any more authentic than their base in religious awareness, experience, aspiration. We have tried—God knows we have tried—to build a great and good city here, always aiming at affluence and clean water, affluence and clean air, affluence and ecology. What's more, we've achieved a measure of affluence for many but not for all—but in almost every case the ecological costs have been exorbitant. We've tried *everything* that high-powered business people, global merchants, and cosmic engineers (all acknowledged status seekers and wearers of approved status symbols) could think of to prescribe—and I for one am grateful for their services, however overadvertised they have been. We are currently trying a different leadership-mix, for which I am also grateful (even if also a mite cynical). What we haven't tried is *religion*—even though there are sociologists who would say of Dallas (as St. Paul said of Athens) that it is a *very* "religious" city. What I mean is that generally speaking, Dallas has tried to keep religion on the level of marginal tastes and preferences (private or group) while focusing on the business of urban development and renewal as our real centerpiece. What I am pleading for is religion as the ground tone of our civic culture—religion as the love of God and love of all humankind—as a truly humane alternative to secular humanism. Here our Puritan forebears were more acute and candid than the Dallas Establishment; for they knew, very well indeed, how "blessed is the nation whose God is the Lord." But it didn't stop there. The Puritans could say and mean it: *Unless the Lord build the house, they who build it labor in vain.*

As well as I can see and foresee, the conclusion follows that the old era of ecclesiastical opulence is over. An era of new and renewed spiritual oases in the very hearts of these human deserts has begun to dawn. The business of religion (and therefore the business of the churches) is the hallowing of life, the resacralization of our cities, the rediscovery of the kingdom of God in our midst—the New Jerusalem at Ross and Harwood (or wherever).

> And then I saw a new heaven and a new earth [the Kingdom within and without]. . . . I saw the holy city, new Jerusalem, coming down out of heaven from God. . . . I heard a loud voice proclaiming from the throne: "Now at last God has his dwelling among men [and

> women, of course]! He will dwell among them and they shall be his people, and God himself will be with them. He will wipe every tear from their eyes; there shall be an end to death, and to mourning and crying and pain; for the old order has passed away!"
>
> —Revelation 21:1-4 NEB

It could even happen here—it has, upon occasion, as I know very well. May it become, even more than ever, *your very special thing*—here at Ross and Harwood! Amen.

# 20

## *Lent and the Challenge of Forgiveness*

### *An Introductory Comment*

The congregation in Pollard Memorial United Methodist Chuch in Tyler, Texas, heard this unsettling, yet comforting sermon on February 27, 1977. Unsettling, because it probes the depth of humankind's sin as does no other Outler sermon. Comforting, because it speaks of God's love, mercy, and grace, the cleansing power of forgiveness, which can calm the unsettling effects of our awareness of sin.

Most unsettling for some will be statements such as: "I know (alas, I know it all too well, for I have some grudges I've come to be almost *fond* of, resentments that I come close to enjoying!) . . . we really do need to repent."

You may say, "How could Outler ever know what a real grudge is? Surely nobody would want to hurt him." However, his strong-spoken convictions on controversial subjects have generated criticism. His acceptance in so many arenas of activity has aroused jealousy and resentment. He has his battle scars!

And yet he says he needs to repent. You may think, "If *he* needs to repent, then I do too."

Colossians 3:1-17 is a heavy dose of Scripture, but it's a lot of gospel too. This is its gospel: that God gives us the power to be gracious toward *others* as he has been toward us. It announces the miracle of being reconciled to others as God, in Christ, has reconciled us to himself. To be a Christian is to share God's grace as we have received it—and to be grateful for all the grace we have been given and all we can share!

This particular passage in Colossians begins by pointing us toward Easter. If we ourselves have shared in Christ's resurrection victory and are therefore facing our own deaths with a sense of being upheld by God's unfailing love, then let us set our affections and values on "things above"—the things that extend our love out beyond our reach, the things that will last long after we are gone—aware that, even now, we are *in Christ* and not just on our own.

Given this premise of trusting faith, the passage then turns to our Christian undertaking to purge our hearts and lives of all needless self-indulgence. It even lists examples of such self-indulgence: (1) sexual infidelity; (2) uncleanness (which, incidentally, is the standard biblical euphemism for homosexuality and other aberrations); (3) enthusiasms and antipathies that have run to an extreme; (4) unbridled appetites (alcohol, drugs, conspicuous expenditures, excessive accumulation); and (5) avarice (a preoccupation with gaining wealth, which blurs one's sense of stewardship in its use and disposition). Moreover—because God so loved us that he gave us his Son, we must, in turn, throttle those sinful inclinations that still remain: (1) temper tantrums; (2) grudges and malice; (3) blasphemy (irreverence toward God and the things of God); (4) abusive language; (5) lies, and other sins.

But these flaws can't just be shucked off and discarded like an old suit of clothes, or washed off like a pair of dirty hands. The Christian life is life in the process of growing new, positive, loving ways to replace the old selfish ones—in the clear realization that we are *all* equally in need of God's mercy (the worst of us and the best of us!)—all equally in debt to God's compassion and Providence. This is why, in Christ, the differences between Greeks and Jews do not matter, nor do any other differences: race, sex, culture, politics, social and economic philosophies. We are all in equal need of

God's grace; we are all in equal debt to God's grace. And this is what the "brotherhood [and sisterhood, of course] of humanity under the Fatherhood of God" really means. This is a truly revolutionary idea, whose social consequences are more far-reaching than many of us could ever guess. Try to imagine a society of people living out their sense of a mutual and equal need of forgiveness; their mutual and equal impulse of gratitude and sharing.

One *becomes* a Christian by accepting God's grace in Christ; by acknowledging God the Father as Creator, God the Son as our Lord and Savior, God the Holy Spirit as his personal presence in our lives and in human life everywhere, and so on. One *grows up* and *matures* as a Christian by the cultivation of Christian habits—and Colossians lists those habits: (1) an instinct for compassion, lodged so deep that you don't *decide* to be sympathetic in the presence of suffering and need; you just *are* compassionate (what you must *decide* is what needs to be done and how best to do it); (2) kindness (which, again, must be a habit and not an occasional outburst); (3) humility (not taking yourself as seriously as you take others); (4) meekness (which does not mean the door-mat syndrome but rather the thankful awareness of how truly dependent we are on so many others); (5) long-suffering (literally, "sturdy endurance without annoyance or frustration"); (6) forbearance (taking others as they are and offering yourself to them as *you* are, without trying to fake it on either side); and (7) forgiveness toward others since you know yourself as a forgiven sinner.

Now, if this dosn't sound like a Lenten sermon thus far, that may be because we have forgotten what Lent was once all about. Our Protestant forebears, generally speaking, abandoned the so-called Christian year—along with the vestments and ceremonies that went with the succeeding seasons of the church calendar. Christmas was repudiated (especially among Puritans), and so were Epiphany and Ash Wednesday and Whitsuntide and Corpus Christi and other special days. Easter, remarkably enough, stayed as a universal holy day—but not Lent or Palm Sunday, Maundy Thursday, or even Good Friday. Lately, as we know, all these have come back, but not always with a full understanding of what, why, and wherefore. The *reason* for the former rejection of these old holidays was that they encouraged people to depend on *outward* ceremonies more than on their inward dispositions. They made it easy to divide up the

Christian life into *segments*, linked to the calendar. Christmas is the *scheduled* time for Christians to be merry; Pentecost is the *scheduled* time to be specially mindful of the Holy Spirit; Advent, the *scheduled* time to be hopeful—and Lent the *scheduled* time (40 days) to repent and do penance.

Here we run into a real paradox. Christians ought *always* to be merry (or joyful), *always* mindful of the *constant* personal presence of the Holy Spirit in our hearts and in the community, *always* hopeful, *always* repentant. And yet, we do need symbols and seasons and hallowed occasions—to focus our attention for a moment on a constant reality and truth. This is why anniversaries are important, and memorial days—even bicentennials!

But Lent was a special paradox—it was so easily construed as a limited time of voluntary self-deprivation, a conscious austerity program when one cuts down on one's sinning, especially one's sins of self-indulgence. "What are you giving up for Lent?" was a typical question for that particular season. It reflects a Christian life-style that vacillates between self-indulgence (when allowed) and self-denial (when forced). We take it almost for granted that carnivals—literally, farewell to meat and good eating—should mean some sort of binge of self-indulgence, since after the carnival comes that long stretch of fasting. Mardi Gras means a "Fat" Tuesday before Ash Wednesday.

Thus Lent took on a gloomy cast—sackcloth and ashes, a forty-day downer with Holy Week as its climax—and Easter became more of a celebration of the vernal equinox than of the Risen Christ. One-on-one, the Easter bunny usually outscores the Empty Tomb!

And this is how we lost the point that Lent is, above all, the Christian's time to prepare for the Easter climax of God's victory over suffering, sin, and death; of Christ's triumph (and ours)—not *over* tragedy but *through* it. And this means that the prime question of Lent is how to make ready in our own hearts and lives for this strange gift of grace, how to get into the habit of receiving God's grace gracefully.

It will never do to say (or even to suppose) that we *deserve* that grace; that anything in our lives or our good deeds has earned God's favor toward us; and that Easter is somehow a vindication of *our own* righteousness. For that is to make a mockery of Jesus on the Cross and the cross that is in the heart of God. Even austerity can be a sort of works-righteousness and, as such, is contrary to the essential gospel message of our salvation as God's forgiveness of our *sins.*

Neither will it do to think of the Cross and Easter as having some sort of magical power, as if salvation were a game of chance and we had happened to score—Bingo! God's grace and mercy are unmerited but they are not happenstance. Our hearts must be prepared to receive his love, gratefully and gracefully. And this is why, in the ancient church and in Eastern orthodoxy generally, Lent began with a special stress on the Christian's forgiveness *of others;* on cleansing one's heart of resentment; on purging one's soul of its enmities, envyings, or contempt. Lent begins with the call for us to forgive others, as God, for Christ's sake, has forgiven us.

The essence of Lent, therefore, is not in our gestures of self-denial (though these gestures are not to be despised or dispensed with). Rather, our special Lenten task is to look *within,* to come clean with ourselves about our feelings of being sinned *against,* of being put upon or put down. We are called to fresh decisions toward those for whom we hold grudges. Can *you* remember being treated unfairly or unjustly lately—by anyone or anything—and do *you* hold a grudge against anybody who has harmed or frustrated you in this way or that?

The answer, of course, is, "Yes, indeed!" We all are *victims* of one sort or another, and we all resent our victimizations in one degree or another. There are thousands of things that have gone wrong in our lives; and "others" are to blame for most of them. And we know who they are! Have you noticed this mood of victimization one finds among most people nowadays? Ethnics are victims of racism; women, of male chauvinism; employees of employers; one nation is victimized by another; one faction by another. All of us are victims of the IRS and of Congress! Besides, there are all those people who somehow have failed to understand us or appreciate our true worth; those who have done us wrong, in thought, word, or deed.

To feel sinned against, or victimized—by others, or by life, or even by God—is to feel resentment: against others, or against life itself, or even against God. And more people feel this way than may admit it, or even be fully aware of it. Else, why are there so many grouchy, ill-tempered, sullen people in the world? Why are so many people angry, "hurt," oppressed, and bent on proving they're O.K.?

The irony of this is that, as long as I am feeling resentment at my victimization and am unreconciled to those responsible—I can never be rightly *repentant* of *my own sins,* of my own victimizings! And yet, without my repentance, there is no forgiveness of my sins; no reconciliation to God, against whom I have sinned either by unfaith or lack of love to his other creatures.

If we are ever to know God's forgiving love, we must let his Holy Spirit cleanse our hearts of our resentments, grudges, hurt feelings, hatreds, motives of revenge—so that our hearts may be turned toward his strange gift of suffering, pardoning love. Forgive us our sins as we forgive those who sin against us; forgive us *our* trespasses as *we* forgive those who trespass against us.

All this is easier said than done, I know (alas, I know it all too well, for I have some grudges I've come to be almost *fond of,* resentments that I come close to enjoying!). Thus it is impossible simply to say, "O.K., here's good-bye to *all* my unpurged resentments." That's why Lent runs for forty days and still leaves us with unfinished business. But the crucial thing is to begin—and that is what this first Sunday in Lent is for: to begin and to go as far as our sense of God's gracious Spirit can prompt and prod us; to let our hatreds and grudges and grumpiness *ease away,* flake off, be assuaged, "get lost." It is a special time to look deeply into our hearts (before God and in the shadow of that Cross that lies ahead) and ask ourselves, as God did of Jonah, "Is it well for you to be so angry?" over what others have done to us, and not to be more contrite over what we have done to others?

We really do need to repent; we really do need a sensibility of sin (*our* sins). This is one of the great, but too often forgotten, Lenten themes. Yet as we stand before God unto whom all hearts are open, *all* our desires known and from whom *none* of our secrets is hid, we really must be willing to let his Holy Spirit cleanse our hearts of all unwillingness to forgive, and to cast away our grudges as if they were emotional *crutches* no longer needed. Then we can more perfectly love God and all our neighbors, really turn to the world and the human family in forgiving and reconciling love (really caring, really concerned). For only thus may we be ready for God's real Easter gift—the gift of gracious pardon, depth of mercy, *amazing* grace (see Col. 3:12-17).

And so may this be to you a blessed, holy Lent and may every day bring to you a foretaste of the Easter miracle!

Will you join with me in our Lord's Prayer, with special emphasis on that part about our trespasses and those of "the others"?

Our Father which art in heaven, Hallowed by thy name. Thy kingdom come, thy will be done on earth, as it is in heaven. Give us this day our daily bread. And *forgive us our trespasses, as we forgive those who trespass against us.* And lead us not into temptation, but deliver us from evil. For thine is the kingdom, and the power, and the glory, forever. Amen.

# 21

# *Living Beyond the Law*

## *An Introductory Comment*

This sermon was first preached to a thousand or more people in downtown Melbourne Central Mission in Melbourne, Australia (also at Memorial United Methodist Church in Thomasville, North Carolina, on February 4, 1979).

Here Albert Outler speaks to the human dilemma: "*Is* there any way to be good without having to try so hard—and forever falling short?" "Life in the Spirit" is his answer.

When we look at Outler's life, we might think that because he has praise and fame, he does not need to try to be somebody, because he already *is* somebody. But he has problems too:

"*My* unsolved problem is where to find the energy, motivation, courage (or humility) to do what I know needs doing. . . . But where am I to get that necessary energy and motivation—if not from the Holy Spirit within; from my willingness to let *him* rule and guide my priorities with his promptings?"

Albert Outler cannot, on his own, solve his problems. His energy and motivation are God's gifts.

# *The Sermon*

The fifth chapter of Galatians is one of those special crystal prisms in the New Testament. It draws up the light of the gospel of Jesus Christ and refracts it over a broad spectrum of insight and understanding. Paul had not yet written his Epistle to the Romans, but he had already plumbed the depths of the moral dilemma which he would later expound in Romans 7: that those of us who try—and try earnestly and honestly—to live by the Law, are still doomed to tragic frustration. For it simply is the case that those of us who dare to flaunt or evade the moral Law, are inescapably damned to equally tragic self-defeat (in this world and the next).

In Paul's world—and also in ours, even if in very different ways—the "shoulds" and "should nots" of customary morality abounded, as signs and symbols of the moral Law, which most people approved—for other people at the very least. The Ten Commandments, then and now, come with nine "shalt nots" and one "shalt." They can be violated all too easily, but they cannot be repealed, and no violation ever succeeds, in God's "long run." There is a universal moral sense, and we know that even when this law is almost universally disregarded—whether in small matters or in actual crime or fraud or outright immorality. These violations leave scars and corruptions in our consciences even when we succeed in observing the Eleventh Commandment, "Thou shalt not get caught."

Here, then, is a profound paradox: We have a moral sense of limits we cannot shake off, and we also have an insatiable hunger for freedom, a radical need to be able to choose and to do as we please, with no let or hindrance from others (especially from customary legal restraints—state, church, school, whatever). Little children are always testing these limits to their liberty—with their parents, teachers, and others. Adolescents are typically obsessed with their need to be free; and wise parents and teachers know that we must treat adolescents as if they were more mature than they actually are, if they ever are to grow on toward maturity. This is why adolescence is so difficult a time—and so anxious a passage, for them and for us. But this hunger for freedom does not ease up in adulthood; each of us, in some degree or other, resents the clogs and hobbles to our doing as we please. (You've seen the two TV ads—the harried businessman who asks, plaintively, "In *this* business who needs *more* paper work?"—and the housewife who, at the end of the day, wriggles out of her apron, a sign that she's had all the motherhood and housekeeping she can take for the time being.)

Hence, the conflict between the moral Law and our drive to freedom is a deadly serious business. The aim of the moral Law is to restrain selfishness. But it's still a no-win situation, because, even if we could succeed in holding the clamps on our self-indulgence, self-assertiveness, we still remain as *self-centered* as before. We may even become *self*-righteous about our *self*-centered victories over *self*-indulgence. (Have you talked lately to a successful dieter or jogger or health-food nut?) We approve the Law and its design—justice, righteousness, equity, fair play—and yet we're caught up in various conflicts with the Law's demands because they cut across our impulses to *do as we please.*

All this points to the radical mystery of human selfhood. As human selves, we are created as unique individuals by the Holy Spirit. We are designed to turn outward in various networks of interpersonal involvements; we are born to live with and for others. And yet there is this tragic drag to turn back onto ourselves as the center of our respective worlds—and this leads to inevitable collisions and jostlings with other self-centered selves. The Law was given to bring order and equity out of this situation—like a traffic cop at a busy intersection. Its business is to define right from wrong and to restrain the reckless from harming others. But there's no way beyond this struggle between the Law and our selfishness, so long as we live self-centered lives in a world with other self-centered people. This is a real dilemma and it is a radical one: Either we disregard the rules that seem oppressive—what Karen Horney spoke of as "the tyranny of the shoulds"—or else we are perplexed over the miscarriages of our good intentions. Either way, we resent the slings and arrows of our outrageous fortunes.

But what alternative is there? Well, the one we seem to turn to most naturally is the assumption that since people disobey the Law *deliberately*, they can, as a matter of course, shape up *deliberately* and become righteous, law-abiding citizens, if only they will try harder to follow the right sort of good advice and counsel. We are forever being bombarded with warnings, reproaches, exhortations—a veritable flood of moral counsel—in our churches, in our schools, from the media gurus. Our moral guides are forever pointing out our personal failures and the failures of our society—always assuming that if we only understood what we ought to do, we already have the innate disposition and power in us to do what we ought. This is the point to all this "consciousness raising," on this issue or that cause—and God forbid that I should discourage any nonmanipulated experience of consciousness raising. But the problems remain. The bleak fact is that racism has not faded straightaway just because it has been exposed for the evil it is. Oppression has not ended when we have identified and denounced the oppressors. Adultery, stealing, lying, price-gouging, and corruption are *not* innocent acts of men and women who *don't know* they're doing wrong.

We go to church, or to this church conference or that—and the all-too-common fare is an orchestrated symphony of celebrations, penitential acts, exhortations, plus a ration of fair-to-middling psychological commentary. We are reminded of the injustices we are party to; we confess our sins (usually in very broad, general terms); we are assured that we're forgiven; we get our usual heavy dose of moralistic, editorial comment, laced with religious sentiments—*all* on the assumption that what we really need is to have our failings (and those of our society) brought to our attention. What then is expected of us are brave, good intentions to change our ways (and to join in with other change-makers)—and the thing is done! The premise here would seem to be that the moral Law of righteousness and justice will rule supreme in our hearts—if only our eyes are opened (by professional eye-openers), if only the way of righteousness is clearly signposted.

None of this works, really, and so we fall back and try harder. The Ten Commandments still are broken, especially Number One. Racism still persists, *and* oppression, *and* neglect of the resourceless and the weak. World peace still eludes us; world hunger still haunts us. Moral sleaziness grows and spreads like a cancer throughout the body social; all the indices of social disintegration still tilt downward. Somtimes it looks as if the malaise of our society were radical—and terminal. The fact is that most of us really *want* a righteous world to live in for ourselves and for our children. But on what terms?—terms we are *disposed* to meet? What wretched men and women we would be if we really understood this deadly paradox of the Law as our ideal, on the one hand, and our despair on the other. *Is* there any way beyond legalism that doesn't slide into lawlessness? *Is* there any way to be good without having to try so hard—and forever falling short?

Actually, these are the questions that lie behind two of the truly wonderful passages in the New Testament: Romans 8 and Galatians 5. We know both chapters, I hope—or we know that we ought to know them (which is itself a comment on our dilemma). Both chapters are focused on a too-often neglected doctrine of the Christian life, as it can be lived in and through the Holy Spirit—God as Spirit, within our human spirits; God as personal, moving and enlightening and empowering us. The activity of the Holy Spirit is to lead us into fuller and more complete understanding of God's self-disclosures in creation and in Jesus Christ; always to inspire us, not just to pious, spiritual *feelings*, but to ethical impulses, motives, and *action.* The work of the Holy Spirit is to make us into better people, to guide us along our pilgrimage—always to the end of salvation, which consists in the restoration of the image of God in which we were created, to which we always are being called and destined. The true meaning of "conversion," "the new birth," even "the baptism of the Spirit," is the transformation (suddenly or by stages) from self-centered life to Spirit-centered life. If any person is "in Christ" (or what amounts to the same thing, "in the Spirit"), that person is a "new creation"—which is to say, that person has a vivid new inner sense of the source and ground of selfhood, a new mood, a new set of attitudes (toward self, others, the world), new motives and dispositions, a *new spirit* (literally). This is our divine inspiration which helps us to *act out our* inspirations, instead of letting all those good intentions we are forever making continue to pave the parking lots in you know where.

This, then, is what we actually need—less legalism, less exhortation; more inspiration, more urgent motivation, more sensitivity to the Spirit's inner promptings and persuasions. To live in the Spirit may, indeed, involve us in more prayer, more gifts of spiritual discernment (it could, indeed, involve us—some of us—in those extraordinary gifts listed in First Corinthians 12, gifts our charismatics cherish—and sometimes claim in special measure). But the end and aim of a Spirit-centered life is the *power to live ethically,* inspired by insights and energy that well up in us spontaneously. Life in the Spirit is not fueled by fear or even by hope of reward; its energies are *love, joy* and inner *peace.* To live in the Spirit means to let the Spirit rule our lives.

We all know the story of the farmer who explained to his more sophisticated son that he wasn't farming, even then, as well as he knew how. We all know how aptly that applies to our own living. *My* unsolved problem is where to find the energy, motivation, courage (or humility) to do what I know needs doing; and to do what a part of me, at least, would *like* to be doing, or at least to see done. But where am I to get that necessary energy and motivation—if not from the Holy Spirit within; from my willingness to let *him* rule and guide my priorities with his promptings? The great good news, which flows from faith in Christ, is just this: that the Spirit who raised up Jesus from the dead is the same Spirit who not only will quicken our mortal bodies but who, meantime, will help us defy the tyranny of sin. For as many as are led by the Spirit of God, they are the sons and daughters of God.

This is why Galatians 5 is so remarkable a clue to the saving mystery of life in the Spirit—life beyond the Law. It begins with the theme of liberation: that is, to live in that liberty from legalism which Christ has gained for us and in which the Holy Spirit has been given to guide us. Then comes a caution—not to *abuse* this special freedom by living "after the flesh" (in a self-centered way). This is followed by a sampling of the works of the flesh (self-indulgence) against which the punishments of the Law are threatened. It's a grim list (and sounds like the evening paper or a soap opera or an X-rated movie script): sexual aberrations of all sorts (including homosexuality—what St. Paul means by his term "uncleanness"); then idolatry, sorcery, hatred, jealousy, outbursts of blind anger, cliqueishness, drunken orgies, and on and on. The one common trait in all these "works of the flesh" is frighteningly clear and simple: It is *self-indulgence.* But, remember, *this* is what the Law was aimed at—the restraint of self-indulgence, especially when it is harmful to others (as it almost always is).

It is not until verses 22-25 that Paul gets to his climax: Those who understand themselves as living in the Spirit are also to *walk* in the Spirit—that is, to allow the Spirit's inspiration to guide their choices and acts. To walk thus in the Spirit is to live above and beyond the Law; life in the Spirit transcends all the Law can do and all it cannot do. The Law is concerned with justice and fair play.

Life in the Spirit is focused on intelligent care for others, on being caught up in good causes so that *their* values dominate our own. To live in the Spirit is to bear the fruit of the Spirit, and Paul tells us what this cluster of fruits includes: love, joy, peaceableness, big-heartedness, gentleness, faithfulness, humility, self-control. I wish we could analyze each of these fruits more fully; each is a special instance of them all—the outward expression of an inner prompting of the Holy Spirit. Notice that none turns back inwardly upon the self: each turns outward; each is concentrated on others; each is a mode of care for the good and well-being of others —starting with those nearest us and reaching out to the whole human family. Love is not a private emotion, even though it is radically personal and subjective. Joy looks outward, too: You know how eager you are to share real joy with others (indeed, it's not real joy until it is shared—and joy always becomes more joyful in the sharing). Peace is also communal. It takes two or more to make peace just as it does to make a quarrel. And so it goes also with large-heartedness, with kindness, gentleness, faithfulness, humility (a distinctively Christian virtue which does not mean self-disparagement or acceptance of one's inferiority, as it did—and still does—in Greek and Roman ethics. It means, instead, the sense of having one's dignity and worth from God, and therefore having no need to show off or to hunger for praise, fame, and ego trips). By the same token, *engkrateia* (self-control) doesn't mean emotional rigidity or the stifling of a person's honest feelings. Instead, it means *self-possession*—like an ambulance driver weaving through traffic with an emergency case, a surgeon concentrating on an operation; like a good businessman planning a realistic deal, a housewife preparing a good meal; like a student at her books, a saint at his prayers. When you're wholly caught up in what you're doing, and if it is really worth doing—*that* is self-control.

The painful truth is that we can't live this way on the strength of our own moral resolves or good intentions. What is more, we can't legislate for or against any of these virtues, *by law.* This is why living in the Spirit is so special: It is the free choice of letting the Holy Spirit within inspire our truest feelings and prompt our actions. You can't compel love, joy, peace, and the rest—and you can't prevent them, either, when people really are thus inspired. This is why Christianity never has been wholly extinguished, even by centuries of ruthless suppression. These fruits of the Spirit are God's personal activity in and through us—God acting in us to make us less selfish and more fruitful, so that his grace may abound in us for all his children. It is the Spirit within who assures us of our security in God's grace, so that we can think of and speak to the Almighty as "Abba, Father." It is the Spirit within who teaches us to pray—to be aware of and responsive to the Holy, in ourselves and in the human community. But it is the Spirit who also prompts us to grace-filled action—inspired living.

You and I must surely know at least some people whose lives seem inspired—some of the time at least—and we know what an inspiration their lives are to the rest of us. These people seem to live beyond all legalistic attitudes; they are free from nail-biting, on the one hand, and self-righteousness, on the other. The main thing, though, is that they are more fruitful, more productive, than guilt-ridden people can ever be—or reckless and immoral people, either. And although such people have ecstatic moments, they do not live by ecstasy; rather, their reliance is always on their inspiration—their "life in the Spirit."

Something like this, then, is what it means to live in the Spirit, beyond legalism but not beyond responsibility. This is the deepest root of unself-centered love, joy, and self-possession. This is where we can find real security for our egos—so that when we score touchdowns in the game of life, we do not need to spike the ball. This is life that is not compulsive, or for sale, or fear-filled.

This sort of life is the great privilege of all those who are born again of Christ, all who allow the Spirit within to be their guiding light and power. This is the great difference between lives struggling to do well—winning a few, losing more—and lives lived out of the overflow inner resources. It is the difference between moralism (and its frustrations) and authentic spirituality (which is, nonetheless, vitally moral).

The Christian gospel is not about any inherent moral power we have within ourselves, or on our own, to obey the Law or to be happy. It is, rather, the joyous good news about a new relationship to God the Father, in Jesus Christ the Son, through the Holy Spirit. It is the good news of the divine power prompting us to love, to rejoice, to be at peace and to live grace-fully. This is life at its best; this is true freedom; this is true spirituality. This is the actual baptism of the Holy Spirit—this baptism by immersion: in the encompassing, pervasive Mystery in which we have come to live and move and have our being, consciously and gladly. How else could we ever really hope for real freedom and serenity in the face of all the changes and chances of this mortal life? Can you imagine any better way, in *this* world, to live or to die?

Wherefore—and this is St. Paul's conclusion in Galatians 5: Walk in the Spirit and you will no longer be in bondage to the lust of the flesh (selfishness)—since, if you are led of the Spirit, you have been freed from the dilemmas of the Law. Stand fast, therefore, in the liberty wherewith Christ has made us free, in the joy and peace that rightly belong to "new creatures." It is in such liberty and such faith that we can live and work and suffer and die—all in the love of God the Father, in the amazing grace of our Lord Jesus Christ, in the holy communion of the Holy Spirit:

> By thine unerring spirit led,
> We shall not in the desert stray;
> We shall not full direction need [lack],
> Nor miss our providential way;
> As far from danger as from fear,
> While love, almighty love, is near.
> —Charles Wesley

# 22

# *Love's Wastefulness*

## *An Introductory Comment*

This Holy Week sermon was preached at Davidson College Presbyterian Church, north of Charlotte, North Carolina, during March of 1980. Albert Outler's single illustrative source for this sermon comes from *A Treatise on Religious Affections* by Jonathan Edwards. Outler emphasizes its thesis: "Love's wastefulness is a world away from the wastefulness of self-indulgence."

Outler himself gives generously of his time for various causes, a long-time habit. At Yale he pastored a church in Wallingford: "This business of ministering to a congregation . . . then going to the Fellow's dinner at Silliman College on Monday evening, and then teaching the next week at the divinity school, and being involved with the Kent and Hazen and Danforth foundations—it was a wonderful sort of spread."

Sandwiched between those types of activities are the casual visits from a variety of folks—students, dignitaries, yard workers. Outler's door is always open.

## *The Sermon*

*Lighten our darkness, we beseech thee, O Lord, that what we hear with our ears may be understood in our minds as thou wouldst have it—and so move in our hearts that they may be illumined by thy truth, through Jesus Christ, our Lord. Amen.*

Our text is that strange story recorded in Mark 14:3-9. This story, by at least two old liturgical traditions, goes with the special readings and prayers for the second day of Holy Week. In those traditions, which have laid great stress on *all* of Holy Week, there has been an annual *reading* of it, although not many notable sermons. In some traditions, like my own, there has been a tendency to leapfrog, liturgically, from Palm Sunday on to Maundy Thursday—and thus ignore this episode. In the Reformed tradition, there, of course, always has been a lessened emphasis on Holy Week as a special season, since every Lord's Day is an observance of all that is material in Holy Week, Easter, and Pentecost.

The result, then, in many cases, is that this Gospel memoir (which appears in two other versions—Matthew 26:6-13 and John 12:1-8) has lost the familiarity it once had—despite Jesus' promise, as preserved by both Matthew and Mark (though omitted in John), that "wherever in all the world the gospel is proclaimed, what she has done will be told about, as her memorial." Here is a prediction, and also an implied command.

But how many times have you heard it told, and what sort of *memorial* does it still signify, for us, in our time? The answer to this question may be reason enough to attempt a rescue of an interesting sidelight in the Passion story from its comparative oblivion.

In Matthew, the woman is not identified; legend has had it that she was Mary Magdalen, or yet another of the women Jesus had saved from shame. Matthew's point was that the anointing was with a *small* bottle of fragrant oil, very costly. Mark also leaves her unidentified, but adds a specific touch to the report about the perfume: It was pure oil of nard, he says (what we would call valerian today). John has a tradition that identifies the woman as Mary of Bethany, sister of Lazarus—and he has also inflated Matthew's *small* bottle to a *full* "*pound* of very costly perfume, pure oil of nard!" This must surely be an exaggeration, as if we were talking about a *pint* of *Shalimar* or *Estée Lauder* or even *Chanel No. 5*.

Matthew and Mark report that it was the whole group of disciples who were aghast at such a wasteful act—such a spectacular instance of consumerism, as our modern jargon has it. This suggests that the first disciples were Methodists—that is, primitive Methodists, schooled in John Wesley's *second* rule for Christian economics, which directed that Christians are to *save* all they possibly can and must eschew indulgence and waste of every kind.

Old-timey Methodists used to *obey* that rule, too; it was Rule 3 they had real trouble with—Give all you can! At any rate, these reported protests of the disciples were at least high-minded: The perfume could have been sold and the proceeds distributed to the poor (and who could fault a concern like *that?*). John, however, knows a tradition that identified Judas as an embezzler and attributes his complaint to base self-interest (he would have had more to embezzle!). But we do not need to take that seriously. For even our own good old Ben Franklin and his Poor Richard would have disapproved such reckless extravagance—Waste not, want not. In any case, unless we stick to Matthew's account about the *small* amount, we have something of a problem here as to whether the woman might have been overdoing it at least a little. Who needs a whole pound of nard all at once—even as a symbolic gesture?

What matters, of course, in all these variations is that the evangelists agree on *how Jesus reacted. He*, at least, responds to a gracious act graciously and gratefully. He recognized in it a symbolic anticipation of his death and burial; he attributes it to Mary's foresight of the looming shadow of the cross. Here was a loving woman pouring out her grief, her whole store of perfume, in a sensitive effort to do *something* to act out her apprehension. And Jesus recognized this, acknowledged it, made it into something significant. It was an instance of *love's wastefulness* and yet it was approved by Jesus and pronounced by him as a fitting and perpetual memorial to a woman who had simply disregarded utility or any counting of the costs. She had even ignored the needs of others—in order to do something special for the doomed Messiah. And this helps explain why Jesus' prediction about her has often been ignored in turn. This reckless anointing tends to offend both the thrifty and those who hate ostentation. But, then, for those who are not bothered by extravagance, the symbolism of this particular act is likely to seem macabre. Self-indulgent people are apt to shy away from any such thing as an anointing for a burial.

Thus we have another example of why it is important to try to sort out from the combined Gospel texts the common core of an actual event and then the later interpretations of that event supplied by the evangelists from their different oral traditions. It seems clear enough, then, that there was some sort of occasion on which a woman pours perfume on Jesus and he takes it as her anticipation of his death and burial—an outpouring of her grief—that should not be forgotten. This is *not* the kind of a story we would expect three evangelists to *concoct,* and so it seems to stand secure in the gospel tradition. Almost the least the interpreter can get by with is some sort of a recollection of a distraught woman, filled with dread of the looming fate of her beloved rabbi—doing, as both Matthew and Mark have it, "what she could," and a great deal more than the disciples had done or even would do when their showdown came on Good Friday.

I would be the last one to speak with any favor toward real waste of any of the disposable goods in a society that once spoke foolishly about "an economy of abundance." Here we are, so addicted to oil and affluence that we are having concurrent inflation and recession. We are already past due a cold-turkey withdrawal from consumerism and a throw-away life-style. We have no sensible alternative but to turn again to using things up (otherwise known as budget cutting). As a nation and as individuals, we are under a holy imperative to become better stewards of the earth and all its resources, to move away from the maximizing of profits to an *optimizing* of human and moral values, to cut back on luxuries and realize that much of what we have become used to as real necessities are, in fact, luxuries we might very well do without. All this is imperative on two counts at least: (1) the notion of an economy of abundance was never better than a delusion; and (2) the specter of world hunger and deprivation is a deepening tragedy, toward which insensitivity or extravagance is sinful.

But that would be matter for another sermon, at some other time. In a church in the Reformed tradition it ought to be enough for now merely to mention the still valid Puritan ethic of thrift, industry, and sobriety. How else did most of us come by whatever it is we may have?

But our present Gospel story has another point to make. Jesus did not reject the disciples' concern for the poor; he had already confirmed them in their concern for relieving poverty and the causes of poverty. That was part of what his ministry was all about. But now he realized it was time to set their priorities and perspectives in a clearer light. In the first place, they needed reminding once again of what they kept forgetting (what they must have wanted to forget)—his approaching death. In this light, they could appreciate such an act of anointing as anticipatory (something as commonplace and yet as basic as the bromide that flowers are for loved ones *before* they are dead, as well as afterward). Beyond that, he was suggesting to them—and maybe to us—that there is a *legitimate* wastefulness in *love* that is very different from conspicuous expenditure or self-indulgence. Love need not resort to penny-pinching in its expressions, symbolic and otherwise. What Mary had done *was* extravagant; but it was an excess of what, in our lives together, is all too often rationed out too sparsely.

True love need not be stingy, or even what we call sensible. Indeed, it isn't. As Paul says, almost as an aside, love is not self-centered; it does not ask What can I get? but What can I give? There is still something noble in the new apothegm, Ask not what you may get from your country, but what you have to give it. And there is still a lesson to be learned, especially by people who have been bred to be reserved and undemonstrative, from that old wheeze about the fellow who confessed that he loved his wife so much it was all he could do to keep from telling her so!

Love is by its very nature *outgoing;* its valid impulse is to give, to honor, to dignify, to enoble the beloved. Love, as all the saints have known, is one of those special treasures in our lives that can be squandered without being thus diminished. A good mother may have one child or five and still have love enough for all, and for each. The good teacher is not impoverished as he shares the love of learning with students. The good doctor does not ask the limits of her duty, but rather about the needs she can serve. And so it goes for every mode of caring and loving and helping in the world.

And yet the world goes on starving for love as much as it does for food. What is worse, this hunger for love is equally as devastating, even if in different ways. Thriftiness in love, carefulness in friendship, selectivity in hospitality—the various ways we have of protecting ourselves against the *risks* of love—all this is very nearly a way of life for too many of us. We are chary of complimenting others for fear of seeming to be flatterers—or soft-headed. We are wary of showing affection—it may seem a sign of weakness, or it might spoil somebody. By now, we have been scared off by all this trendy business about touching and feeling and group encountering, so that we often draw back to the opposite extreme. Because we have seen what happens when libertines let it all hang out, we have failed to make the crucial distinction between exhibitionism and real affection. And this is too bad in the case of Calvinists, for one of the greatest volumes by the greatest American theologian (Jonathan Edwards) is *A Treatise on Religious Affections,* in which he makes this distinction abundantly clear. But it is equally unfortunate for Methodists, since John Wesley abridged, published, and distributed a popular edition of Edward's *Treatise on Religious Affections!*

And so we come back again to the memorial of the woman who anointed Jesus with all that perfume—and maybe to the recognition that love's wastefulness is a world away from the wastefulness of self-indulgence. Jesus promised that she and her heedless outpouring would be remembered—and that the implications of it all would be pondered by Christians in later ages. For even though the hungry need food, they need more than food alone. They need love and dignity and Christian fellowship. Love has always to reach out beyond self-interest, beyond ostentation, to anoint people in their sufferings, and their prospective sufferings. To love God above all, and all else in God, is to unstopper your heart and open up your loving without stint, and sometimes even without heed.

Let us now share in a memorial to a loving person who lived long ago; and let this be, in its turn, a reminder of the death of Christ for which that love was poured out. Then let us take to pondering what it would mean for us to combine the gospel imperatives to provide for the poor, to liberate the oppressed, and yet not ration out our love to others as if it were in short supply.

It is no accident that the very next incident in each of the Gospel stories, after this one about love's wastefulness, is the story about Judas and his decision to betray the Master on whom he had once pinned such high hopes. Judas was a zealot, a freedom fighter, a man who stood for social justice, political liberation, and the violent overthrow of the hated Romans. He must already have been deeply frustrated by Jesus' gentleness. And the sight of Jesus' acceptance of such gracious, wasteful love may actually have been the last straw. And so he acted, on quite sincere convictions—such as all zealots have, or claim to have. And in that action to force a decision, he lost all he had already risked on Jesus as the revolutionary leader he had once believed in.

Can you imagine any way the evangelists could have made more clear the ironic and tragic contrast between love's wastefulness and the empty-handed revolutionary? Surely, Mary's way was better than that of Judas! And—it still is!

Let us pray: Almighty God, whose love for us in Christ surpasses all our understanding, teach us to love without thrift and yet also without self-indulgence. So create in our hearts a memorial to that loving woman who anointed Jesus for his burial that we, now in the time of his risen glory, may offer up our own lives as memorials to thy grace, by giving them into thy keeping and for thy service, through Jesus Christ our Lord. Amen.

# 23

# *Easter Faith and Human Hope*

## *An Introductory Comment*

The 1980 Easter crowd that came to Davidson United Methodist Church near Charlotte, North Carolina, heard this message on hope: "The Easter faith, then, is the font of a program for Christian *life*, and *work*, and witness. And out of *that* hope, comes the promise and prospect of the serenity and courage that can face transience and death without slackening our commitments or diminishing our joy."

The scriptural account of the resurrection of Jesus Christ, plus other Scripture alluding to that experience, are Albert Outler's authority for this belief in the resurrected Christ. This is no mere proof text; it is life. Experience validates his faith.

Outler's hope, grounded in the Resurrection, gives him courage to tackle his work. He sometimes describes himself as a bridge-builder. When we look at his accomplishments, he is indeed that: He has built bridges between Christianity and psychotherapy, Christianity and philosophy, Christianity and culture, Christianity and separated churches, and so on and on.

# *The Sermon*

*Traditional Easter Greeting: The Lord is risen! He is risen indeed!*

There can be no doubt about the fact that it was the Easter faith that turned a tragedy into a triumph, that transformed a devastating disenchantment into a religious movement that has changed human history. Without the Easter faith, the whole episode of Jesus' life and teachings would simply have dropped from interest and memory—and his disciples would have melted away into the sea of anonymity from which they had come. What turned a small group of insignificant and craven men (who had not even dared to show up for the crucifixion and who had lost what cohesion they ever had) into a close-knit body of faithful people, thereafter emboldened to respond to Jesus' commission to be his "martyrs" (witnesses) "in Jerusalem and all Judea, and Samaria, and in the uttermost parts of the earth"? Is there any way to account for the rise of the Christian church except by an appeal to the fact, and the meaning, of the Easter faith of those first Christians?

The Gospel accounts of the Easter events differ—as we should expect them to, considering that the events they were reporting were so startling and so unique. These differences in detail don't really matter very much, but some of them are interesting. For example, I grew up with a picture in my mind of that huge stone the Romans used to seal up the tomb, and which would take a crowbar to move. Then one day while rummaging on my own in a seldom-visited part of northeast Jerusalem, I came upon the remains of the tombs of an ancient royal family of The Kings of Adiabene (which makes quite a story in itself). And there I discovered the type of stone that had been designed to be rolled away! It was not a huge boulder which only giants could handle, but a millstone-type wheel in runnels, which even I could roll.

But one of the most remarkable details in the four Gospel stories is in John: There Mary Magdalen fails to recognize Jesus—until he speaks her name and she responds with the Hebrew diminutive for rabbi—rabboni! *We* do not discover Jesus; it is *he* who discloses himself to *us.* And yet that one disclosure was enough to send Mary back to the group of faint-hearted disciples, to stir up their flagging spirits and raise a new hope that their adventures with and for Jesus were not yet over.

This brings us to a profound message in these stories of the Easter faith. It is best illustrated for me by a remarkable pair of sculptures in a Washington cemetery that some of you may know. In Rock Creek Cemetery (not Rock Creek Park) there is the Adams Memorial, a sculpture by Henri St. Gaudens which depicts the inconsolable grief of Henry Adams after the death of his wife. It is a hooded figure of a woman and is called *Grief.* On her face is profound resignation, deep bereavement—a grief without transcendence or redemption. Not far away (about fifty yards) is another sculpture by Gutzum Borglum, a representation of Mary at the tomb at the precise moment she recognizes Jesus. Remnants of grief are still visible in her face. She looks up and there stands the Risen Lord. She says, with the gift of joy also visible in her face, "Rabboni."

Here is a striking contrast. In the Adams Memorial we see noble and heroic *resignation* to the fact of tragedy and death—but no living hope. Courage, stoic fortitude—yes—and what is now called grief work by the psychiatrists. But heart-lifting hope, no. Here is human dignity at a very high level, but without a quickening hope or a renewed conviction that God had wrought life out of death and a new peace out of infinite pain. But in the other sculpture, we see the birth of hope out of despair, faith born of the unexpected, courage as the gift of a new future.

The Easter faith, then, is not just the joyful awareness that spring has come back round once more, that in these vernal glories all around us we have new promse of yet another season of growth and harvest. It has always interested me that the early Christians were presumptuous enough to reset their Christmas and Easter calendars to coincide with two of the great pagan festivals—of the winter solstice and the vernal equinox—and then try to transform their meaning. This bold venture has never been more than partially successful: the cults of the Easter bunny and the Easter egg (both older than Christianity) have survived and are still doing well.

The Easter faith is something different, and its bearing on our human hope strikes far deeper into the mystery of God's grace and Providence. In the natural order, transience and death are inevitable aspects of life itself.

> Time, like an ever-rolling stream,
> Bears all its sons away;

They fly, forgotten, as a dream
Dies at the opening day.
—Isaac Watts

And death is there for us all, a grim and unwelcome robber. Whatever comes to us that we would like to keep forever—in a frozen moment of arrested joy and pride—passes on relentlessly and fades (not only in the memory of others but in our own as well). The mountaintop experience may be very well, but it will not last—and life winds down with all the indignities and disabilities of accidents, disease, and old age. And the end of it all is death, for each of us.

Now, sensible men and women in all ages have known this, and in their better moments they have been able to rise to real heights of fortitude and acceptance of the inevitable—they have learned to make the most of every human circumstance. But this is not real *hope,* not a truly serene confidence that "God is within the shadows, keeping watch above his own."

The Easter faith rises *above* this, even for those of us not so high-minded and resigned. What God did in Jesus is both promise and proof to all who live and suffer, to all who grieve and die, *in Christ.* And this is the ground, not only of our hope for our future, and the human future, but also for our faithfulness in any given present. This is the point and the conclusion to one of Paul's most impassioned passages of the Christian's deathless hope, *in Christ.* He asks,

> How can some of you say there is no resurrection of the dead? If there be no resurrection, then Christ was not raised; and if Christ was not raised, then our gospel is null and void, and so is your faith. . . . If it is for this life only that Christ has given us hope, we of all men are most to be pitied.
>
> But the truth is, Christ was raised to life—the firstfruits of the harvest of the dead. . . . As in Adam all men die, so in Christ all will be brought to life; but each in his own proper place: Christ the firstfruits, and afterwards . . . those who belong to Christ.
>
> —I Corinthians 15:12-14,19-20,22-23 NEB

There is, as you know, much more to St. Paul's argument in that fifteenth chapter about God's sovereign grace, about the mystery and the certainty of resurrection. There is that familiar and triumphant paean at the end: " 'O death, where is thy victory? O death, where is thy sting?' For the sting of death is sin, and sin gains its power from the law; but, God be praised, he gives us our victory through our Lord Jesus Christ!" (I Cor. 15:55-56).

And what does all this amount to? Not to a merely sentimental celebration of returning spring, or even our natural delight in the flowers and the feasts and our rising expectations after the passing of the winter of our discontent. It is, instead, a direction not only for dying but for living as well: "Therefore, beloved, stand firm and immovable, always abounding in your work for the Lord [work without stinting] since you know that, in the Lord, your labor cannot be lost."

The Easter faith, then, is the font of a program for Christian *life*, and *work*, and witness. And out of *that* hope, comes the promise and prospect of the serenity and courage that can face transience and death without slackening our commitments or diminishing our joy. To share the Easter faith is, therefore, to share the surest of all human hopes. Let us pray:

Almighty God, who on that first Easter day brought Jesus Christ from the dead, stir in our hearts by thy Holy Spirit, to renew our own Easter faith and so also our human hope, in this world and in the world to come. Through Jesus Christ our Lord and Savior. Amen.

# 24

# *On Getting First Things First*

## *An Introductory Comment*

In this sermon, preached on October 18, 1981, at First United Methodist Church in Beaumont, Texas, Albert Outler speaks about God's rule of righteousness: "Jesus calls us to seek and find the kingdom of *God,* the rule of the kind of righteousness that roots in love rather than coercion."

Outler calls us to make this life-style our top priority, the atmosphere in which we see, feel, think, and make our decisions. He says, "It comes down finally to a radical choice: life under the Rule of Grace *or* life under the rule of self-interest. Under the Rule of Grace our lives are acknowledged as gifted, and lived out in basic trust in God's upholding love." All of life's secondary values are accepted as useful, even necessary—but never paramount.

Outler did not put personal comfort high enough on his list of values! For many years during the hot Texas summers, he drove George, a Plymouth Duster with no air conditioner. Many of his friends hoped that one day he would enjoy the comforts of a larger, better-equipped automobile. When told he *deserved* it, he cringed at the thought that his friends never heard that grace cannot be deserved. But it was a graceful cringe!

# *The Sermon*

Our text is a single verse from the Sermon on the Mount: "But seek ye *first* the kingdom of God and his righteousness and all those other *things* will be added unto you" (Matt. 6:33). This exhortation, as you can see, comes as the climax of the first two-thirds of our Lord's great Sermon. It is the hinge on which the whole argument turns: What *really* stands highest in our life's priorities, and how can we get those priorities in the right order? But, in order to understand this verse in its context, I would like to offer a sort of paraphrase of the preceding eight verses, so as to make clearer how Jesus led his hearers to this conclusion. I hope some of you may be intrigued enough to check out the whole Sermon for yourselves. *That* result, just by itself, would make our time together worthwhile.

Our various human loyalties, said Jesus, cannot be equally divided. You cannot serve the true Creator God and the god of *things* with equal fidelity. And so you must ease off being anxious about *things* —money, food, drink, clothes, and so on. Life is more than the *things* it takes to sustain it, even though things are needful *in their place.* Look around you—at the birds and the lilies, for example—how lovely they are and how amply they are provided for by our heavenly Father. He is at least as concerned for *you* as he is for them. Moreover, by being anxious or by wishing, can any of you add a foot to your height or a year to your life-span? Why then so much anxiety about food and drink and *things*—as if God didn't know or care about such things, too—*as secondary?* What matters most is that you put God's kingdom and his righteousness at the very *top* of your priorities, governing all the others. Then, and only then, will you have put first things *first.* Once this is settled, then "second" things can be put second, and so on for third and fourth! And your anxieties will shrink back down to size!

What must have struck some people in the crowd was Jesus' use of the phrase "kingdom of God and his righteousness" as a prescription for the reduction of anxiety. In those days the bare notion of *king* or *kingdom* was bound to stir anxiety and fear, or ambition and scheming. Now that the kings and queens and princes of this world are so tame and ornamental, it is hard to remember that in Jesus' day, kings (even the petty client-kings of the Roman Empire) wielded raw power, ruthlessly and by whim. Both in fact and symbolically, they stood terrifyingly aloof, far above the multitide, and wielded the choice of life or death over the people. Even good kings were intimidating and the bad ones were truly dreadful. Just to be near a king, or to be dependent on his pleasure or wrath, was cause for anxiety and caution. Many of us—even in our vaunted freedom, equality, and fraternity—still feel something of this kind of anxiety around the boss (whoever he or she may be!), or in the presence of some powerful or rich person who could make or break us. Now multiply this tenfold or more, and you get something of the atmosphere that surrounded the ancient idea of *kingdom.* Then, add the element of *divinity,* and you get a glimmer of how radical a challenge to customary concepts Jesus had produced with his vision of "the *kingdom* of *God.*" For earthly kings die, or are overthrown, or at least you can keep as far out of their reach as possible.

But *God* is eternal; rebellion against him always fails; and there is no hiding place from his wrath and judgment. Thus, when Jesus came preaching "The Kingdom of *God* is at hand; repent and believe this strange good news," it was bound to sound startling. And when he proceeded to describe God's kingdom, it began to sound even more astounding. For instead of a kingdom of unchallenged and irresistible power, with strict rules of equity and rigid pecking order, Jesus kept on talking about God's rule of unmerited favor and compassion—about a whole new climate or atmosphere created by this sort of rule and order in human life. Instead of rigid laws, strictly and sternly imposed, Jesus spoke of the kingdom as the rule in human hearts of God's compassionate *grace.* To repent and to claim one's citizenship in *this* kingdom was not merely to confess your faults, feel remorseful and guilty, but to let your mind and heart be changed, from self-centeredness to God-centeredness, and so to keep *God* ahead of things and creatures and self-interest in your life. Let the kingdom or rule of God's grace and *his* righteousness stand first in your life and then, but only then, all your other priorities will find their subordinate places in due proportion.

This idea is revolutionary because it displaces the patterns of power—the pecking orders that govern our lives in earthly politics, economics, and culture—with the patterns of *grace:* the rule, guidance, and control of that special *divine* love that prompts and sustains that special sort of *human* love that we might call *gracious:* By *gracious* we mean generous, unselfish, sensitive to human dignity; the sort of love that disdains coercion and relies upon persuasion instead. I do not need to tell you how our lives are forever perplexed by the question of priorities—and most of all, by the question of which priority governs, guides, and shapes all the others. For most of us, most of the time, it seems that our priorities are assigned to us by *others,* or by chance or necessity. For so many, what we call "making a living" (and what that involves) is our top priority—which is to say, most people seem to suppose until you are "making a good living," you don't begin to live well.

You may know the story of the oil man in Midland who wanted to be buried in his favorite Cadillac—and when he was, one of his old friends standing by the oversized gravesite said to another old friend, as the crane was lowering the car and the corpse: "Hoo, boy!—now *that's* what I call *really* living!"

There are so many things in life that *do* matter and that rightfully demand attention: getting ahead, expanding our comfortable or stylish life-styles, paying off our debts and paying back our enemies, staving off illness and old age or coping with them as best we can—you can go on and on with these "needs" and God knows all of them *are* important, in their way and up to a point. But the basic questions about our priorities are: What comes *first?* What matters most? Where are we coming from and where would we like to stand when the bottom line is added up? We know people who put their *jobs* first. We know people who put *pleasure* first. We know people who put their ideologies and ideas ahead of anything else. We know people who say Amen to John the Baptist's exhortation to fair play and justice—but who remain locked into the network of injustice and deprivation that still blight the lives of all too many of God's children.

This is why it is so hard to hear Jesus' demand that we should seek *first* the kingdom of God and his righteousness as the *top* priority that will put everything *else* in its proper place. And that phrase *"the Kingdom of God"*—it sounds so familiar and yet so vague, or so pious, or so impractical. Thus the notion of setting God's kingdom as our top priority takes on a negative tone. It suggests putting one's self down, forfeiting one's freedom, reining in one's appetites and ambitions with harsh rules and unwelcome regulations:

There was a young man named Augustine
Whose conduct was simply disgustin'.
He said, "Lord, make me pure, but don't hurry the cure;
Your grace in this matter, I'm trustin'."

There are people who try to put *morality* first—and try to identify *their* view of morality with the kingdom of God and *his* righteousness; who seek first what they *want* rather than what God demands of us. The great philosophers have taught us to seek first the kingdom of the Good, the True and the Beautiful—and many of us have agreed *that* would be ideal if only we could bring it off. This is why Jesus tried so hard to help us see what the kingdom of God and *his* righteousness really are like and what putting them first would really mean in our lives. And he tried to suggest that the kingdom is not a *code* or a constitution, but a fascinating *mystery*. This he conveyed in parables which give us some inkling of what he meant us to see and respond to.

These epigrams and parables are not statements of abstract principles; rather, they are prods to new insights and new horizons. In all of them (and they would be well worth special study) the common hint is that the kingdom of *God* is *different* from all other kingdoms; that it is not like other domains of arbitrary power and coercion. It is, in essence, the domain of *grace*, of persuasion and voluntary commitments. Thus Jesus tells us how blessed (or "happy") the poor in spirit may be because theirs is the kingdom of God—for instance, the kingdom belongs to men and women who have won an essential independence from the tyranny of *things*. This is a clue to the difference between grace and coercion or clout or manipulation—how different from other patterns, with their pecking orders, their legalism, and their utopianism. It points to a realm in which we may live by the power of God's unmerited, outgoing favor—by his enabling, ennobling love, by his spontaneous generosity. Grace is *God's* gift of outpoured love; it is God's gift *to us* of the equivalent power to love *others* without cost-benefit analyses. Grace is the power and disposition, as in a good family, to treat every person appropriately, rather than according to some abstract rule of misguided uniformity.

Thus, the parable of the sower and the soils suggests that the sower spreads his seeds generously, but that the results are not in exact proportion—that grace, therefore, does not confine its generosity to those projects whose success is assured. Grace takes loving risks. Thus, the parable of the tares in the wheat is a rebuke to those people who cannot abide blemishes in others. It is a reminder that if we demanded perfection of others—or of ourselves—then in the course of *justice,* none of us would see salvation. The flip side of this insight comes with the parable of the mustard seed: Grace pays unexpected dividends, out of all due proportion. And so also in the case of the leaven—a little goes a long way and, in any case, is not a matter of strict proportion. Then the parables of the hidden treasure and the pearl merchant move us toward an awareness that the choice, between the kingdom of God and any other kingdoms—of things, or idols, or self—is not a matter of a little more here or a little less there: Putting God first is double or nothing. The pearl merchant will risk all to get all. Finally, the parable of the fishermen brings us back to the realization that the Rule of Grace is not murky or reckless, but that in the end and overall, Grace chooses the best and discards the worthless.

There is, of course, much more about the Kingdom of Grace in the New Testament. But this may be enough to suggest to us what it might mean to live by grace, to have the Rule of Grace (God's Reign) as our first and governing priority in *all* of life. What comes clear is that the Rule of Grace is not rigid or harsh. It is not even equitable in the ordinary, legalistic sense. It is not merely proportional. It is the rule of God in our hearts—God, to whom we pray "*Thy* Kingdom come" (in place of all *these* other kingdoms in which we now live—kingdoms of chance; of coercion; of subhuman, impersonal legalism). A good parent's love is not always orderly or measured out in strictly equal chunks. It is understanding, accepting, affirming, the right mix of pressure and patience which helps *everybody* to be themselves and to grow *together!*

This, then, is why Jesus calls us to seek and find the kingdom of *God,* the rule of the kind of righteousness that roots in love rather than coercion—and to make *this* lifestyle our *top* priority, the atmosphere in which we see, and feel, and think, and make our decisions. This puts *first* things first—with *everything else* secondary and in due proportion.

It comes down finally to a radical choice: life under the Rule of Grace *or* life under the rule of self-interest. Under the Rule of

Grace our lives are acknowledged as gifted, and lived out in basic trust in God's upholding love, with all life's secondary values arranged in their due course—as useful, even necessary—but never *paramount.* Under the rule of self-interest, which is our alternative, success may seem more promising, but is, as we know from every human testimony on this point, finally self-defeating (even in the short run). And so we have a question to answer: *What* stands first in our life? What *is* the prevailing weather in our heart? And how do we really, deep in our hearts, want our lives to be?

Jesus' formula for those who wanted to get first things first does not say: Decide to do this or that. Rather, he says, repent—"Let your heart and mind be changed in their basic orientation"—"Let God's design for your life become *your* basic design for your life, too." *This* is the good news that saves: that the Rule of Grace is as close and as open *to us* as we are willing to accept it as our rule of unselfish love and to let this unselfish love govern our lives.

The Rule of Grace is not really depriving! In it we lose nothing that is *really* essential or even really important. God's righteousness is not stifling or barren of joy. Indeed, this is where joy and happiness come from—the upwelling sense of being centered in the Center, of being upheld by an unfaltering Providence, of living without greed *or* fear. Living in God's kingdom, as Jesus said, is like living in a house built on a rock-solid foundation. For then, despite life's storms and tumults, the house and all who live in it are secure in the grace on which we can count unfailingly in every time of need. And so may it be with us, as we set God's Rule of Grace first in our hearts and lives—confident that all we really need will be added unto us. God, give us the faith to embrace this great good news as the power of grace and mercy and peace in our lives! Through Jesus Christ Our Lord. Amen!

# 25

# *Wesley's Covenant Service, and Ours*

## *An Introductory Comment*

This sermon was preached on January 3, 1982, at Oak Lawn United Methodist Church in Dallas.

Its thesis is laid out by Outler: "The decisive contrast between all natural religion and biblical religion is the basic notion, in the Bible, that the divine-human relationship is, indeed, governed by God." The Bible illustrates God's nature through his covenants: those with Adam and Eve, with Noah, with Abraham, with Moses and the people of Israel; and "the prophetic covenants, the messianic covenant—and finally, the climax of them all, the New Covenant in Christ."

Albert Outler's use of Richard Alleine's covenant service gave his audience the background for Wesley's Covenant Service, as well as the modern adaptation. In his introductory comments, Outler called the occasion a "solemn hour," yet his light touches of humor made the solemn hour uplifting. According to Psalm 2:4, "He who sits in the heavens laughs." And he who sits in the pew and listens to Albert Outler laughs, too—laughs the laugh of God.

## *The Sermon*

From before recorded time, men and women have been fascinated and stirred by their awareness of an encompassing Mystery in which they lived and moved and had their being. Much of life's business (beyond food, shelter, and survival) had to do with this dreadful and exciting relationship; indeed, much of the business of food, shelter, and survival was interlaced with this sense of mystery and with better and worse ways of responding to it.

But, in all such natural religion—in both its primitive stages and its modern obsessions—we see the crippling effects of fear and greed. Primitive religions are full of rituals for avoiding divine wrath and disfavor—and nowadays we hear people speak of keeping in favor with the Man Upstairs "or else"!

Over on the other side, there is a distressing show of cunning and superstition. Its essence is the expectation of being able to plug into the divine powerline, and then wire that power into our own appliances or purposes. It is faith not only in good luck, but in our control over Lady Luck. Our human hunger is to be *super*human!

We know how lives burdened by fear and dread and guilt are stultified—"cribb'd, cabin'd and confined"—or even driven mad. People turn up at Parkland and Terrell Hospitals with disabling fears or guilt feelings; people walk the streets, or ride in fine cars, with unbearable loads of anxiety or frustration. And as for our obsession with using religion—or positive thinking—to our own advantage, every paper or magazine advertises some course or conference or book that promises the secret of *self*-fulfillment, and *self*-salvation. Here then, we see the fatal weakness of natural religion; of these blends of fear and superstition. Each has a single concern: that we do something or other that will *affect* God (get him off our backs and into our pockets!).

The decisive contrast between all natural religion and biblical religion is the basic notion, in the Bible, that the divine-human relationship is, indeed, governed by God—not by his wrath or seduction, but by an overarching moral law and by contracts and covenants, drafted *by God* but shared in, freely and faithfully, by his human creatures. The story of Adam and Eve is the story of a covenant between God and humankind. It ends in tragic failure, but

God is not one to abandon a promising experiment. He makes another covenant with Noah (that the earth will continue in an ecological equilibrium, *if* . . . ). The story goes on and on—the covenant "with Abraham and his seed forever," with Moses and the people of Israel. There are the prophetic covenants, the messianic covenant—and finally, the climax of them all, the New Covenant in Christ. This climactic covenant embraces the good essence of all that went before, but now stands as God's final offer of a fully mutual relationship with his human family. God's revelation in Christ is not his *only* revelation—but it is the *full* revelation of the meaning and truth of all his other revelations, everywhere and at any time. "God, who in other times has dealt with us in partial and varied fashion through the prophets, has now finally come to us in his own Son." Beyond this, covenant making cannot go.

The essence of the covenant between God and humans, in any of its variations, is *not* equality but *mutuality.* God is God—and we are human—and there is no equality between the infinite and the finite, between Creator and creature. It is the very essence of sin to resent one's creaturely limits, to rebel against the God who made us as we are. This is to suppose that we exist by some intrinsic right, as if God could not get along very well without *us!* The truth is that we do not exist by any law of metaphysical necessity but by the sheer mercy, grace, and favor of our Creator-God. All covenants come from God's initiative, from his stubborn insistence on bringing us into faithful, obedient relationship, so that we can be happy and so that he can delight in our happiness. "I *am thy* God," he says, "and I *will be* thy provident, gracious Lord, Sustainer, and Deliverer *if* you will cast your dependence upon my Providence and live up to my rightful expectations of you (which do not exceed your created powers and potential). I will lay no demands upon you that are beyond your capacities to respond—and, in your respondings, you will find your self-fulfillment as a gift. What I want from you is what you would want of yourselves, if you knew your own full potential. I do not ask you to be *angelic,* but only truly and fully human."

But what does being truly and fully human really mean? For most of us—and this is the sign of our alienation from God—it means to be free and powerful, self-sufficient, and unfrustrated. At the heart of these impulses is *pride,* our preoccupations with self, our hunger for more for ourselves than we demand for others. But this is not what being truly and fully human means at all.

Being truly and fully human means being truly and fully dependent upon God's provident grace; it means the free acknowledgment that we exist *from* God, *for* God, *to* God. It also means the happy and glad acceptance that this is the true state of being human—for ourselves and for all others, as well.

Thus, it is not *our* part of covenant making *to bargain* with God, but rather to acknowledge him *as God,* to trust his grace as we see it revealed and made human in Jesus Christ, to confess our inability ever to deliver ourselves from this human bondage to appetites and selfishness, to dedicate ourselves to that rule of righteousness that God expects of us. This, then, is the way of salvation, a conscience awakened by the Holy Spirit, the human spirit humbled by self-knowledge, which comes as the gift of faith and the assurance of God's unmerited pardon of all our sins, for Christ's sake. It is the sense of being reconciled and upheld, together with our free and full commitment to the risks of love and the tasks of love. This is what has brought us together in this covenant-making service on the verge of this new year—to remember, to renew, to make a fresh beginning.

Most of you may already have realized that I have been summarizing one of John Wesley's favorite themes—and that this covenant service is a continuation of a regular, annual practice in the Methodist Societies from 1755. In 1780, Wesley published a separate tract entitled *Directions for Renewing Our Covenant with God.* And as we know, Wesley felt free to provide his own people with treasures that others have produced: In this case, his source was a jewel of seventeenth-century Puritan spirituality—the *Vindiciae Pietatis (Vindication of Godliness),* written by Richard Alleine in 1663 (when he was refused a license to publish it, and the sheets were sent out to the palace kitchens to be burned!). Wesley had already published this rare book, in extract form, in his *Christian Library* in 1753 (vols. 30 and 31; the "covenant" text that Wesley abridged is in vol. 30, pp. 320-27). Wesley's 1753 version was republished four times in ten years and, after Wesley's death, in a series of revisions that lasted throughout the nineteenth century. What finally came out of these revisions is the so-called modern adaptation which we shall be using (it dates from the 1920s). I wish we could compare Alleine's original with Wesley's extract—and both of them with our present text. It would help us to see the continuities in our tradition as well as our recent tendencies to water down the Puritan emphasis on sin and self-examination—and to obscure Wesley's intense concern for a really robust program of moral and spiritual discipline.

But since we can't do *that,* let me carry you back to some of the passages in the older text, for a taste of what lies behind the text we shall be following as we renew our own covenants with God, rededicating ourselves to *his* glory and to the service of *his people:*

> As you consider this covenant of grace proposed to us by God [said Alleine], yield yourselves to the Lord Christ; give up the dominion and governance of yourselves to *him.* . . . Those that yield themselves to Sin, and to the World are saying in their hearts, "*Sin,* I am yours—*World,* I am yours—*Riches,* I am yours—*Pleasures,* I am yours!" But he who makes covenant with God must say, "*Christ,* I am *yours,* as an instrument of thy righteousness." . . .
>
> But this giving of yourselves to Christ must be such as supposes that you are heartily contented: (1) that *he* appoint you to your work and station. It is, therefore, necessary, my Beloved, to sit down and consider what it will cost you to be true Servants of Christ, to take a thorough survey of this whole business of Christianity, and not to engage yourselves hand over head to what you know now. First, you must see what it is that Christ expects and then yield yourselves to his whole will. Do not insist on making your own terms with Christ. *That* is not allowed, to you or anyone else.
>
> Go to Christ and tell him: "Lord Jesus, if thou wilt receive me into thy house, I will not stand upon my own terms. . . . Command me what thou wilt, put me to any task thou seest as good. . . . I will be no longer my own, but give myself up to thy will in all things. . . . Lord, set me where thou wilt: let me be a vessel of silver or gold, or of wood or stone—so I be a vessel of honour. . . . If I be not the head or the eye or the ear, let me be the hand or the foot . . . so be it I may be serviceable. Rank me with whom thou wilt, put me to doing or suffering. Let me be employed for thee or laid aside for thee, exalted or abased *for thee.* Let me be full, let me be empty; let me have all things, let me have nothing."
>
> *This* is closing with Christ, as your sovereign King and Lord, and in this is included your renouncing the devil and all his works, the

> flesh and all its lusts—together with consenting to all the Laws and Ordinances of Christ and of his providential government.
>
> Beloved, such a close with Christ as this is wherein *the essence of Christianity* lies—when you have chosen God to be *your* portion and happiness, when you have laid up your whole interest and all your hopes with Christ. . . . Christ will be Saviour to none but his Friends and Servants—and he will have no Servants but by consent. His people are a willing people . . . he will be all in all or he will be nothing.[13]

But then, in order to assist putting these matters into practice, Alleine gives five directions to observe:

> First, set some time apart, frequently, to be spent in secret before the Lord: a. in seeking his special assistance . . . ; b. in considering the conditions of the Covenant; c. in searching your hearts (for unrepented sins, for Christ's commands not yet obeyed). Be honest in this; see that you do not even try to deceive God. Secondly, compose your spirits into the most serious possible frame, suitable to transactions of so high an importance. Thirdly, rely on God's promise of giving you grace and strength whereby you may be enabled to perform *your* promises. Trust not in your own strength . . . but take hold on *his* strength. Fourthly, resolve to be *faithful.* Having thus engaged your hearts, having formed your purposes into words, *to the Lord,* resolve yet further, *in his strength,* never to go back or fall away. And lastly, seek out a convenient time to set apart for such a renewal—in the most solemn manner possible—as if the Lord were as visibly present before your eyes as he is invisibly present in your hearts. There and then, open your hearts to the Lord in a suitable form of words.[14]

This is what we are about to do. As God is our God, so may we acknowledge Alleine's Christ as Lord of our lives. As Christ has lived and suffered for us in love, so may we live and suffer for him—and for his other brothers and sisters for whom he died. As the Holy Spirit gives us the powers of discernment and action, so may we use them to God's glory and in outpoured service to all to whom we can in any wise be helpful.

Here is Alleine's doxology—319 years ago! It sounds quaint in our ears but we can still make it our very own, as Wesley did, and as millions of other Methodists have done since:

And now, glory be to thee, O God the Father, whom I am bold from this day forward to call *my* God and *my* Father: that ever thou shouldst find out such a way for the recovery of undone sinners. Glory be to thee, O God the Son, who hast loved me and washed me from my sins in thine own blood and art now become my Saviour and Redeemer. Glory be to thee, O God the Holy Ghost, who by the finger of thine almighty power, hast turned my heart from sin to righteousness.

O dreadful Jehovah, the Lord God Omnipotent—Father, Son and Holy Ghost—thou art now become my Covenant-Friend; and I, through thine infinite grace, am become thy Covenant-Servant. Amen. So be it. And the Covenant which I have made on earth, let it be ratified in Heaven—this night and forever![15]

[Bishop John Russell then led the congregation in "An Order for Such as Would Enter into or Renew Their Covenant with God," from *The Book of Worship for Church and Home,* pp. 383-88.]

# 26

# *The Measure of Greatness*

## *An Introductory Comment*

This sermon was preached at Denton United Methodist Church in Denton, Texas, on October 17, 1982. In it Outler shows that while the disciples wanted a greatness derived from power, Jesus preached a greatness experienced in servanthood, in response to God's grace.

When we look at Albert Outler, we see an educated man. He has a classical education, the only kind one could get at Wofford at the time—a major in Greek and minors in Latin, English literature, and European history. He has a working knowledge of seven languages and more degrees than he cares to mention.

But Outler sheds a different light on his education: "Besides my parents, it was my older sister who was my first teacher and probably the best one I've ever had. My formal education was quite standard—which is to say, inferior. But my informal education was rich and exciting."

His parents had a summer home in the mountains of North Georgia, and his growing-up years in and about Young Harris still inspire him. This Appalachian Mountain "high" followed him through Wofford and Yale, to Duke and back to Yale, and then to Southern Methodist University.

# *The Sermon*

Honor and joy be with you on this happy and hopeful occasion. The joy and pleasure of being with you, old friends and new ones, in a congregation that cherishes its heritage, poses an interesting perplexity for me: How to integrate three themes into a single sermon—your 125th anniversary, the Gospel lection, and the launching of your financial campaign—and keep all this within the allotted time? So, if what you are about to hear sounds a bit more disjointed than you might expect, set it down to all those different concerns at the same time.

One of the reasons I feel at home with you here in this remembrance of your past 125 years, is that I myself have lived through the better part of that period. The survivors from my generation have experienced more successive "future shocks" than any other group of people in any equal span of human history. My memories reach from my early marvelings at telegrams and electric lights to my stupefaction in the face of the electronic revolution that looms upon us. My experience at Corpus Christi with a Lincoln Continental that constantly talked and blinked information was almost too much to handle. This was typical: too much change too fast, for too many of us to react and appropriate with anything more than superficial cultural adaptations.

The shadow side to all this excitement has been that the technological changes have not brought with them a proportional improvement in the quality of life. All the indexes of social health are pointed downward. Most of our expectations of the future are diminished—even when they are not abandoned. Some of us are hysterical about the fateful possibilities (as seen in current versions of the end-of-the-world syndrome). As reconciled as I am to the computer revolution, I keep wondering when the printouts will not be sprinkled with misspellings, barbarous grammar—when will their messages become more lively or profound? The speed with which banalties can be reproduced, or communicated, is not what we used to mean by *progress.*

What is important in these past 125 years, then, is not technology (as crucial as it may be), but the human achievement (the struggles for human dignity and community), the widening horizons of the human potential (*under grace*), the growing sense of the single human community to which we belong (as children of one heavenly Father), and the sense of identity and freedom in the community of the people of God (the upholdings of faith, the sunbursts of hope, the joys of beauty and love).

We have our dates, official rosters, and descriptions of public occasions. But I have the growing impression, even as a historian, that conventional historical records may not measure human greatness—may not indicate the full human share in history—in its proper terms and perspectives. I have no wish to diminish the luster of those who have been reckoned great among us in times past. My concern, however, *is* to call attention to unremembered greatness that also has gone into the makings of this occasion and others like it.

Fame is one thing; true greatness is another. Popularity and power leave their mark; the virtues that enrich human character are not so readily apparent. In the official records of this church there are entries that ought properly to be there. But it would be fitting also on this occasion to acknowledge the unrecorded services of the unnamed, the unsung—the unpretentious contributions of men and women and young folks whose part in this church's life has been crucial, in good times and bad. Thomas Grey's point, in his "Elegy Written in a Country Churchyard," is commonplace: "Some mute inglorious Milton here may rest." But he could have made another point too—and nearly did by implication—the paths of service that our forefathers trod have opened the future to many who may not even know whom they ought to thank.

*This* is the burden of our Gospel lesson for the day (Mark 10:35-45). It is the record of an incident and idea that lodged deeply in early Christian memories—for variants of it are to be found also in Matthew 20:20-28 and Luke 22:24-27. And still another echo of this point about the measure of greatness is heard in John's Gospel (the foot-washing scene, 13:4-17). One reason the idea spread so widely and stuck in so many memories was that it was so strange and so challenging to the ways of the world they knew and took for granted.

We notice first that the incident comes late in Jesus' public ministry, as the disciples were looking down the way ahead and realizing that in the coming kingdom there would have to be some organization; that it would matter who was head honcho in such an outfit in its eschatological future. In the Marcan story, it is James and John who take the initiative in bidding for the top spots, emphasizing their willingness to serve in any higher office, any field of wider opportunity—which, being translated, usually means anything with more clout! In the earlier (Palestinian) version in Matthew, it is their *mother* who puts her sons' names in nomination (a slight indication that the church has not always been male-dominated!). Jesus reminds them of the difficulties and risks of higher office, but they claim to be prepared for that. Both Matthew and Mark record the irony of the resentment of the other ten Apostles—not that James and John had been pushy, but that they had gotten the jump on *them!*

This jockeying for election to the Great General Conference in the Sky came after all those teachings in which Jesus had tried to show and teach those men about the unique quality of God's kingdom and the rule of his righteousness—in the parables and in his own works of love and mercy. And his reason for this was to help them shake loose from a social order, in their world, which always had depended on stable pecking orders of dominance and submission, on pyramids of power. From time immemorial, the perpetual threat of social chaos had been staved off by the seizure of power and the imposition of social control—by force or by the threat of force. Centuries earlier, the priests of Sumer and Egypt had come up with the idea that kingship would be more effective if it were recognized as divinely sanctioned—and the idea of divine-right monarchy and theocracy was born (or developed—it may have been born in Ebla and Ugarit) in the very dawn of civilization.

At any rate, it was understood by everyone that the social contract in secular society called for the dominance of the many by a few as the price of public order. The bluff old centurion (in Matt. 8:5-13) understood this as a matter of course: "I do what I am told by those above me in the pecking order and those below me do what *I* tell *them*—that's the way the world goes around." In such a society the measure of greatness is how many more people are *below* you than above you in the power pyramid. Supreme greatness is being on top alone. This was the immemorial form of social, economic, and political order. It even shaped their theological images of divine sovereignty; their mythologies are full of stories about power struggles among the gods and goddesses and the difficulties of the head god in fending off his challengers.

And who would we be—even now that the older patterns of divine-right monarchy are gone—to criticize those old patterns of pecking orders, pyramids, and rule by intimidation? Are we not still engaged in the same power struggles to succeed—and do we not still define success by reference to one's rung in one or another pecking order? Who is the greatest among us? The one nearest the top of his or her pyramid, the one with the most inferiors—all this in the face of our devoutly believed dogma of human equality? We are taught to dress for success (dress up or dress down, upon occasion). We study how to gain dominance by the way we walk and stand and sit; how to win by intimidation or charm (but to *win!*). There are all these courses in assertiveness training; hundreds of signals in our culture send the same message: Toot your own horn or hire it tooted—else there will be a dead silence! These concepts of pecking orders and pyramids are not confined to the military or to the world of business; they show up in politics, the professions, on the campus, and (in some special forms) in the church—amongst clergy and laity alike! I have a friend whose front door has on it a sign in four-inch letters: James Smith, *Ph.D.* We have bishops whose electoral campaigns were political works of art. We also have many episcopal also-rans whose lives were thereafter blighted by their near-misses. We have groups that protest their oppression, and I could not agree more that they must be freed from it. But I wish I had more confidence that liberated men and women would go on being liberat*ors* and not become oppressors in their turn.

In these incidents in the Gospels (and there must have been many) Jesus begins by acknowledging this universal tendency in society . . . and then rejects it, flat out. "You know," said he, "how the *archons* of the people [the power wielders, or power brokers] love to lord it over those below them in the pyramids, and how their *megaloi* [big shots] love to assert their authority and have it recognized." This is the way of the world—its moral essence is that every gain of mine is somebody else's loss; the dignity of one person is bought at the expense of an indignity to others. This radical selfishness shows up in George Orwell's *1984,* when O'Brien explains to Smith that power consists in being able to humiliate somebody else without fear of retaliation. We hear it in Camus' novel *The Fall:* "Power is the privilege of venting your irritations with impunity."

But, said Jesus, "It shall not be so among you. In the kingdom of God [and in the community he is building on the earth] the one who would be greatest among you, let him [or her] become the most helpful servant of all." Preeminence among the friends of Christ is measured not by their power (to coerce), but by their service in the manifestation of God's grace to others.

Clearly, the images here go back to the great-servant images of the Old Testament, but chiefly they refer to Jesus himself and his ministry in their midst. "For the Son of Man has come not to be ministered to but to minister and to give his all in sacrificial love—a ransom for many. . . . I am among you as one who serves." And in John 13, there is that vivid example of Jesus washing *their* feet rather than being served as a messianic hero.

This, then, is the measure of greatness: how much of your talents, time, and concern are invested in others and in good causes, without a thought of adequate compensation. And we know this, if we stop and think, from our own experience of those who have given us more than we ever gave them in return. I think of the handful of really great teachers I have had who left a generous portion of themselves in me; of church folk, lay and clergy, whose investment of time and talent and fortune were aimed more at need than notoriety; of the psychiatrist I know who makes just enough money in his practice to support his community-service projects; of the retired businessman who runs a dental clinic in West Dallas. We know of Mother Teresa in Calcutta and Dom Helder Camara in Recife—and they are truly great. But how many others are there who also give themselves without stint and who also are great, by Jesus' standards? These are the people who actually hold the world together, without the plaudits of the crowd; they build our churches and schools, and widen our horizons of mission and witness and service.

This role of servant-ministry—this avenue to greatness in God's eyes!—is open to all, but it cannot be chosen (or at least sustained) by our moral choice alone. A self-serving effort to be great in this way can lead to two alternative temptations. One is self-punishment (the shadow side of *pride*), the thought that if we debase ourselves as servants, God will exalt us and we will still come out ahead. This is self-denial without grace and it is just that; graceless and often fruitless. But then there is the temptation to make our servanthood a matter of rivalry so that we can excel in the greatness of servanthood. The Benedictines tell of the boast of their brother monk: "I can out-humble any man at this table."

Greatness comes from giving ourselves away, but we cannot become great *just* by giving ourselves away—for we cannot decide how best to give ourselves away just by our own self-centered choices. Servanthood is a role that comes with faith in God, and from our sense of gratitude to him for his gift of love in Christ and for his continuing presence in our lives in the Spirit. Servanthood is gratitude at work—grace in thoughtful action—caring for others because God has cared so much for us. Servanthood is our self-identification with Christ, who emptied himself and took upon himself the form of a servant!

The ministry of servanthood takes on many forms. It is, always first and last, the gift of ourselves—but that also means our talents and our share of this world's goods. And it includes our servant ministry *in* the church and *for* the church and *through* the church, for Christ's sake and in his name. Wesley had a neat formula for this which Methodists have found at least two-thirds acceptable: (1) Gain all you can—without harm or discredit to yourself, to others, or to God (which also means to God's creation and to the natural balances in the world). This rules out many forms of gain; what it rules *in* is productivity, diligence, and usefulness. (2) Save all you can—by thrift and careful use. Consumerism and conspicuous expenditure are *not* part of the Christian ethic. Have you seen John Brooks' ironic essay *Showing Off in America?* As I read it, I thought of Wesley and his eighteenth-century examples of competitive display as badges of greatness. "Gain" (or wealth), for Wesley was always *for use*—and yet not for use on oneself, beyond what he called "one's necessities and conveniences," and *these* were fairly modest. Rule No. 3 followed from No. 1 and No. 2, but was the hardest: *Give* all you can. Put your surplus accumulation to some good cause. The Christian, said he, is neither wastrel nor miser. If you gain *wealth,* you must *use* it or it will ruin you!

As Christians, we are called to greatness. This means *our* acceptance of God's gifts of talent and creative world goods, and their utmost development. It means our recognition of such gifts and aptitudes and their cultivation, and enjoyment in their use. It means an ambition for greatness, guided by the sense of true greatness as we see it in Jesus and in those who bear his Name, in intelligent, fruitful, responsible *service.*

Let the world have its *archons* and big shots—and their fatuous dreams of fame and greatness. It shall not be so among us; for in our tradition at its best, greatness is measured by preeminence in service and self-giving—and joy and gladness in such a servant-ministry. This is the spirit in which we can celebrate our past 125 years and our opening future, made possible as it has been by the servanthood of others (known and unknown). It is also the best way to ensure the future—of the Church and of its servant-ministry in the world.

Blessed are the gracious and the generous, for in them we can see God's grace and generosity made fully human and the fully human made truly joyful. And this, said Jesus, is what life is all about! Amen.

# 27

# *The World So Loved by God*

## *An Introductory Comment*

John 3:16 has been one of Albert Outler's favorite "themes and variations." This sermon was given as an Auburn University Leith Lecture on October 25, 1983; variations were preached in Sydney, Australia; Shreveport, Louisiana; Albuquerque, New Mexico; and at the South Georgia Conference.

Here there is no hint that Albert Outler has unraveled one stitch of the mystery of God's love and grace, or even tried. While more mystery remains than he or anybody understands, enough knowledge of God's love and grace is available to change lives that can change the world.

*Experience* is John Wesley's addition that completes the quadrilateral. (He borrowed *Scripture, reason,* and *tradition* from the Church of England.)

Outler continues to emphasize the *experience* dimension of Wesley's doctrinal statement, and this emphasis accounts for his rejection of all types of legalism, no matter how well-intentioned their proponents. When the radicals among liberals and conservatives attempt to legalize grace, Outler is ready with: "For God so *loved* the world that he gave . . . ."

# *The Sermon*

One trouble with a familiar text like this (John 3:16-17) is our easy supposition that, just *because* of its familiarity, it has been milked dry by generations of exegetes, preachers, and pious Christians. Hence the temptation for us to try for a novel twist to tweak our jaded reactions. There are, however, at least two good reasons for putting such a temptation by. The first is that many of the old familiar texts of Scripture aren't all that familiar to "modern" people anymore (to Methodist congregations, at least). Nowadays, they often strike new ears as fresh, with exciting new "insights."

I remember a rap session at Davidson last spring, after a class discussion of the picture in Hebrews of Jesus as High Priest. The point is that I was mildly astounded when a very bright junior chimed in: "I've gone to church all my life, and I'm a religion major, too—but this is the most of the Epistle to the Hebrews I've ever read—and even in the parts I've read, I'd missed all this emphasis on Jesus' *humanity*."

This opened the way for an oral quotation from my late great and good friend, Professor Samuel Sandmel, one of the truly great Jewish scholars of our century, to the effect that Hebrews seemed to him a sort of *fifth* Gospel because of its interest in the historical Jesus. At this point, several in the group spoke up in half-surprised agreement. That experience (and others like it) have sharpened my awareness that, even in the Bible Belt, the Bible has far more "new twists" for modern churchgoers than they are likely to expect. If you doubt this, try it out on your friends, or even on—yourself!

Another and even better reason for returning, time and again, to the grand old texts is simply that however familiar they may be, they are nonetheless inexhaustible. We can probe them repeatedly and they will still reward us with new insights, or with new angles on old insights. This is why they came to be "familiar" in the first place. And of all the grand old texts, none is grander or more familiar than John 3:16-17: "For God so loved the *world* that he gave his *only* Son [*monogené* means *a son* in a unique relationship to his father]—that whosoever believeth in him should not perish but have *everlasting* life. For God did not send his Son into the world to *condemn* the *world* [or more precisely, to *judge* it] but that the *world* might, through him, be *saved!*"

Yes, yes—we have heard all that before; what are we to make of it now? Well, for starters, let's ponder the contrast between John 3:16 and John 1:12. *There,* it says that "all who received him [the Logos and Light of the *world*] also received power to become the *sons* of God" (plural—*and generic!*). If Jesus were God's Son in some special way (*monogené,* as in 3:16), and then if *we* are God's son*s* and daughter*s* in a more general way (as in 1:12), then how is Jesus' status as *unique* Son to be correlated with *our* status as faith-begotten children of God?

Let's leave this question dropped like a seed in the topsoil of our minds—reminded, though, that any glib answer to it would be wrong! While it's sprouting, let us go on to some further questions about Jesus' *double*-relatedness to his Father *and* to us. This is not a merely speculative question: It is an issue of life and death for Christian faith from the beginning till now. In and with Jesus of Nazareth, we have to do with the Living God, in grace and power—nothing less. And yet the New Testament appears everywhere to take Jesus' *humanity* for granted, and as an ingredient in the faith that saves. *This* paradox—of divinity and humanity in one actual, historical human being—this defines the problem of Christology, which is to say, Christian reflection on the biblical witness to Jesus Christ as "the man of God's own choosing" (Acts 17:31) for *his* project of reconciling the estranged world to himself. This will be the hinge-question on which all these thoughts will be turning.

There is, however, a much more obvious point in our text. It is a brave, bold declaration of God's wondrous love for this world, a love so gracious as to involve his own best-loved—to *save* the world rather than merely to *judge* or condemn it (as the Jewish Messiah was expected to do)—and notice the old assumption in the root meaning of to *judge* that is also meant to *condemn.* This is the only text in the New Testament that uses "the world" in quite so positive a sense. Elsewhere, even in the Fourth Gospel, Christ's kingdom is not of this world (John 18:36); it is a world Jesus came neither to save nor to judge but to overcome (16:33); and so, therefore, must Christians (I John 5:4). This world is not our home; it has its own princes (I Cor. 2:6, 8; John 12:31) and rulers (Eph. 6:12); it even has its own god (II Cor. 4:4). Friendship with "the world" is enmity against *God* (Jas. 4:4). If any man *love* the *world,* the love of the

Father is not in him (I John 2:15). Here, then, is a series of texts that *seem* to clash directly with *our* text.

This is why the negative connotation for the term *world* has come to sound normal in Christian ears. We speak readily enough about a worldly person, and about worldliness. But then most of us would not want to be labeled as otherworldly, either—and for most of us it simply would not be accurate. And so we have a problem: How *are* we to understand and value "this world" in which we live? How are we to follow St. Paul's exhortation not to be conformed to it and still love it? John 3:16 says that *God* loved it a lot! May *we?* If not, then why did God? And if we *may* love it, then *how* should it be loved? Just how *worldly* may Christians be and not have their "friendships with the world" amount to "enmity against God"?

Our practical or implicit answers to questions like these show up not only in our lingo but even in our life-styles. They may not even be conscious! Many professing Christians, as we know, are just as cosy with the world as they possibly can get—they are not concerned to judge it *or* save it—only to enjoy it to the hilt. Here are people, often professed Christians, who go on consuming more than their share of the earth's limited resources, who go on laying up more treasure on earth than they can put to good use in fruitful, loving service. So, how and why did *God* so love *this* world and deal with it so differently than we do? God was in Christ reconciling the world to himself (as if the world were more tragically estranged from God than God was estranged from the world). What does *this* tell us about the saving mystery of Jesus Christ?

All of us have seen that remarkable view of our planet Earth taken from one of the Apollo spacecrafts returning from the moon. From *that* far out, we look beautiful! Most of us have seen the beauty of the earth from an airplane window, or from a car window when we have driven off the interstate, or from a mountaintop in summer, or when lost in rapture in a symphony hall. "For the beauty of the earth," and all that. How often have you thought how *detached* this sort of beauty is—how subtly it defines the difference between our feelings about the beauty of the earth *from afar* and our feelings about the human scene *up close?* Dallas from a helicopter is an impressive sight, or even from Thanksgiving Square. But West Dallas, seen at ground level and up close, is so shocking that few of my friends ever go there willingly. I never leave one of the wards in

Parkland Hospital without a trauma of my own. Southern Methodist University has some handsome vistas, but inside our classrooms and laboratories and residence halls there are human problems that daunt even the most cheerful counselors and teachers. There is much bustle and zest in downtown Dallas—but there is also so much frustration and jungle-style infighting that I am always glad to escape—although if I end up on one of our freeways, I realize how unfree they are. This is why that TV horror that slanders our fair name is so popular: It helps people identify with high-level human meanness, with self-defeating selfishness. Mrs. Outler and I live in a quiet, peaceable neighborhood, and we take long walk-talks in and about a five-square-block area almost daily. Over the years we have come to know many of our neighbors—and the better we get to know any one family, the more we learn of the tragic *admixture* of human happiness and wretchedness in a setting that looks as if it were as favorable a human environment as one could find. There is not a single family in our area, as far as we know them, without its heartbreak. *This* world, then, at a safe distance is lovely; up close it is *less* lovely and lovable, on a scale that generally runs from not too good to horrible.

Why on earth, then, could *God* so love this world that he would go to such lengths to save it? What on earth is he doing about its teeming wretchedness? Why did he ever embark on such a paradoxical venture as this human creation—which seems so often and so perversely at enmity with His purposes?

The Christian answers to such questions must come finally to focus in Jesus Christ—in God's self-revelation in Jesus, in his proclamation of the kind of righteousness that would make of this world a peaceable kingdom. This is what the Bible stories all add up to—the creation of so beautiful a *world*, but a world so tragically gone astray from its original design—and yet a world the Creator seeks to save through his resourceful initiatives. "God was in Christ reconciling the world unto himself" . . . and still that world, in large part, is unreconciled. The history of salvation is the tragic story of a world in wrack and ruin, of the miracle of God's gracious offer of redemption, and of God's strange forbearance in holding that offer open. But why on earth would God go to so much bother? Why should he continue to hold his offer open? He is not all *that* dependent on the outcome of this one experiment with a human creation—or *is* he?

Well, if he is not *dependent,* he at least has been obstinate. This is the plot in the biblical scenario: from the Fall, the Flood, the Exodus, the tedious strayings of Israel, to the Incarnation and the first chapters of church history. It is the story of God's repeated rescripting the storyline even as he holds fast to his unrevised design. This is the essential drama in church history: from its shaky beginnings through all the paradoxes in which either success or failure has led to one sort of distortion or another. And yet God's design remains unaltered and God's interest in his implausible experiment continues *un*withdrawn. Why?

The beginning of an answer lies in just precisely this divine perseverance. What God has made was well-made; and even in its tragic ruins there is a human project worth salvaging. And Jesus is the proof of that divine recognition that God's investment in the human family is far too valuable to pull the plug on. "Like as a father has compassion on his children, so also the Lord has compassion on all who acknowledge his Lordship."—"Oh, love that *has* not let us go—and *will* not."

Clearly, then, in God's eyes and in his unswerving purpose, the human experiment is surpassingly important, and Jesus is the proof of just how much store God has set on us. For God loved the world *that much*. . . . Thus, Jesus on the Via Dolorosa and on the Cross. God loved us *that* much, too. There has been, and can be, no greater love. And therefore, no world so loved can be thought of as worthless. No such world can be treated as a grab bag—or as an oyster to be opened and gulped down.

Yet it is equally clear that this world, so much beloved, no longer reflects God's original design except in a shattered, distorted way. God's love of the world is not requited from and by the world. The New Testament speaks of the world as lying in darkness and wickedness—and we are reminded of this almost every evening when we see the newscast on television, or whenever we scan the daily papers. This world, as it now stands, is not yet subject to Christ's gracious rule; it *is* under the dominion of sin and of evil forces (the rulers of the darkness of the world); it is racked by inhumanity and subhuman wretchedness; the whole world (as it seemed to St. John, and to us) lies in darkness. But this is to pass judgment on the world, although passing such a judgment has its place (as St. Paul tells us in I Cor. 6:2, where it says that the saints—and that means us—are to *judge* the world by God's authority and power). Even so, our judgments of the world are not definitive. What the world needs most is not merely judgment—or self-salvation either. It needs to be saved—saved from its unhappiness, from its wretchedness, from its failures to fulfill God's design for his human children—that we should be holy and happy, all together.

And if there is one thing that is tragically certain, it is that the world cannot save itself. No human being nor even the whole of the human community has achieved, or can achieve, the human potential by human efforts alone—of any kind. This is the essential fallacy (or delusion) of the so-called human-potential movement and of all these cults of self-salvation that have sprung up about us in our currently psychologized society.

But if there is no salvation in human effort, how can there be *any* salvation for human beings that will not be a mere salvation by fiat or by some arbitrary divine act that would so stultify human freedom as to diminish the full *humanity* of the saints? This is St. Paul's question in Romans 7: "Oh, wretched man that I am; who shall deliver me from this body of death?" His answer, the answer of the Christian gospel in every age from the apostles down to our own time, is given in Romans 8.

Our only salvation is by grace, and this is St. Paul's essential gospel, the grace of God in Christ shed abroad in our hearts by the Holy Spirit. We cannot be saved by having the thresholds of heaven lowered so that our compromised lives can sidle over them, while St. Peter looks the other way. There is no heavenly admissions officer to stamp an O.K. on our falsified transcripts! We can be saved only by God's active, morally honest, life-changing love—which is only to say again that we are *saved by grace.* But how can we receive this grace, this love? By *faithing* it, by accepting it in repentance and deep humility and with firm assurance. But how is any such faith confirmed? And *this* gets us back around to our text: God *so loved* us that he gave us his very best gift—and in this gift is both the reality of saving grace, and its confirmation. We will not be saved, in any first instance, by *our* love—only by God's love, manifested in Jesus.

No such world so loved by God can be despised. If God found it lovable, then so must we—and in the same sense that God found it lovable. We must love what reflects God's image and purpose. No world so loved can be treated mainly as a target for exploitation and *self*-interest. Gods outgoing, sacrificial love calls for our own best love—outgoing and sacrificial. The world is not merely to be judged, or exploited, but to be saved, and we must seek out our various supporting roles in God's great drama of human salvation.

But we will never understand the drama as a whole, in any scope or depth, until we have understood its central character. This is why our faith in *Jesus Christ* must search out and reach for an adequate understanding. *This* is what Christology is all about—as adequate an understanding as we can manage of the mystery of the One who was as truly human as any of us and yet also truly divine. This is, indeed, an inexhaustible mystery. But there are better and worse ways of understanding it, and it makes a crucial difference for Christian *living* that the *better* ways be sorted out from the worse. This, then, will be our project from here on.

But the quality of any *analysis* depends upon what is to be analyzed—and in Christian experience, this must be the living faith of Christians in Jesus Christ as Lord and Savior to the glory of God the Father. This is the faith that has been summed up in our text—and in its mate in Second Corinthians 5:

> For God so loved the world—and so loved *us*—that he gave his first-born Son, that whosoever believes in him [faiths him, puts life and destiny in his hands and grace] shall not perish, but have life everlasting. For God was in Christ reconciling the world to himself. *Therefore, be reconciled to God* through Christ—not only to be saved, but to live in the world as Christ lived in the days of his flesh.

Now we know what God has done in and for the world, out of his love for it (and for us). So, what then are *we* going to do, in and for this very same world? Perhaps there are answers to these questions (or clues at least) in an old prayer the Wesleys knew by heart:

> Almighty God, Father of all mercies . . . we bless thee for our creation, preservation, and all the blessings of this life, but above all for thine inestimable love in the redemption of the *world* by our Lord Jesus Christ, for the means of grace, and for the hope of glory. And

we beseech thee, give us that due sense of all thy mercies, that our hearts may be unfeignedly thankful, and that we may show forth thy praise, not only with our lips, but in our lives, by giving up ourselves to thy service and by walking before thee in holiness and righteousness all our days; through Jesus Christ our Lord, to whom, with thee and the Holy Spirit, be all honor and glory, world without end. Amen.[16]

# 28

---

# *The Sainthood of All Believers*

## *An Introductory Comment*

When the Sunday morning crowd arrived at St. Stephen's United Methodist Church in Houston on May 27, 1984, little did the people realize that they would leave as saints—that is, they would leave as saints if they loved others out of their response to God's love for them.

Albert Outler says that "outward holiness is the fruit of inward holiness—of our love for God in response to his love for *us*, our faith and trust in him, our sense of radical dependence upon his grace and bounty, our eagerness that his will be done here on earth."

He asks, "But, where does all this end? When can we think we have arrived at some state of perfect love? The answer is that love—of God or of neighbor—does not run by calendars or meters or rules." It "never ends" (I Cor. 13:8).

Then he adds that none of us has arrived at a state of perfect love. We are all in the same boat. But we can be as saintly as anyone who ever lived, *if* we love others as God loves us through Christ. That love, lived out, is always perfect.

## The Sermon

"You, therefore, must be perfect, as your heavenly Father is perfect" (Matt. 5:48).

This text, with its "therefore," is the conclusion of Jesus' extended comment about the various ways so many religious people try to be "good *enough*" without overdoing it.

Few people object to goodness in moderation. Most people would profess themselves to be in favor of decency, fair play, generosity, neighborliness, altruism, social justice—up to a point! This was the righteousness of the Pharisees (the most conscientious and religiously observant people in Jesus' day). And this has always been the righteousness of the best of the Gentiles: doing as little harm as possible, doing as much good as may be convenient, observing at least the more obvious religious rituals and obligations.

There was a well-meaning man in John Wesley's time named Joseph Trapp, who preached and published a series of very popular sermons on *The Folly of Being Righteous Overmuch*—denouncing the notion of demanding too much of oneself and others by way of moral and spiritual discipline. Some of you may be surprised to hear that Trapp's target was the Methodists, then a small but vigorous group of people who had started a new religious movement in the Church of England.

Since then, we have managed to avoid such charges, but the tradition (that Methodists are called to more than conventional goodness) lingers on. Wesley has a wonderful comment about people who are just religious enough to have a bad conscience and be miserable about it, but not enough faith and grace to make them happy, joyful, and really useful.

This notion of there being no limits to our loving God and neighbor (which, *together*, define the essential meaning of perfection or holiness or wholeness, here and elsewhere in the New Testament) is a mite unnerving, aware as we are of all the other limits and bounds of life—time and space and talent and wisdom and all the rest. For many of us, "pretty good" is very good, indeed—and for God to ask us for more may be asking too much.

One thing we do agree about, however, is that all of us who are baptized, practicing Christians—even of the most moderate sort—belong to "the *priesthood* of all believers," as members of the general ministry of the people of God. We are, each of us, entitled to pray, to read the Scriptures, to live as witnesses to others of our faith, to express this faith in acts of love and mercy, to share in the world's work and weeping, to do at least a little to set this upside-down world right side up again (as much as we can and wherever we can). And this is right and good as far as it goes.

Typically, though, we have misunderstood this traditional notion of the *priesthood* of all believers, even while believing in it devoutly. We tend to think of it as a license to be priests *for ourselves*—to pray directly to God without mediation (other than through Christ and the Holy Spirit); to read the Scriptures on our own and decide not only what this text or that means, but also which parts of Scripture we like and don't like, what grabs us and what leaves us cold—in short, to be solitary Christians and to look after our own spiritual needs, even as we expect others to do the same. Actually, as Wesley said emphatically, solitary religion is a travesty—and invalid. For the work of a priest or minister is always principally *for others*—to pray for *them*, to study the Scriptures with *them*, to help share and bear *their* griefs and burdens. Jesus was *the* man for others; John Wesley was also a man *for others*. And so should we be, in Jesus' name and Spirit.

But Jesus, and John Wesley as a faithful interpreter of Jesus, added something more to this image of the *priesthood* of all believers—the *sainthood* of all believers. Unless our goodness and lovingkindness reach beyond ordinary bounds of religious observance, we are still falling short of our spiritual capacities; we are still settling for less than our best. Christians are called to be *priests;* we are also called to be *saints.* Such a notion will take some of us aback—"Who, *me*, a saint? You've got to be kidding! Who wants a halo? Who wants other people suspicious of one's piety? Who can live with such religious pretension? Who, indeed, can measure up to any such expectation? We know what human nature is, don't we? And we also know that nobody's perfect, don't we?"

Well, yes, if by *saints* and *sainthood* and *perfect love* we mean something finished, complete, and unsurpassable. If you think of saints as people without flaws who never fall short of the glory of God, clearly there are few of *those*, if any. But the New Testament word for *saint* does not refer to a person without flaws. Indeed, it is fairly candid about the flaws among the people who are called saints. The New Testament saint is a person who is openly and freely dependent on the grace of God for pardon and forgiveness, whose love of God is forever reaching out beyond bounds and whose love of neighbor surpasses all self-interest or even altruism.

One of the distinctive things in the Methodist *tradition* was this insistence of Wesley's on the *sainthood* as well as the *priesthood* of *all* believers. He taught a doctrine of salvation as a process of growth in grace from the earliest dawning of conscience through the successive stages of repentance, forgiveness of sins, reconciliation with God, regeneration (new birth, conversion, "change of heart"), on through the growth-process of loving God more and more until we love him most of all (above all else!), *and* of loving our neighbors more and more until we come to love them just as we ought to love ourselves—that is, not without egotism or self-centeredness but as a reflection of our love of God. We love ourselves properly because we are children of God, wholly dependent upon God's grace and favor, and *therefore* worthy of our own self-respect and intelligent care. And so also we should love God's other children, our neighbors. *This* is holiness, according to the New Testament and John Wesley. When Wesley was asked what the special design of God for Methodists was, his reply was characteristic: "To reform the nation, particularly the *church*, and to spread *scriptural holiness* over these lands."

What is scriptural holiness? Wesley's reply: "love of God" (*inward* holiness, he called it) and "love of neighbor" (*outward* holiness—or, as we might say, social action). And who is our neighbor? Wesley's answer: *every* child of God in every place, in any real need or distress that we can ameliorate or relieve. Our neighbors live next door—they may be easy or hard to help, and they may or may not reciprocate. But our neighbors also are down there in the inner city, in blighted sections of rural slums, in El Salvador, in Beirut, in Moscow. And we are to love *them all* as we love ourselves—and spend as much time and money and concern on *them* as we do on ourselves and our families. Wesley's teaching here is interesting and based on a sliding scale of *needs*. At the top of that scale stand luxuries, followed by conveniences, necessities, and extremities. And the law of love, for Wesley, is that our luxuries and conveniences must give way to our neighbor's necessities (*any* neighbor's) and that even our *necessities* must give way to our neighbor's *extremities.* There is something both ironic and hypocritical about our church leaders flocking to Baltimore, or wherever, to proclaim their solidarity with the poor, while they live well on generous expense accounts.

John Wesley identified himself with the poor by living among them and helping in all sorts of ways, and yet he dispensed loving care to a hundred good causes: clinics, welfare centers, orphans' homes, and the like. He fought against social injustices and their root causes in the social and political life of Britain. He fought against slavery abroad. A large fortune went through his hands during his ministry; but none of it stuck, and next to none of it was spent on overhead. When Methodist saints, in the old tradition, spoke of caring, and of liberation, of justice, and of setting human affairs to rights, they were reflecting their actual commitments to unselfish, hands-on service—the self-denial that comes from love; the self-oblation that goes with love. It is a travesty of Christian social action when any of this love of neighbor turns into self-serving, or when any but the needy are profited thereby.

But outward holiness (sainthood) cannot be sustained by moral concerns alone, and certainly not by good intentions or emotive rhetoric. Outward holiness is the fruit of inward holiness, of our love for God in response to his love for *us,* our faith and trust in him, our sense of radical dependence upon his grace and bounty, our eagerness that his will be done here on earth—as it is done as a matter of course in heaven—and done by *us,* to the utmost of our powers. Inward holiness is the state of at-oneness with God in Christ, at-homeness with God as the indwelling Holy Spirit. It means searching the Scriptures, formal prayer and informal prayer, meditation and spiritual discipline (inward communion with the Spirit of God in the soul), and corporate communion with Christ in his Holy Supper.

But, where does all this end? When can we think we have arrived at some state of perfect love? The answer is that love—of God or neighbor—does not run by calendars or meters or rules. Love, as Paul said, "*never* ends" (I Cor. 13:8). We love because God first loved us and because his love always antedates our love (this is what Wesley meant by *pre-venient* grace: God always is acting, before we can even re-act—indeed, in order that we *can* re-act). *Then* we can go on loving (God and neighbors) as long as we are responsive to God's love, which, from his side, is forever.

And so, as Methodists, we are called to the sainthood of all believers—to the vocation of Scriptural holiness—to the joyous and peaceable life-style of loving God *and* neighbor, of grateful and gracious devotion to our *best* selves (i.e., the image of God in the human soul). We are, you might say with St. Augustine, *condemned* to an eternal disquiet in our souls until we find our proper quiet and peace and rest in God—who has made us for Himself and in whom we truly live and move and have our being. To set our sights lower than this is to betray our fear that the grace of God may not be quite sufficient after all, that the powers of sin and death have the last word in our lives. And *this,* as a bottom line, is *unbelief.*

Our calling, then, is to forget what is behind, and to press on to what God's grace makes possible: the prize of God's high calling to life in Christ Jesus. Wesley's way of phrasing his summons to this higher life ran like this:

> Now, then, do all diligence to walk in every respect according to the light you have received. *Now* be zealous to receive more light daily, more of the knowledge and love of God, more of the Spirit of Christ, more of his life, and of the power of his resurrection. *Now* use all the knowledge and love and life and power you have already attained. . . . So shall you daily increase in holy love, till faith is swallowed up in sight, and the law of love is established to all eternity![17]

Amen.

# 29

## *Who the Holy Spirit Is*

### *An Introductory Comment*

Preached on March 10, 1985, at First United Methodist Church in Denton, Texas, the first of four Hopkins Lectures, this sermon witnesses to the identity of the Holy Spirit and helps to explain why the old hymn "In the Garden" is not one of Albert Outler's favorites. Indeed, he will paraphrase it irreverently: "And he walks with me and he talks with me, and he chuckles me under the chin!"

Views of God like this will prompt a thirty-minute lecture on how people are misled into a false intimacy with the divine.

While Outler admits he does not understand the mystery of the Holy Spirit, he knows who the Spirit is, and he is sure the Spirit does not stagger beside us like a servant or act like a pal in a buddy system.

The Holy Spirit is the "Lord of life! Giver of life! Guide and Consummator of life!"—the agent of God's goodness in creation.

Mushy sentimentalism regarding the Holy Spirit sends Outler up the wall. Gratitude to God for bringing alive the spirit of Jesus Christ through his Holy Spirit—that attitude gives him a sense that the "gospel-light" is dawning.

To speak of *spirituality* is to speak first of all of God's spiritual activity—in creation, history, society, and personality. It is not high-mindedness, or meditation, or navel gazing. There is, of course, something radically *subjective* about spirituality and the spiritual, but something even more radically *objective.* The inner self interfaces between Holy Spirit and human spirits.

The absence of a formal doctrine of pneumatology in the Scriptures in the early church is a paradox. Along with such an absence of a doctrine about the Spirit, it is obvious that Christians in every age since Pentecost have lived by the Spirit and have had their identity as *Christians* sustained by Him.

Since Pentecost, the Holy Spirit's unique ministry has re-presented Jesus to individuals and to the church body. He is *the* Divine Witness—God making himself manifest within, without coming in range of *our* grasp or management.

Now we must turn to a crucial distinction between spirituality and all self-help techniques; between true Christian spirituality and *unitive* mysticism; between participation in God (*metousia Theou*) which keeps us open to the Spirit, and the various projects by which we try to gain some spiritual superiority that can be turned to our own advantage. To live in the Spirit is to be led by the Spirit—as St. Paul reminds us—but he does not lead us to become shamans, with special powers over others. The gifts of discernment—yes; magical or miraculous powers—no.

Let us begin where all Christian reflection properly begins—the Holy Scriptures (*holy* because they are inspired by the Spirit; because it is in them that we encounter the Spirit of God who is also the Spirit of Jesus Christ). There are many biblical *images* of the Holy Spirit: (1) wind—breath (expiration, inspiration, aspiration, respiration); (2) extraordinary powers—God present in *episodes;* (3) a brooding presence, encompassing Mystery; (4) flight—wings (the descending or ascending dove); (5) internal witness to God in Christ within the human heart (Emanu-el); (6) dispenser of extraordinary *gifts;* (7) dispenser of *ordinary fruits;* (8) source of authenticity and valid meaning in Holy Scripture—inspiring witness to the *Word* of *God* in Scripture; (9) agent of the grace of our Lord Jesus Christ in all its aspects and influences; (10) the energy and agent of *communion.*

The concept and the emergent doctrine of the Holy Trinity (in Scripture and tradition) expresses the ultimate paradox: God's absolute and unqualified unity, history, and personal existence. The notion of "Trinity" tries to explain how God can be utterly transcendent, yet also *self-communicating* and *compassionate*—thus also redemptive and purposive, with an explicit purpose to restore in each human being the image of God in which he or she was designed.

The fact that there is no separate essay on the Holy Spirit by the early Fathers is due partly to no controversies or heretical misinterpretations about him.

In Christian *worship* the Spirit reveals himself as: our teacher in prayer, the agent of grace, the giver of gifts, the consecrator of priests and ministers, the consecrator of the sacraments, the Spirit in the church. In Christian life the Spirit makes for aspiration, inspiration, and respiration.

We can round out this exploration of the identity and office of the Holy Spirit with a quick overview of a remarkable fact in the history of the church's creeds and confessions of faith. It is a fact—and one not often enough reflected upon—that there is a strange *silence* about the Holy Spirit in the earliest summaries of Christian teaching and belief. When Christians were made aware of Jesus Christ's re-presented presence in their midst, they did not often speak of the Holy Spirit as the agent of this mystery: the perennial re-presenting of the absent Jesus. It is almost as if they had taken Jesus' comment—that the Holy Spirit would not speak of *himself*—almost too literally and supposed that *they* need not speak of him *explicitly,* either. You will be spared a detailed history of these references, if for *our* purposes today you are willing to trust my generalizations about them.

The earliest text of the forerunner of the Apostles' Creed ends almost abruptly: "And also in the Holy Spirit." Later versions add phrases until we have the Spirit associated with Holy Church, with the forgiveness of sins, with the resurrection of the body and the life everlasting. There are somewhat more fullsome references to the identity of the Spirit in Irenaeus, Tertullian, and Origen, but always as if his presence and energy were *assumed.* By contrast with their controversies about the nature of God as Creator and about Jesus as both human and divine, the reality and identity of the Holy Spirit were taken for granted. Even in the first text of the creed of Nicea (A.D. 325), the focus is on the mystery of Father and Son, Creation and Redemption—and the last line is almost an anticlimax—"And in the Holy Ghost."

Even in the *Te Deum Laudamus* there are fullsome references to Father and Son, but then comes the cryptic line: "And also the Holy Ghost, the Comforter." Indeed, this is one of the ways we can *date* the *Te Deum.*

In the mid-fourth century, however, there were those in the larger Christian community who began to downscale the nature of the Holy Spirit, to suggest that the *Spirit* is a pious personification of the spiritual world in general—which is to say that the Holy Spirit was in danger of disappearing into the prevailing Greek mysticisms of the time, in danger of becoming a "personification" of the invisible and supernatural world round about us.

Christians don't like to cudgel their brains about doctrinal mysteries unless they must—until they are confronted with unacceptable distortions of the tradition. But this denial of the equal deity and dignity of the Holy Spirit, as personal manifestation with Father and Son, stirred a reaction. Thus when the Nicene Creed came up for revision—at Constantinople in 381—the official form of the doctrine was set down in creedal language:

> And we believe [*pisteuomen, credimus*] in the Holy Spirit, the Lord and Giver of Life [*Dominus et Vivificator!*], who proceeds from the Father and who, with the Father and Son [*Filioque* is not in any of the original texts or the present Orthodox texts] is to be worshipped and glorified, who spoke through the prophets [i.e., the Spirit-inspired writers].

Who then is the Holy Spirit, and what is his unique office in the mystery of the Holy Trinity? He is God in continuing personal action, in the church and in the world, calling all men and women, in any age that yet may be, to attend to the mysterious reality, God's climactic self-communication in Jesus Christ, and to what *that* still means to you and me and to all God's children!

Lord of life! Giver of life! Guide and Consummator of life! One God in Three Persons, Blessed Trinity. This is the basic reality of Christian spirituality from the beginning and in every generation since. And so may the communion of the Holy Spirit of God be with you all, always. Amen.

# 30

## *The Promise of the Paraclete*

### *An Introductory Comment*

Those present at First United Methodist Church in Denton, Texas, on the night of March 10, 1985, came to know the promise of the Paraclete as expressed in John 14:16, 26 and Romans 8:26, translated from the original by Albert Outler. The Holy Spirit comes to the aid of our human frailty and limitations. We do not even know how we ought to *pray*, but through our inarticulate groans and stumbling speech, the Spirit himself is pleading for us, and God, who knows the secrets of our innermost hearts, hears our prayers, because the Spirit pleads for God's people in God's own way.

Outler says he finds himself oftentimes speechless before God in prayer. He *knows* about the nature of God through Jesus Christ, through the works of God in history, and through the works of his Holy Spirit. But there are moments during prayer when his mind reaches the point of nonthinking and simply *is*, with the Holy Spirit carrying the prayer load.

He knows he has not even made a beginning in expressing the mystery of prayer. He usually ends his sermons with a prayer, and when he sits down, he seems to fall silent. Could it be then that his prayers are too deep for words?

# *The Sermon*

The texts of John 14:16, 26; 15:26-27; and 16:5-15 contain encouraging words. Seen from any human angle, the prospects of early Christianity were bleak. Those first Christians composed a small religious sect that had sprung up around the brief public ministry of an obscure and unauthorized rabbi from Galilee (of all places), and they were facing an indifferent (and often hostile) world, with a strange message: Jesus Christ—crucified, dead, buried, risen, ascended—Messiah come in the flesh, even now to be confessed as "Lord and Savior, to the glory of God the Father." They were prepared to quote Paul: "God was in [Jesus] Christ, reconciling the world unto himself. Wherefore, be *ye* [the world] reconciled!"

In practical terms, they were in the process of being excommunicated from their Jewish matrix. Their Messiah was Jewish, but their claim that he was Messiah incarnate was incredible and scandalous to *Jewish* orthodoxy. They were equally at cross-purposes with their environing secular culture. We call it Hellenism, but it was actually a hodgepodge of mystic divinity, polytheism, and popular religion, along with religious philosophies like Stoicism and Epicureanism which offered a sort of worldly wisdom that seemed to ameliorate the human condition by at least a little. Paul had this situation in mind when he explained to the Christians in Corinth that Christian preaching—of Christ crucified—was a *skandalon* (a doctrinal apostasy) to the Jews and a *morian* (theoretical nonsense) to the Greeks.

At first—and, in a sense, all along and still—Christians believed their present age had an imminent culmination, just ahead. This expectation of a Second Advent bolstered their hopes for a divine vindication of their preaching and its truth-claims, "any day now." All this was summed up by the seer of Patmos who, in his vision, heard the promise of the glorified Christ: "Lo, I come quickly"—and they responded, in fervent faith, "Even so, Lord Jesus, come quickly." But history kept unrolling and the Apostles kept being gathered up to glory—and the memories of Jesus in the days of his flesh kept fading. New crises of faith kept threatening the church's survival. Most of the other nonstandard-brand Jewish sects had not survived the destruction of Jerusalem (in A.D. 70); in the Hellenistic world, sects and religious movements came and went, with a couple or three generations their normal life-span. We know how this is: Who among us remembers much now about Billy Sunday, or the Keswick Movement, or Moral Rearmament, or George Albert Coe?

In short, and again humanly speaking, Christianity could not have sustained itself for long on the strength of its historical *memories* of Jesus of Nazareth—nor by the wisdom of his sayings, nor by the good ideas enshrined in that wisdom. Socrates had lived and taught wisely, had died courageously, and had left an even larger body of memorable sayings. But his movement had barely survived, and only in a bleached-out and esoteric fashion. It is not accidental that Socrates had no crucial role in Neo-Platonism! His wisdom (sadly altered) was still enshrined in the minds of a select few, but it was no great cultural force in the world of late Hellenism.

By contrast, Christianity not only survived; it actually continued to reach out and spread—from Jerusalem and Judea to Samaria, Antioch, and Rome; from the Euphrates west to the Gates of Hercules; from Egypt to Gaul. We have a letter from the second century that describes the Christian life-style as it was being lived out in cities, towns, and countryside "over the entire inhabited world" (*oikumene*). The fact is that church history never came to either of its expected ends: the Christians' expectation of a dramatic apocalyptic ending, or the secular expectations that so insignificant a movement would run its course and fade away, along with the fading memories of Jesus of Nazareth. We need to understand this survival and learn from it, since it holds the key to Christianity's continuity in and through time and history and cultural change, and its preservation of its identity, its essence in continuity with that of Apostolic Christianity. And it also holds the key to our own problem of the continuity and identity of Christianity today, in an unimaginably different world. It is the key to our own Christian self-understanding as confessors and witnesses to Jesus Christ as *our* Lord and Savior, to the glory of our gracious heavenly Father.

What happened, of course, was a different sort of Second Advent than the average Christian had ever been able to envision. This came at Pentecost—after the tragedy of Good Friday, the miracle of Easter morn, and the confusion that followed. Its consequence was that Jesus became alive again, and powerful, and forever thereafter *present,* wherever two or three are gathered in *his* Name. *Now,* they could give thanks to God for his gracious gift of his love incarnate in Jesus. Now they could more clearly understand the puzzlement of the disciples during Jesus' earthly life. Now their memories could be recharged with meanings that had not been there before. Jesus was no longer a "has been." He was, and would always be, a living, revealing, reconciling, redemptive presence and energy in the hearts and minds of the faithful—Jesus Christ, yesterday, today, and forever. Now, when they gathered at their Holy Meal in remembrance of his death and passion, they could speak of it as a *eucharist,* and could unfeignedly believe that the Risen Christ was *really* and truly present in their midst.

They were even enabled to remember how Jesus had tried to prepare them for this renewal of his presence in history, and they began to gather together their freshly relevant memories of his farewell discourses and to set them down.

This is why our double texts are so important together. In the Fourth Gospel, chapter 15 is meant to remind all subsequent disciples of what discipleship really means—in fellowship and service. But thenceforth the disciples would not be forlorn or left on their own:

> But when the Paraclete is come, whom I will send to you from the Father [which is to say, the Spirit of Truth self-revealed, who proceeds from the Father and will be given to you], he will bear witness to me [he will explain, interpret, re-present *me* (Jesus)]. And this will enable you to become witnesses to me also—and because you have been with me from the beginning, your witness will ring true.

And then, in the next chapter in verse 13, the explanation is rounded out:

> And when this Spirit of Truth will have come among you, he will guide *you* into the fullness of the truth [about me, my Father, his Kingdom of Grace and Righteousness]—for he will not be talking about himself [the Paraclete does not call attention to himself, but to Jesus and his import as the Christ]. It is, therefore, expedient [Jesus tried to explain this to dispel their dismay] for me to go away so that the Paraclete will come in my place—to convict the world of its sin and alienation [to bestir human consciences] and to call the world to true righteousness and full humanity. It will be the Paraclete's office and ministry to guide you into further truth and

> fuller freedom, for your real hope lies in the promise that the truth about me, as you come to know and understand it from the Spirit, will make you truly free!

But what could he have meant with these veiled references to a Paraclete and a witness and a guide to truth?

*Paracletos* has many meanings in Greek, just as the Holy Spirit has many offices and ministry in the world, in the church, in persons. *Kleteo* is a Greek verb that looks two ways: It is both a legal term and also an interpersonal one. In a courtroom, it means to serve as a witness, to give faithful evidence to the *truth.* On the interpersonal level *para* (i.e., with) *kleteo,* means to stand by a friend, to give aid and comfort (which is to say, *strength*—since *con-fortare* means to strengthen someone by standing with that person in a crisis or difficulty). The Paraclete is our divine witness to the truth as it is in Christ Jesus. He is our divine aid and advocate in our spiritual up-reachings for grace and peace and joy.

This is the way it was at Pentecost: The Christians received compelling evidence of *the truth*—not only of what Jesus had said and done, but of who and what he was—and also the power to pass this evidence on, to be witnesses to it. So it has been in the life of the Christian church. The Holy Spirit is not God in the absence of Jesus; he is God making Jesus *present,* again and again, as historical memory recedes and as history continues to unfold in its endlessly ambivalent way.

And so it is with us. Jesus is a memory for many people—dim, distorted, and largely ineffectual (look at the perennial interest in the *Holy* Land—e.g., the Church of the Holy Sepulcher!). And for the believing Christian *in any age,* led by the Paraclete, Jesus is always much more than a memory. He is a living presence, a companion on life's way. He is to us what he has been to every generation before us: God's unique and plenary self-communication. For Jesus was careful to direct the attention of his disciples to the fullness of God. Thus the Spirit of Jesus, the Spirit of Christ, the Holy Spirit (and not just our historical memories) points us to Jesus as God's indwelling, redemptive presence in our lives, in the church, in the world. By the Spirit, through the Son to the Father!

This is the point to St. Paul's insight (in Romans 8) that it is the *Spirit* who comes into our hearts to clarify our "knowledge" of God and of our relationship to him, in and through Christ. "The Spirit," says he, "bears witness to our spirits that we are beloved *children* of God." His caring love has been manifested in Christ—so that instead of standing before him *only* (high and lifted up, with the typical reaction: "I am undone!"), we can also realize that he is one with our Father, whom we can address with the assurance of trustful children.

> For all who are moved by the Spirit of God are children of God. The Spirit you have received is not a spirit of bondage leading you back into a life of fear, but a Spirit who makes us aware of God's relation to us, so that we can address him as "Abba, Father" and behave accordingly. In such an awareness, the Spirit of God joins with *our* spirits in testifying that we are God's children. And if children, then heirs! Thus we [in and by the Holy Spirit] are God's heirs and co-heirs with Christ—if, that is, we share his sufferings now and do not just rest content to share his glory hereafter.
>
> —Romans 8:14-17

This is not to minimize the crucial role of Jesus Christ as the self-presentation of God in an actual, historical, personal existence. Without the Jesus of history, the Christ of faith would be an abstraction, an ideal, a timeless truth. And this is the heresy of docetism, of Gnosticism—of salvation by human wisdom and human values.

Nor must we ever forget that the Lord God Almighty *is* high and lifted up and that his majesty *does* fill earth and sky and all things, visible and invisible. Awe and reverence *go with* a sense of trust and assurance in his presence. Getting chummy with the Deity is false religion, since it is only a step away from trying to manipulate God, and that is idolatry! True spirituality is the wonder of feeling at home in God's felt presence, in awe and reverence (what the Bible calls "godly fear"), *not* on the score of *our* merits and good works but because of his grace and blessing.

This is the essence of prayer and meditation and devotion. It is also the prime motivation of Christian social action as well. Let St. Paul give us a closing word about the Holy Spirit as our Comforter, Guide, and spiritual Director—the intimate God who is still not the manipulable God, just because he is "within."

Thus, we read in Romans 8:26:

> In the same way, the Holy Spirit comes to the aid of our human frailty and limitations. We do not even know how we ought to *pray*, but through our inarticulate groans and stumbling speech, the Spirit himself is pleading for us, and God, who knows the secrets of our innermost hearts, hears our prayers, because the Spirit pleads for God's people in God's own way. In this way he cooperates for good with those who love God and are called according to his purpose.

Wherefore, unto God the Father, who created us, unto God the Son, who has redeemed us, and unto God the Holy Spirit, who upbuilds us in our full humanity in his own image, be, as is most due, all glory and honor, all faith and trust—now and forever. Amen!

# 31

## *Gifts and Fruits in the Spiritual Life*

### *An Introductory Comment*

In this Hopkins Lecture, preached in First United Methodist Church at Denton on March 11, 1983, Albert Outler spoke about the gifts of the Spirit and the harvest of those gifts in Christian living. Listing the gifts, he gives his own unique interpretation of their Greek meanings, then does the same for the harvest of the Spirit. He hones those meanings down to a fine understanding of the workings of the Holy Spirit.

Outler would like to continue his work and participate as much as ever. The spirit is willing, but the flesh is weak, and he frequently comes home exhausted. After returning from one lecture circuit he told this Hal Luccock story: "After a long preaching circuit at some colleges and universities, Hal came home one afternoon and wanted to rest. Mary said, 'There is a good lecture down at Woolsey Hall.' Hal answered, 'Mary, I am just worn out. I'm too tired. May be a good lecture. I just don't want to go.' Mary told him, 'Hal Luccock, your tongue is going to wear out before your ears do.' "

Very early on, St. Paul set out the essential logic of Christian spirituality: "*If* the Spirit is the *source* of our life [of our distinctive *human* life, as special creatures in God's creation], then we should allow the Spirit also to *direct* the course of our lives" (Gal. 5:25). There is a play on words here: *zomen* (life welling up from a source so deep down as to be beyond self-consciousness) as opposed to *stoikomen* (life in its daily rounds and routines—self-conscious, more or less, all the time). Christian spirituality is taprooted in the very source of our identities as unique and individual persons. It manifests itself in those self-conscious rounds, routines, and rituals. "To *be* in the Spirit" is "to *walk* in the Spirit"—and to have it *show!* This suggests a double-sided pattern in the Holy Spirit's guidance, both in our peak experiences and in our daily rounds. Such patterns are delineated by St. Paul in his early writings (I Cor. 12 and Gal. 5). In First Corinthians 12, the Apostle speaks of the *gifts* of the Spirit; and then, in Galatians 5, of the *harvest* of those gifts in Christian living. And the gifts of the Spirit are to be tested by their moral fruits.

The fact that Galatians was written before the Corinthian letters, as we have them, does not signify that Paul himself thought of *fruits* and *gifts,* in *that* order. And the men who put the canon together seem to have understood this. The logical sequence is: first the *gifts,* and then the *fruits,* which are their "harvest." This is the canonical order and we shall stick to it in our study. We have a lot of Scripture to deal with, and I hope you will not be dismayed. The fact is, these two chapters are the classical source of valid Christian spirituality in all the ages, and in all the later classics of Christian devotion. If First Corinthians 12 and Galatians 5 are already familiar territory, listen again. If not, then open your minds to what the church has received as nourishing spiritual food.

Paul begins by reminding his Corinthian readers and hearers that when they were Gentiles, they already had a sort of spirituality—an inclination to seek the favor and power of certain spiritual influences and to be led by them (the first-century equivalent of contemporary spiritualism!). But, says he, those impulses were not all that truly spiritual. They were attached to "voiceless idols"—which is to say, to projections of their own human spirits, directed and controlled more from within the human self than from the Holy Spirit, within and beyond the self.

He proposes, instead, that an acid test of truly spiritual gifts can always be applied: how they relate a person to Jesus. It is not primarily whether a "spiritual experience" makes us feel good or emotionally uplifted. But if someone is disposed to say or think, "Jesus doesn't really matter," this is a sure sign that person is not under the guidance of the *Holy Spirit.* Nobody can be a Christian who says, "*Anathema Jesus.*" By the same token, no one can profess that *Jesus is Lord,* and really mean it, without power and direction from the *Holy Spirit.* All spiritual gifts in the Christian life are Christ-referenced, Christ-centered, and Spirit-bestowed.

Now, obviously, there are many different kinds of gifts; and it is important not to rank them in any order of priority. None is better or worse; they are all different. And yet, as St. Paul says repeatedly, they all come from the same Spirit. Note, in passing, the correlations between spiritual gifts and ministries of service *(diakonia).* Spiritual gifts are not given merely (or even mostly) to be enjoyed. They are designed to provide talents and tools for *service.* For all the differences in their ways of working, it is the same God who is working in them all; and each is aimed at enriching the gifted person with spiritual rewards and anointing the koinonia with spiritual blessings. And what is St. Paul's listing of them?

Gift No. 1: *Logos sophia*—a wise understanding. This includes not just *information,* but wisdom; not just the smarts, but the power to see things steadily and whole. The world has many people who are rich and powerful and clever; they seem to have everything they need, *except* a sufficient sense of how to put their money or power or cleverness to responsible good use. All of us know bright and articulate people who lack the breadth and height of great ideas, people who know "what's what" in their field but not the "so-whats." The world is drowning in a flood of information; it is perishing for wisdom. The real problem about artificial intelligence is not so much whether it represents real *intelligence* as that it is *artificial* and neither human nor humane in and of itself. The real challenge of the computer age is not whether it will enlarge our horizons. Of course it will; it has already. But how much wiser will it make us? The jury is still out on that one, but the evidence seems skimpy.

Gift No. 2: *Logos gnoseos*—the word of inner self-understanding.

Here is the difference between *sophia* and *gnosis: Sophia* is the large view; *gnosis* is the inward look. Neither is better or worse. But they *are* different. The wise need to learn from the mystics.

Gift No. 3: *Pistis*—the willingness to trust. The experience of swimming may be the best analogy of this gift. A good swimmer *trusts* the water.

Gift No. 4: *Charismata hiamaton*—gifts of healing. These have always included an understanding of the healing processes and powers and, most of all, the real meaning of health and wholeness. It is God who heals, typically through "natural processes." It is the role of "spiritual healers" to be "channels" and "partners" and, above all, to do no harm.

Gift No. 5: *Energemata dynameon*—control over natural and paranormal forces (i.e, the "power of miracles"). One may doubt the human power deliberately to *cause* "miracles"—as in *Green Pastures,* when God "rared back and *passed* a miracle" any time he chose. But there are people in whose presence the unexpected and the inexplicable often happens, to the glory of God and the edification of his people.

Gift No. 6: *Propheteia*—the power of articulating divine truth (forthtelling, rather than foretelling).

Gift No. 7: *Diakriseis pneumaton*—"discernment of spirits," the ability to distinguish between false and true spirits, between true inspiration and "enthusiasm" (and here Wesley had the right idea: "enthusiasm" is overeagerness for results without the equally eager acceptance of the necessary means).

Gift No. 8: *Gene glosso*—various kinds of "tongues" (i.e., ecstatic utterances in praise of God). Consider Paul's emphasis on having ecstatic utterances "interpreted" to the congregation. Such utterances, or tongues, are properly addressed *to God,* and are not disguised addresses to other persons.

Gift No. 9: *Hermeneia glosson*—the power to interpret those same ecstatic utterances in discursive language. This is a gift for which no rules are given; a gift that, in orthodox circles, always appealed to "standing revelation." When either glossolalia or hermeneutics proposes something essentially *new*—not a further and deeper understanding of the truth already "known" in Jesus—you can count on it being false.

With the enumeration of these nine gifts, the point is stressed again and again: These are so many different gifts from the same Spirit. Verse 11 repeats the theme: "But all these gifts are the work of one and the same Spirit, who bestows them respectively on those he wills, expecting each gifted Christian to put them to their best use."

But what *is* their best use? Clearly not to show them off in spiritual pride, or to use them as stepping stones to self-aggrandizement in the community of faith. That way lies self-righteousness and spiritual arrogance. The gifts of the Spirit are all given for their use in the building up of the body of Christ, promoting its unity ("one single body with many limbs and organs, members one of another"). Spirituality is not a private affair, or an advantage that the introverts among us may enjoy. Notice how none of the gifts of the Spirit looks *inward* or involves self-contemplation. They all look outward; they all invite unself-conscious concentration on something more than one's own affective states. They are spiritual gifts from the Holy Spirit to the human spirit, which means they are turned intensely inward (but are distorted when turned into an outward show). Their positive and constructive aim is to reorient the self away from itself, to some loving end or other; to be concerned with the well-being of others and the Christian community.

This is why St. Paul could end this special chapter on spirituality with a decisive upward move—from any and all these marvelous gifts of the Spirit, which all believers have and should put to their *best* uses—to a still better way to participate in the life of the Spirit: the way of love. Thus, it turns out that this whole essay on spirituality is nothing more than a lead-in to First Corinthians 13!

Now, I would like you to hold First Corinthians 13 as background in your mind as we now turn to Galatians for the logical, moral, spiritual climax to the way the Spirit's gifts lead to the Spirit's *karpon* (harvest). For here we see spirituality as a manifestation of the Holy Spirit, energizing Christian men and women to their human best (which is to say, to their manifestations of the "virtues" of the Spirit—incarnate in Jesus). Incidentally, if you find any of this at all interesting, I hope you will test it for yourself by reading and pondering these chapters (I Cor. 12–13 and Gal. 4–5), verse by verse. You'll find that a fruitful experiment!

In Galatians 4, Paul poses the same idea that will reappear in Romans 8 (or, by canonical logic, already has appeared in

Romans 8). "To demonstrate how truly you are God's children [says Paul], God has sent *his* Spirit—the Spirit of *his* Son—into our hearts to enable us to address the Sovereign God as 'Abba! Father!' . . . You, therefore, are no longer mere subjects, but children—and by God's utterly free action, you are heirs of Christ eternal." This is salvation by grace through faith.

He then plunges into the controversy over the extent to which Christians are bound to the ritual laws of religion (in this case, Judaism—but the principle holds for them all, including Christianity). And he triumphantly concludes with a claim for Christian *freedom.*

"You, my friends, were called to be free men and women." But there is a grave danger here: that humans will *abuse* their freedom in Christ, instead of using it aright. St. Paul's basic metaphor here, and elsewhere, is what he calls flesh—what was later called human nature, or what the Lutherans still speak of as concupiscence. The paradox of freedom is that if we indulge our unredeemed appetites without restraint, the results are always *self*-defeating. Instead of leading to enjoyment and satiety, they distract us from our true self-realization.

St. Paul sets this life after the flesh against life in the Spirit in stark contrast. It may even be too stark, since by God's own design, the human body and mind are interdependent and cannot exist apart. "Flesh," then, must be understood as a metaphor for unbridled appetite, self-indulgence, sensual pleasures. For, in St. Paul's mind, apparently, sensuality can be classified into four clusters: (1) sexual promiscuity (of *all* sorts); (2) idolatry and sorcery, including their sophisticated forms of false religions; (3) the typical rough and tumble of self-serving politics: "of quarrels, contentions, envy, unbridled anger, selfish ambitions, dissensions, party intrigues and jealousies" (as in Texas politics and business, or in a typical "United" Methodist Annual Conference!); (4) intemperance in food and drink—usually mislabeled as "good times." These various life-styles have one thing in common: They stifle the influence of the Spirit—and hinder the coming of the kingdom.

True spirituality—life in the Spirit—looks outward and upward and brings with it a distinctive "harvest" of spiritual virtues that amount to a typically Christian life-style. Notice how Paul correlates spirituality and gracious living and also how both these reach beyond the realm of any enforceable *law.* You can't legislate for or against love or joy, peace, patience; you can't enforce them or interdict them. But, if you do truly "live in the Spirit," such virtues grow up and ripen as fruits of a life that has used its spiritual gifts wisely and well.

Here then is the *karpon* (harvest) of the Spirit—and it is described as a series of Christian dispositions (in 5:22-23). We can take it as a capsule summary of the moral character of a mature Christian, shaped and brought to true self-realization by the grace of the Holy Spirit, within and among us:

No. 1: Love—and here we are back again in the atmosphere of First Corinthians 13: Love is a better "way" than any other (including loveless spirituality!).

No. 2: Joy—this is the *feel* of grace in the heart, the unsummoned upwelling of happiness. Christian joy is very different from success or satisfaction. It is more nearly delight in God's goodness and grace and in the good and gracious things that happen to us in the course of the Providence of God.

No. 3: Peace—not just the absence of conflict but the upholding sense of *serenity,* even in stressful times and circumstances. Peace is more than a surcease from anxiety and strife. It is that special poise and inner calm that comes from unfaltering trust in God's care and safekeeping.

No. 4: Patience—and we do not always think of patience and spirituality as correlates. In the Greek, the term is *macrothumia,* which the King James translators turned into *long-suffering,* but which, more literally, means *large-heartedness.* It is the tendency to see the good in others and emphasize that, rather than fixing on their flaws.

No. 5: Kindness—from a Greek noun that connotes a comfortable, comforting temperament, a trait that resembles whatever we mean by "user friendly." A kind person, in this sense, is one who is easy and comfortable to be around. And in Romans 2:4, we are reminded that it is the *kindliness* of God (rather than his awesomeness) that leads us to repentance and faith.

No. 6: Goodness—which is like and unlike kindness. Goodness points to a settled character of wishing well (benevolence) and doing well (beneficience).

No. 7: Fidelity or faithfulness—the moral habit of standing by one's word, one's commitments and promises. Spirituality is not the business of following the winds of spontaneous feeling, but of holding fast to what is good.

No. 8: *Prautes*—This word is something of a puzzle. It does not mean *meekness* (as in the Authorized Version) or *gentleness* (as in the New English Bible) or *tolerance* (as in Phillips), but rather the desire to get a thing *done,* but with the least degree of *self*-assertion possible in order to be effective. It is something like a phrase such as "keeping a low profile while doing all one can." It is the Spirit's way to lead rather than to drive, to comm*e*nd rather than to comm*a*nd. The power of the Spirit is, by God's design, less awesome than winsome.

No. 9: *Engkrateia*—This word does not mean *temperance* (as in the Authorized Version) or *self-restraint* (as in Weymouth) or even *self-control* (as in the Revised Standard Version and the New English Bible). It really is that spiritual state of affairs in which a person is so fully "caught up in the Spirit" in some project for which the self is capable of using all its powers and concentration *without* self-consciousness. A mother tending a child, a scientist intent upon an experiment, an ambulance driver concentrating on her mission (and what it takes), a scholar at his books, or a saint at prayer—these are instances of the sort of engrossment we see when dedicated people are doing well in the spirit of self-forgetfulness. This is *true* spirituality: to be led out of yourself into some worthwhile enterprise—losing yourself, and then discovering you have found more than was suspected.

Notice that there is not a whiff anywhere in any of these four chapters about *ecstasy.* St. Paul was not opposed to ecstasy—he was an occasional ecstatic himself and not ashamed of it. He was always wary, however, lest ecstasy should be preferred above the ethical virtues. To live in the Spirit is not to be three feet off the ground or "out of this world." It is rather to be a living witness (visible also to others) to the Spirit of Jesus in and through a life of love and service.

Here, then, is a Christian plumb-line for appraising one's spirituality. Are you aware of *your* spiritual gifts? Have you received them *as gifts,* with gratitude? Are you cultivating *your* gifts, without wishing for something other and different? And are you aware of the challenge to grow in grace and in the enjoyment of these fruits of the Spirit? In your spiritual disciplines, are you aware of how these fruits are turning you more and more away from self-concern and toward a more and more intense God-consciousness on the one hand and, on the other hand, toward more and more engrossment with others and *their* needs?

This, or something like it, is what it means to live and walk in the Spirit, to live by the Spirit—and in the process, to become more truly and fully human, one's own actual best self. After all, this is what God designed for us to be; it is for this that he reserves his "Well done, good and faithful servant. Enter into the joy of thy Lord!"

# 32

# *Christian Spirituality in a Wesleyan Perspective*

## *An Introductory Comment*

In this last of the Hopkins Lectures, given at First United Methodist Church in Denton, Texas, on March 12, 1985, Albert Outler traces the spiritual formation of John Wesley.

When asked what he would like to accomplish during his lifetime, Outler said: "If at all possible before I die, I hope to convince a fair number of able people about this conviction of mine—about Wesley being an interesting theologian as over against being an eponymous hero.

"What is interesting in him is not merely the fact of his popular impact. There were people in his time who were as popular as he, and there were people who were better preachers than he. And I don't think it was the organization that made the thing tick as much as it was the message.

"That message is quite unique. It is rational and coherent, but not a systematic way of understanding and expressing the Christian faith and the vision of the Christian life. If that is so, then he deserves better than he has had from Methodists on the one hand and non-Methodists on the other. If that's not so, then I have wasted thirty years.

"Can I convince enough competent witnesses, a large enough jury, to see Wesley as a competent theologian?"

Indeed, many who read these sermons will be convinced!

## *The Sermon*

*These all died in faith, not having received the promises but having seen them afar off, and were persuaded of them and embraced them, and confessed that they were strangers and pilgrims on the earth (Heb. 11:13).*

The church has lived, through the centuries and through crisis after crisis, in and by the power of the Holy Spirit, through the devotion of now faceless and nameless Christians who continued as faithful witnesses to Jesus Christ as Lord, at whatever cost. The real church history cannot be written, for it is a story of the prayer-life of Christians, and that cannot be cast in narrative. But the prayer-life of Christians does have its harvest in ethical fruits, by which its gifts and quality can be measured and evaluated.

John Wesley understood this very well, and he tried to teach his people to pray and to live in the Spirit, to appreciate their spiritual gifts and to share their spiritual harvest. Part of the point to the nickname Methodist was its reference to people who were methodical and disciplined in their prayer-life, in their Scripture reading and study, and in their use of *all* the means of grace. Methodists have more to learn from Wesley on this score than on almost any other, save doctrine—and so I invite you to review with me Wesley's understanding of Christian spirituality.

Wesley has no claim to be ranked with the great theologians (like St. Augustine and St. Thomas or even Luther and Calvin). But he does not deserve the theological limbo into which he has been cast by the generality of other theologians, and even by his own Methodist people. None of his ideas was original, but what is truly new is his special synthesis of the great Christian ideas, gathered from many traditions into a coherent view of Christian existence that could be expressed in plain terms for plain people. He was, by choice, a folk-theologian: a people's theologian, not a theologian's theologian. He was a learned man who divested his sermons of most of the technicalities of theological discourse and fashioned an eclectic theology that sought to rise above the snarls and tangles of doctrinal controversy.

His career spanned the whole century that followed the tumults of a civil war brought on partly by religious polarizations and followed by an epoch of decadence in the so-called Stuart

Restoration. At issue all through the eighteenth century was the tension between a concept of God's sovereign grace (as viewed in the so-called Five Points of Calvinsim, more easily recalled in the acronym TULIP: Total depravity, Unconditional election, Limited atonement, Irresistible grace, the final Perseverance of all true believers), and another perspective of that same sovereign grace viewed as the divine *ac*tion in which human *re*action makes a decisive difference.

The seventeenth century had been so violent and demoralized that most nominal Christians in the century following were quite willing to purchase peace in the church at almost any price. The result, in the eighteenth century, was a climate in which deism could flourish, in which rationalism was fashionable, in which "latitudinarianism" was more acceptable than orthodoxy because it was less divisive. Spirituality was still cultivated by private persons and small groups. But the state church was careful not to press its coercive powers, to rely instead upon the means of grace as channeled through the church and its ministers in the form of a sort of soteriological monopoly.

Wesley was a child of his time. He grew up with the gospel of moral rectitude (as it had been preached and practiced in his family and in those of most of his contemporaries). But a succession of four "conversions" (not just the one at Aldersgate that we all know about) brought him to a new version of spirituality, at the core of which was a distinctive doctrine of grace, taprooted in his understanding of the special offices and ministries of the Holy Spirit.

In 1725 (under the influence of Thomas à Kempis and Jeremy Taylor), he was converted from the conventional lightheartedness of his college days to a new sort of seriousness toward God: to a conscious dedication of himself to a devout and Spirit-filled life. Two years later (1727) he had yet another conversion—this time a spontaneous illumination of God's surpassing glory.

> The light flowed in so mightily upon my soul, that every thing appeared in a new view. I cried to God for help, and resolved not to prolong the time of obeying Him as I had never done before. And by my continued endeavour to keep His whole law, inward and

> outward, to the utmost of my power, I was persuaded that I should be accepted of Him [in the Final Judgment], and that I was even then in a state of salvation.[18]

These two conversions are too often underestimated because so little tangible fruit seemed to follow from them. Thus they have been overshadowed by conversion No. 3—his so-called Aldersgate experience. This came on May 24, 1738, when he felt his heart "strangely warmed" by the inner witness of the Holy Spirit, and "an *assurance* was given him that God had taken away *his* sins, even *his*, and had saved *him* from the law of sin and death." This was no new doctrine, but a new existential sense of grace and a new spirituality, based now more on assurance and trust than on hope and piety.

But the full force of his powers as a witness to Christ was not yet released. He set off to visit the Moravians in their homeland, and found their spirituality impressive, but their sentimentality offensive. In turn, he was received by them as an immature Christian, not yet fit for their full fellowship. Accordingly, they fenced him from their Communion table.

In the following October he was much affected by the account he read of the Great Awakening in New England (by Jonathan Edwards) and found himself driven back—not to Luther and Calvin but to the *Anglican Homilies*, which he promptly abridged into a theological charter that served him well for the next five full decades. But his seriousness and illumination and heartwarming never turned into a fully fruitful ministry until the following spring (of 1739) when, very reluctantly, he took his gospel of justification by grace through faith into the fields and out to the marginalized people of Bristol and Kingswood. Their response transformed Wesley's faith and self-confidence. Thereafter, his spirituality took on a vital power it had not had before.

Here then was an example of perceptible grace, the action of the Holy Spirit in his heart and will, changing him from a stuffy and obnoxious pietist into a grace-full and therefore effectual minister of Christ and servant of God's people. And at the heart of it all was his discovery of the correlation between the presence and activity of the Holy Spirit and the rule of grace. The focus of all this was the theme that would preoccupy his preaching and teaching for five decades: the interaction of the Holy Spirit and the human spirit.

For Wesley, grace is God's benevolence and mercy in all its ramifications, directed chiefly toward his human family, which stands without any other remedy, in utter and total dependence upon that benevolence and mercy. God's grace is manifest in creation, in Torah, in the vision of the prophets—and in all other revelations of God. It is the vision of God's unmerited mercy that none of his human children has been left "without a witness" (to his omnipresent Spirit, in whom we live and move and have our being). But grace was finally and fully revealed in Jesus Christ, whose life and death and triumph are the *meritorious* cause of our justification (instead of the *formal* cause, as the Calvinists insisted). The Holy Spirit is seen as God's active and intimate self-communicator. The Spirit bears witness, with our spirits, of God's reconciling pardon of our sins and of Christ's merits imparted as a transforming power, neither inherent nor infused. Here is a notion of an *absolute* divine initiative in each and every good human action, from the first awakenings of the spiritual life to its highest reaches, but never without an authentic human *re*action, participating positively or negatively. The Lutherans and Calvinists had taught that the human condition, apart from grace (what they called natural man) was truly hopeless. Wesley agreed with their conclusion, but disputed the premise:

> [There] is no excuse for those who continue in sin, and lay the blame upon their Maker by saying: "It is God only that must quicken us; for we cannot quicken our own souls." For allowing that all the souls of men are dead by *nature*, this excuses none, seeing there is no man that is in a state of mere nature; there is no man, unless he has quenched the Spirit, that is wholly void of the grace of God. No man living is entirely destitute of what is vulgarly called "natural conscience." But this is not natural. It is more properly termed "preventing grace." Every man has a greater or less measure of this, which waiteth not for the call of man. . . . So that no man sins because he has not grace, but because he does not use the grace which he hath.[19]

The key image in John Wesley's anthropology is the *imago Dei.* In sin, this image has been not destroyed, but disfigured. The effects of sin are less that they alienate *God from us,* but rather that they alienate *us from him* (and so also from our true selves). God *was* in Christ reconciling the world to himself; not reconciling himself to the world. Wrote the younger Wesley:

> The whole world is indeed, in its present state, only one great infirmary. All that are therein are sick of sin, and their one great business is to be healed. And for this very end the great Physician of souls is continually present with them, marking all the diseases of every soul, and "giving medicines to heal its sickness."[20]

This theme of *therapeia psyches* continues and develops throughout his theological lifetime. "But," young Wesley had added, "as perfect holiness is not found on earth, so neither is perfect happiness: some remains of our disease will ever be felt, and some physic be necessary to heal it."[21] Later he would come to believe that healing grace has no such limits. Instead, he taught that Christians may, and should be, perfected in love *in this life.*

The order of salvation, for Wesley, encompasses the entire span of the life of faith and yet it proceeds by stages to its final end of glorification in the life of the world to come.

> Salvation begins with what is usually termed (and very properly) "preventing grace," including the first wish to please God, the first dawn of light concerning his will, and the first slight transient conviction of having sinned against him. All these imply some tendency toward life, some degree of salvation, the beginning of a deliverance from a blind, unfeeling heart, quite insensible of God and the things of God.[22]

It should be added that this is not the only sense in which Wesley uses *preventing,* or the phrase *prevenient grace.* All grace is prevenient in the sense that God's initiatives are always, and at every level, antecedent. Wesley coined a metaphor about the human soul as having a "spiritual *sensorium,*" designed by its Creator to be able to *re*act to the Spirit's stimuli, but latent and passive except as such stimuli are initiated from beyond. But the Spirit's prevenient actions can be inhibited or resisted by the human spirit. The grace and power of the Creator (e.g., natural laws and physical processes) may not be resisted. The graces of the Holy Spirit may be. Such a view is not as subjectivist as it may seem—or as it has been interpreted by some in this narcissistic culture of ours. Authentic spiritual experience is not self-originated; it is an inner experience of an actual reality over against ourselves even if also within ourselves. The Spirit may possess us—but always and only to *his* ends and purposes, which are spiritual and moral, through and through. Wesley tries to explain this in his further delineations of the order of salvation:

> Salvation is carried on by "convincing grace," usually in Scripture termed "repentance," which brings a larger measure of self-knowledge [of our need of grace], and a farther deliverance from the heart of stone. Afterwards, we experience the proper Christian salvation, whereby "through grace" we are "saved by faith," consisting of those two grand branches, justification and sanctification. By justification we are saved from the guilt of sin, and restored to the favour of God; by sanctification we are saved from the power and root of sin, and restored to the image of God. All experience, as well as Scripture, shows this salvation [this restoration of the image, which is the human power to respond to God's initiatives] to be both instantaneous and gradual. It begins the moment we are justified, in the holy, humble, gentle, patient love of God and man. [For Wesley, early and late, the essence of sanctification is the gift, power and fruit of love—love to God above all else, and love to neighbor—that is, *every* child of God in all the world to whom we can be loving.] It gradually increases from that moment as a "grain of mustard seed . . . but" gradually "puts forth large branches," and becomes a great tree; till in another instant the heart is cleansed from all sin, and filled with pure love to God and man. [Note that Wesley consistently defines sin as the violation of known laws of God—which is to say, *voluntary* and deliberate.] But even that love increases more and more, till we "grow up in all things into him that is our head"; "till we attain the measure of the stature of the fullness of Christ."[23]

Here, we have grace characterized by a gamut of qualifiers: preventing grace, convincing grace, justifying grace, sanctifying grace. There are others: accompanying grace, the grace of assurance, the grace of wisdom, the grace of perseverance, uncreated grace, created grace. But always the constant meaning is that grace is sheer mercy, unmerited gift and blessing. And the appropriate response to such grace, in any of its measures and modes, is gratitude and graciousness.

In one place, Wesley coins a metaphor about the *ordo salutis,* which I have not seen elsewhere: He speaks of a porch of true religion as *repentance*—repentance for John Wesley is not merely "being sorry," or self-reproachful attrition in the forensic sense. It is chiefly self-awareness: of one's distortions and disfigurements of the *imago Dei* (and therefore of one's *true* humanity). Its function is to bring us to an honest acknowledgment of our need of healing by *grace* (rather than by justice or bare acquittal). Its function is to "hide pride from man" (as he puts it, quoting Job 33:17) and so prepare the heart and mind for a saving trust in God's pure, unbounded love, revealed in Jesus Christ.

Justification is God's act of imputing the unmerited righteousness of Christ to a believing sinner and of imparting the righteousness of "a new creature in Christ." It is pardon, forgiveness, assurance, and heart-cleansing. It is what God does *for* us, in restoring us to a proper relationship with God. And it is by faith alone. It is sheer mercy, grace upon grace, an ineffable gift—to be received, accepted, turned to its proper ends of hope and love.

Sanctification is the living-space of true religion in which Christian life goes on growing toward maturation. Like all else, sanctification is the work of the Holy Spirit: an eventful process in which grace and "the means of grace" achieve their aim and goal. It is, therefore, what God the Spirit does in us and with us and through us, insofar as we are responsive and faithful to the Spirit's prompting presence in our lives.

Classical Protestants had always had a problem with the linkage between faith and good works. They were rightly terrified of "works-righteousness." Wesley's concern tilted the other way. His pet phobia was antinomianism (i.e., faith without good works as its fruitage). The grace of assurance and the grace of participation are identified in one of his favorite biblical tags: "faith working by love" or "faith energized by love" *(fides caritate formata).*

Thus, spiritual formation and the processes of "growth in grace" are two different perspectives on the same dynamic reality: the enhancement of the believer's participation in the divine love that is the essence of God's gracious providence. "All who desire the grace of God are to wait for it in the means which he hath ordained."

The first of these ways is *prayer:* prayers of adoration, of thanksgiving, repentance, petition, and intercession—"prayer of every kind, public and private and the blessings annexed thereto." A second appointed means of *waiting* for grace is *"in searching the Scriptures."* Wesley disregards the grammatical question posed by John 5:39. He takes it as a command: *Search* the Scriptures; and live in them and think with them more as a whole than about this text or that. As an aside, he comments that Christians are not to neglect the Old Testament.

> Thirdly, all who desire an increase of the grace of God are to wait for it in partaking of the Lord's Supper. . . . [This is not] a bare permission only, but a clear explicit command. . . . Is not the eating of that bread, and the drinking of that cup, the outward, visible means whereby God conveys into our souls all that spiritual grace, that righteousness, and peace, and joy in the Holy Ghost, which were purchased by the body of Christ once broken and the blood of Christ once shed for us? Let all, therefore, who truly desire the grace of God, eat of that bread and drink of that cup.[24]

Wesley denounces the doctrine of spontaneity in desiring sacramental Communion; it is an efficacious means of grace, of which all Christians are commanded to avail themselves without being overly concerned about one's own moral "fitness" or that of the administrant. What one really should be concerned about is Christ's living, gracious, *real presence.* Wesley's doctrine of sacramental presence was realistic but emphatically unanalytic: Christ is really and truly present in the Eucharist, but this is a mystery with no fully rational explanation or theory.

There are other means of grace and "spiritual formation": Christian conversation, the aid of good spiritual directors, the reading of "serious books," and methodical meditation. And since all the means of grace are aimed at holiness, one must never forget that there is no holiness except social holiness—that one cannot grow in grace without disciplined self-oblations of love and service to others, and most especially to Christ's poor and disadvantaged. The way of holiness is the way of self-denial and cross-bearing—to the end always that the kingdom of God may come on earth and that his righteousness will be done in earth, as of course is the case in heaven.

In "The New Birth," Wesley speaks of spiritual maturity as the fullness of life:

> And now [in the life of prayer and pure intentions, the true believer] may properly be said *to live:* God having quickened him by his Spirit, he is alive to God through Jesus Christ. . . . God is continually breathing, as it were, upon his soul [as in Gen. 2:7], and his soul is breathing unto God. Grace is descending into his heart, and prayer and praise are ascending to heaven. And by this intercourse between God and man, this fellowship with the Father and the Son, as by a kind of *spiritual respiration, the life of God in the soul is sustained.* [See also "The Great Privilege"]: The Spirit or breath of God is immediately inspired, breathed into the new-born soul; and the same breath which comes from, returns to God. As it is continually received by faith, so it is continually rendered back by love, by prayer, and praise, and thanksgiving—love and praise and prayer being the breath of every soul which is truly born of God. And by this new kind of *spiritual respiration,* spiritual life is not only sustained but increased day by day.[25]

Here, then, is a concept of God's gracious love and mercy which sees it as a truly personal self-communication offered to all by a gracious God "whose mercy is over all his works." Grace is as much a climate as an activity. It is love energizing human freedom without licensing it to self-indulgence. And this, according to Wesley, is what it means to live in the Spirit, to walk by the Spirit, in life's high moments and also in its daily rounds.

As the peroration of his thirteen sermons on our Lord's Sermon on the Mount, Wesley sums up his vision of the Christian life in grace. For all its quaintness it might be edifying for us to hear—as the conclusion of this meditation—a godly exhortation from John Wesley to us all:

> In a word: let thy religion be the religion of the heart. Let it lie deep in thy inmost soul. . . . Be serious. . . . Let thy soul be filled with mildness gentleness, patience, long-suffering towards all men, at the same time that all which is in thee is athirst for God, the living God; longing to awake up after his likeness, and to be satisfied with it. Be thou a lover of God and of all mankind. In this spirit do and suffer all things. Thus show thy faith by thy works: thus "do the will of thy Father which is in heaven." And as sure as thou walkest with God on earth, thou shalt also reign with him in glory.[26]

Amen.

# 33

## *God's Part, and Ours*

### *An Introductory Comment*

This sermon on "working out your own salvation" was preached at First United Methodist Church in Winter Park, Florida, on September 8, 1985— one of that church's Great Preachers series. This is no neatly outlined plan of salvation, simply because none of Albert Outler's sermons are neatly outlined.

After one of Outler's sermons at Yale in Marquand Chapel, Hal Luccock said, "Al, that was one of the most remarkable *tours de force* I have ever heard. If they can convict a beggar of having no visible means of support, they could convict you of being able to get from one premise to another without any bridge!"

Outler responds, "For Hal, preaching was always the reasonable building up a set of building blocks with illustrations and allusions. The sermon was always to come out symetrically smooth. For me, a sermon is an effort at getting in enough different angles of insight to allow the hearers a kind of diaphorous medium—a medium they can see the light through, but cannot be allowed to suppose they have a clear delineation of the mystery.

"I try to help the hearer see what I think I see, or fail to see and wonder why I thought I did. It is a kind of interplay with the audience, not to snow them—they do not have to take it on my authority—but to make it confirmable to anybody who will take the pains to check it out."

# *The Sermon*

Our text from Philippians 2:12, "Work out your own salvation with fear and trembling," is particularly appropriate for this occasion. For I do believe "it is God who is working in you, inspiring both goodwill and good deeds, to his own chosen purpose."

The unmerited honor to be in this company quite naturally opens the door for me to express my belief in the great gospel doctrine of justification by faith—and I have long since learned to recognize useful analogies between the comforts of the unmerited favors of *God,* and such unearned and unmerited honors as this. There have been a few times in my seven decades-plus that I have received less than I felt I deserved. Most of the time, though, as with most of us, it has been the other way around—much more has been given than I had any right to *expect.* And so, I have gone through life feeling grateful for the bounties of Providence—and now this visit to Winter Park adds yet another proof of the bonuses of grace.

But it is just precisely this experience of your gracious welcome that has prompted further reflection on the crucial issue in Christian self-understanding raised in our text, an issue that lies at the heart of the gospel. Do we live generally and from day to day by *our* own merits, or by God's grace; by human initiatives, *or* by divine prevenience? Is the human tragedy, reported endlessly in the daily media, the fruit of sin? *Or* is it the outcome of unfortunate social circumstances? Are we *saved* in this life and for the life to come, by *our* good works and merits? Or by God's sheer mercy accepted in and through faith and trust? Is human virtue innate, *or* is it the fruit of the Holy Spirit in our hearts and lives?

These are ancient either/ors. We meet them in Jesus' parables and preeminently in Paul's letter to the Romans—but also in the recurrent theological controversies in the centuries ever since. There would seem to be something almost instinctual in our human tendency to take the credit to ourselves for whatever good we do—or enjoy—and by reverse psychology to shift the blame for what evil happens to us—or what evil we commit— on to somebody else or something else. Maybe it was Adam who got it started. He bucked the blame over to Eve and *she* passed it on to the serpent, who seems to have been struck speechless by such outrageous buck-passing! It took a tornado to convince Job that life is more mysterious than all those futile efforts of his friends to explain it all in simplistic and moralistic terms of merit and demerit.

This problem of God's free grace *and* of human free will has baffled both learned and plain people down through the ages. There has never been a lack of theoretical explanations for this in human terms, and none has been successful. Genes versus culture? Satan versus God, as in Job? Incidentally, this long-standing perplexity is a sure sign of a really profound problem—one that keeps on turning up to trouble the hearts and minds of succeeding generations. These great problems are always too profound to be "solved" in any given age, by the theories of *that* age. Take, for instance, the moralistic notion that since we human beings have the ability to obey the moral law, it is *our* part to obey God's will, and then it is God's part to grade us on our performance, and on that basis to reward and punish us accordingly. That seems fair enough, doesn't it? Well, yes—until you see the way St. Paul lays out the depths of the human dilemma in Romans 7—with his discovery that "the good that one part of me would like to do, I fail to do; and that the things I do that are wrong, or unexpectedly harmful, seem to have happened despite my good intentions."

This paradox troubled him so deeply that he comes to the end of the chapter with a doleful question: "O miserable creature that I am. How may I be rescued from this tragic dilemma?" His answer, as we know, is the crux of the true Evangel: that *God in Christ* can do for us what we cannot do for ourselves; that he *has* done it already, in principle, for all. We are saved by the grace of God in Christ, through the faith that accepts that grace and lives by it. This is the kind of faith that is energized by love! This is the kind of energy that is sanctified by grace.

Nowadays, the pendulum of religious and ethical opinion has swung heavily over onto the moralistic side. We are, most of us, acutely aware of the human predicament: the mystery of iniquity in which human beings who obviously were made to be happy *and humane* are so often *unhappy* and *inhumane.* And so, we seek a moral and psychological formula for success (there's bound to be one, isn't there?). We want to know the secret of liberation from the shackles of our frustration and lack of meaning. We thirst for the magic potion of happiness. One of the largest sections in any of the bookstores in our town is about self-help, self-improvement, self-salvation (how to be happy though human). We have shrinks not only in their offices but invading our dens and bedrooms, on TV and radio. Many of the sermons I hear seem based on the premise that if people only *knew* what was right and good (in personal and interpersonal relations; in national and international affairs; in social, economic, and political questions), they would readily do their part in serving the general good as a matter of being human. And so, we are *told* what is good and right in all manner of very complex issues, by men and women who set themselves up as public oracles (aided with a dash of Scripture here and there, along with large doses of *ideology* and editorial rhetoric). Most of it rests on the Pelagian premise that God has created us all with the capacity to save ourselves, provided only that we are well enough informed and highly enough motivated.

And yet, in the world we know, for all the good advice we get, despite all the glittering promises dangled before us, for all the hectoring and heckling from our self-appointed prophets of justice and peace—this same world is awash with misery. It teeters from the brink of one catastophe to another. We are bombarded on every side by self-righteous subjunctives: "*If only* we had done thus and such"; "*If only* we would do thus and such." Marxist or socialist solutions are proposed as panaceas for all our problems, but rarely with the plain indicative that not a single Marxist or socialist country has solved *any* of the great *human* problems. We are offered hypothetical capitalist solutions, which might work, *if* only people were ungreedy, nonpredatory, immune to the prejudices of race, class, sex, nationalism. *If* only one generation were unwilling to mortgage the human future in favor of its own present advantages; *if* only men, women, and children in the so-called Judeo-Christian tradition had not abandoned the work ethic for the shirk ethic.

But this goes against the grain of economic history. It was Adam Smith himself who taught that the *Wealth of Nations* comes from systematic exploitation of *self*-interest. And more Methodists accept the tenets of Adam Smith than those of John Wesley. (They were, by the way, contemporaries.)

And yet, there is so much unhappiness that cannot be traced to poverty or to political oppression. There is so much unlived life, so much half-lived life, so much disenchantment, disappointment, frustration. Freedoms *denied* make for human misery; freedoms *abused* make for human decadence; and the bitter fruits of decadence in all dimensions of our society are all too apparent.

There is a bottom line here, and it is hard to accept: *Self-salvation is not a human* possibility. If human life is to have truly human meaning and fulfillment, if human beings are to have authentic faith and fortitude for life, in the face of suffering and death, all of human life must be recognized as a gift from God, life's Source and Sustainer and Redeemer. Our salvation is from the Lord God Almighty, by whose love we are redeemed, in knowledge of whom standeth our eternal life, and whose service is our perfect freedom.

If *this* is so, whence then, can come the faith that will turn our hearts and wills to God in repentance? From whence may come the assurance of sins forgiven, and of grace bestowed, for holy and happy living?

We cannot, by ourselves alone, *choose* to turn to God unless God himself turns us toward him and we turn freely. This is what is so truly amazing about grace—it is *from* God, in and for us and others. This, of course, is the paradox posed by Paul in his Philippian letter which we read for our text. The gospel does not say that we can save *ourselves* with God's help, but rather that God can, and does, save us with our faithful participation in *his* saving grace. This is very much more than a play on words! Work out your own salvation with fear and trembling (with no final reliance on your own power or virtue). And you are free and able to do this because God is already and always working in you, inspiring your goodwill and good works according to *his* good purposes which you can make your own.

The initiative in all things that really matter to us comes from God. "In *the* beginning, *God* . . ." But this is true in all beginnings, and continuings, and endings: *God* first, last, and always. It is God's part to *act*, to take and hold the initiative. It is our part to *re*act to God's initiatives and prevenience. And the essence of sin is to try to reverse this order—to act as if what we did could *merit* God's approval. And the consequences of these dispositions to act on our own rather than *re*act to God's gracious initiatives are tragic. We are not, in point of plain fact, free to initiate any truly moral action on our own, for the very simple reason that any radically *self*-motivated actions of ours would be *self*-interested, *self*-serving (*selfish* in the most literal sense) and so would be corrupted and corrupting, from the beginning. But we *are* free to respond to God's grace as it is given us, preveniently (which is to say, in advance), by God's Holy Spirit, present and active in our hearts and consciences, in our minds and wills, in our faith and hoping and loving. *This* is what it means for us to be *at work* in *our own* salvation. We can do this because of God's prevenient grace working *in* us—inspiring us and filling our hearts with joy and confidence and courage, in proportion to our willingness to have this happen and our eagerness to share God's *unmerited* grace—amazing and efficacious.

John Wesley understood this mysterious paradox as well as any other Christian thinker since St. Paul. His ideas about it are summarized in a sermon on our Phillippians text—and it would richly repay your reading and pondering. As a taste of it, I offer you his conclusions as our conclusion for our hearing of the Word today:

> "But," say some . . . "Is there not rather a flat opposition between the one [notion] and the other [that God works *and* that we work, too]? If it is God that worketh in us both to will and to do, what need is there of our working? . . . For if we allow that God does all, what is there left for us to do?" [He has already rejected the notion that *we* can work out our salvation on our own.] . . .
>
> But . . . if we consider the matter more deeply, we shall then see there is no opposition between these . . . but on the contrary the closest connection, and that in two respects. For, first, God works [in you]; therefore, you *can* work. Second, God works [in you]; therefore you *must* work. . . .
>
> If he did not work it would be impossible for you to work out your own salvation. . . . It is equally impossible for us to "come" out of our sins, yea, or to make the least motion toward it, till he who hath all power in heaven and earth calls our dead souls into life. . . .
>
> [And this he does by what] is more properly termed "preventing grace" [grace that is offered even *before* it is sought]. . . . No man sins because he has not grace, but because he does not use the grace which he hath.
>
> Therefore inasmuch as God works in you [as the power of the indwelling Spirit], you are now able to work out your own salvation. Since he worketh in you of his own good pleasure, without any merit of yours . . . it is possible for you to fulfil all righteousness. . . . We know indeed that word of his to be absolutely true, "Without me ye

can do *nothing!*" But on the other hand we know every believer can say, "I can do all things through Christ that strengtheneth me!" . . .

God has joined [this paradox] together. [His part to act; our part to react to his gracious leadings.] . . . Therefore we must take care [never to put it] asunder. We must beware of that mock humility which teacheth us to say, in excuse for our wilful disobedience, "Oh, I can do nothing." [It *is* true that you cannot save yourselves; but God is willing and able to save you, if you put your trust in him and seek to live by his grace.] Stir up the spark of grace which is now in you, and he will give you more grace. . . .

God worketh in you; therefore you *must* work . . . otherwise he will cease working. . . . Even St. Augustine [agrees that] "he that made us without ourselves, will not save us without ourselves." [It is our part to respond to God's unmerited mercies with gratitude and good works, both of love and mercy, of our own. And this will bring to us the happiness, the sense of meaning, the assurance and confidence, in life and death, that nothing whatever, in all creation, can separate us from the love of God which is in Christ Jesus.]

"Labour" then, brethren, "not for the meat that perisheth, but for that which endureth to everlasting life." Say with our blessed Lord, though in a somewhat different sense, "My Father worketh hitherto, and I work." In consideration that he still worketh in you, be never "weary of well-doing!" Go on, in virtue of the grace of God preventing [going before], accompanying, and following you, in "the work of faith, in the patience of hope, and in the labour of love." [And be assured that labors such as these are never in vain, *in the Lord.*]

And "the God of peace, who brought again from the dead the great Shepherd of the sheep"—Jesus—"make you perfect in every good work to do his will, working in you what is well-pleasing in his sight, through Jesus Christ, to whom be glory for ever and ever!"[27]

Amen.

# *Albert Outler: A Biographical Profile*

1. Methodist Parsonage Born and Bred:

Youngest child of John M. and Gertrude Outler; born in Thomasville, Georgia, November 17, 1908.

2. Education:

Elementary and secondary education in Thomasville, Dawson, Savannah, and Americus, all in southern Georgia; B.A., Wofford College 1928 Phi Beta Kappa (English major, minor in classics and English literature), honorary D.D. 1952, honored by Outler Professorship in Religion 1968, Distinguished Service Award 1987; B.D., Emory University 1933 (major field, psychology of religion), L.H.D. 1968; Ph.D., Yale University 1938 (specialization, patristics).

3. Pastoral Experience:

Rural circuits, South Georgia Annual Conference 1928-33; inner city church (Macon) 1934-35; ex-urban church (Wallingford, Connecticut) 1947-49.

4. Academic Service:

Duke University (instructor, assistant, associate professor) 1938-45; Yale University (associate professor, Timothy Dwight Professor of Theology) 1945-51; Southern Methodist University (professor of theology) 1951-79.

Visiting Professorships: Princeton 1957-58; Davidson College 1980; Texas Wesleyan College, 1983-84.

5. Denominational Service:

North Texas Conference 1952-77; chair (successively), Board of Social Concerns, Board of Ordained Ministry 1958-70;

delegate, General and Jurisdictional conferences 1960-76.

6. United Methodist Church:

Preacher, Uniting Conference 1968; chair, Doctrinal Study Commission 1968-72; vice-chair, Commission on Ecumenical Affairs 1964-68.

7. World Methodist Conference:

Plenary address (London) 1966; plenary address, Conference on Evangelism (Jerusalem) 1974; lectures, World Methodist Conference (Honolulu) 1981; World Methodist Executive Committee 1976-82; plenary lectures, Oxford Institute on Methodist Theology 1962, 1981, 1987; Oxford Institute for Theological Studies 1982.

8. Ecumenical Involvement:

Delegate, Third World Council on Faith and Order (Lund, Sweden) 1952; chair, North American Section, Faith and Order Study Commission on Tradition and Traditions 1953-63; delegate, plenary address, North American Conference on Faith and Order (Oberlin College) 1957; delegated observer, Second Vatican Council 1962-65; delegate, Third Assembly World Council of Churches (New Delhi) 1963; delegate, Fourth Assembly WCC (Uppsala) 1968; vice-chair, Fourth World Council on Faith and Order (Montreal) 1963; Academic Council, Ecumenical Institute for Advanced Theological Studies (Jerusalem) 1965-71; Bilateral Conversations (Methodist/Roman Catholic) 1965-81; board of directors, *National Catholic Reporter*, 1978-83.

9. Professional Societies:

Duodecim Theological Discussion Group 1938- ____; past president, American Society of Church History 1938- ____; past president, secretary, American Theological Society 1940- ____; past president, American Catholic Historical Association 1960- ____; Fellow, American Academy of Arts and Sciences 1968- ____; Texas Institute of Letters 1974- ____; Academy of Senior Professionals, Eckerd College 1986- ____.

10. Endowed Lectureships (more than 80):

Yale, Harvard, Duke, Emory, Pacific School of Religion, Loyola, Earlham College, Isthmus Institute, "Cato Lectures," New Zealand, Australia, Southern Methodist University, etc.

11. Service at Southern Methodist University:

Intramural: Regular class-loads and committee assignments; chair, Graduate Council on the Humanities; Faculty Planning Committee on Graduate Education 1956-60; Faculty Committee on the University's Master Plan 1963; charter member, president, Faculty Senate.

Extramural: Visiting preacher, Sunday school teacher in local churches, pastors' schools, spiritual retreats, ecumenical celebrations, etc.

12. Community Involvements:

Thanksgiving Square, Isthmus Institute, Goals for Dallas, Greater Dallas Community of Churches.

13. Honors:

Fourteen honorary degrees; the Outler Professorship in Wesley Studies at Southern Methodist University, endowed by Texas Annual Conference 1983; honorary Fellow, Wesley College, University of Sydney, Australia; a Festschrift—*Our Common History as Christians: Essays in Honor of Albert C. Outler*, ed. John Deschner, Leroy T. Howe, Klaus Pengel (Oxford University Press: 1975); Pax Christi Award, St. John's Abbey and University 1987; *Perkins Journal* special issue (Spring 1974), containing a virtually complete bibliography of Outler's published writings to that date; The Outler Prize in Ecumenical Church History 1986-____, awarded by the American Society of Church History.

14. Publications:

*Psychotherapy and the Christian Message* (New York: Harper & Bros., 1954); *John Wesley: A Library of Protestant Thought* (New York: Oxford University Press, 1954); editor, *St. Augustine: Confessions and Enchiridion*, Vol. VII, The Library of Christian Classics (Philadelphia: Westminster Press, 1955); *The Christian Tradition and the Unity We Seek* (New York: Oxford University Press, 1957); *That the World May Believe* (New York: Women's Society of Christian Service, 1966); *A Methodist Observer at Vatican II* (Westminster, Md.: Newman Press, 1967); *Who Trusts in God? Musings on the Meaning of Providence* (New York: Oxford University Press, 1968); *Evangelism in the Wesleyan Spirit* (Nashville: Tidings, 1972); *Theology in the Wesleyan Spirit* (Nashville: Tidings, 1975); editor, *The Works of John Wesley*, Vols. 1-4, *Sermons* (Nashville: Abingdon Press, 1984-1987).

The bulk of Albert Outler's publications has consisted of "occasional pieces," written upon invitation or assignment—essays, reports, forewords, reviews. When he served as pastor of Baxley Circuit he aided Caroline Miller in the writing of her Pulitzer Prize-winning novel of 1930, *Lamb in His Bosom.*

# *Notes*

1. *Morte d'Arthur.*

2. From "The Ritual," *The Book of Hymns* (Nashville: The United Methodist Publishing House, 1966), p. 12.

3. Ibid.

4. *The Book of Discipline of The United Methodist Church, 1984* (Nashville: The United Methodist Publishing House, 1984), p. 70.

5. "Elegy Written in a Country Churchyard."

6. Leon Joseph Cardinal Suenens, *A New Pentecost?* trans. Francis Martin (New York: Seabury Press, 1975), p. 101.

7. *Book of Discipline,* pp. 70-71.

8. Ibid., p. 58.

9. Ibid., p. 70.

10. Suenens, *A New Pentecost?* p. xii.

11. Author's transcription from Suenens' Perkins Lectures at First United Methodist Church, Wichita Falls, Texas (March 1975).

12. The Reverend and Learned Cotton Mather, *Magnalia Christi Americana: Or, The Ecclesiastical History of New-England,* ed. Richard C. Robey, Research Library of Colonial Americana (London: The Bible and Three Crowns, 1702; New York: Arno Press, 1972), "A General Introduction," Para. 1, 3.

13. John Wesley, *A Christian Library,* Vol. 30, "Vindiciae Pietatis" (Bristol: 1753), pp. 320-27.

14. Ibid.

15. Ibid.

16. *The Book of Worship for Church and Home* (Nashville: The United Methodist Publishing House, 1984), p. 181.
17. *The Works of John Wesley,* Vol. 2, *Sermons II,* ed. Albert C. Outler (Nashville: Abingdon Press, 1985), Sermon 36.III.6.
18. *The Works of John Wesley,* Vol. 1, *Journals 1,* 3rd ed. (Grand Rapids: Baker Book House, 1978), May 24, 1738, Par. 5.
19. *Works of Wesley,* Vol. 3, *Sermons III,* ed. Albert C. Outler, Sermon 85.III.4. Copyright © 1986 by Abingdon Press. Used by permission.
20. Ibid., Sermon 109, p. 533.
21. Ibid., p. 534.
22. Ibid., Sermon 85.II.1.
23. Ibid.
24. Ibid., Vol. 1, *Sermons I,* ed. Outler, Sermon 16.III.11-12. Copyright © 1984 by Abingdon Press. Used by permission.
25. Ibid., Vol. 2, *Sermons II,* Sermon 45.II.4; Vol. 1, *Sermons I,* Sermon 19.I.8.
26. Ibid., Vol. 1, *Sermons I,* Sermon 33.III.12.
27. Ibid., Vol. 3, *Sermons III,* Sermon 85.III.1-8.